D0847532

WITHDRAWN
FROM THE RECORDS OF THE
MID-CONTINENT PUBLIC LIBRARY

782.421642082 W842   FEB 0 6 2004

The Women of country music

MID-CONTINENT PUBLIC LIBRARY
Smithville Branch
205 Richardson
Smithville, MO 64089   SM

THE WOMEN OF COUNTRY MUSIC

THE WOMEN OF COUNTRY MUSIC

A READER

EDITED BY
CHARLES K. WOLFE AND JAMES E. AKENSON

THE UNIVERSITY PRESS OF KENTUCKY

MID-CONTINENT PUBLIC LIBRARY
Smithville Branch
205 Richardson
Smithville, MO 64089

SM

MID-CONTINENT PUBLIC LIBRARY

3 0001 00964376 0

Publication of this volume was made possible in part
by a grant from the National Endowment for the Humanities.

Copyright © 2003 by The University Press of Kentucky

Scholarly publisher for the Commonwealth,
serving Bellarmine University, Berea College, Centre
College of Kentucky, Eastern Kentucky University,
The Filson Historical Society, Georgetown College,
Kentucky Historical Society, Kentucky State University,
Morehead State University, Murray State University,
Northern Kentucky University, Transylvania University,
University of Kentucky, University of Louisville,
and Western Kentucky University.
All rights reserved.

Editorial and Sales Offices: The University Press of Kentucky
663 South Limestone Street, Lexington, Kentucky 40508-4008

07 06 05 04 03   5 4 3 2 1

Library of Congress Cataloging-in-Publication Data

The women of country music : a reader / edited by Charles
Wolfe and James Akenson.
     p.   cm.
Includes bibliographical references.
   ISBN 0-8131-2280-5 (paper : alk. paper)
   1. Women country musicians—Biography. 2. Country music—History
and criticism. I. Wolfe, Charles K. II. Akenson, James Edward, 1943-
ML394.W65 2003
782.421642'082—dc21   2003005310

This book is printed on acid-free recycled paper meeting
the requirements of the American National Standard
for Permanence of Paper for Printed Library Materials.

Manufactured in the United States of America

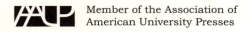 Member of the Association of
American University Presses

CONTENTS

INTRODUCTION

This publication marks our fourth annual effort to collect modern country music scholarship in book form under the auspices of the University Press of Kentucky. Starting with this volume, the *Country Music Annual* title will no longer be used, as it suggests a certain point in time and does not really reflect the timelessness of the discussions in *Country Music Annual 2000, 2001,* and *2002.* The eclectic nature of these three *Annuals* will be replaced with this volume as a thematically oriented series. We hope that this sharper focus will allow an exploration of one subject in greater depth and generate additional interest among the readership.

The Women of Country Music: A Reader obviously explores issues related to gender in country music. It has been a neglected chapter in the music's history, rife with stereotypes and vapid generalizations—often by male historians. This began to change some ten years ago, with the landmark study by Mary Bufwack and Robert Oermann, *Finding Her Voice: The Saga of Women in Country Music.* This monumental and well-researched history brought hundreds of new facts and artists to light, and inspired a new generation of scholars to look at the history of country music from a new perspective. This perspective, and others developed out of it (or in reaction to it), provides the conceptual framework for this present collection. It is appropriate that this book is being published on the tenth anniversary of the Bufwack-Oermann study. The diversity of scholars and topics found here suggests that a great deal of work has been done, but points to a continuing labor by scholars sifting through the historical and contemporary structures that give country music its identity.

Any collection of articles that includes the quotation "It's a great life for dogs and men but it's hard on women and steers" is bound to stimulate thought. It also suggests that this reader includes the work of scholars who may be new to the country-music research community. Rebecca Thomas certainly provides worthwhile insights with that quotation, not to mention her analysis of "The Cow That's Ugly Has the Sweetest Milk." Linda Daniel's work on women in Canadian country music evolved from her doctoral dissertation and brings insight to the Canadian country-music scene as well as to the difficulties facing women as country-music artists. Gloria Nixon-John also gives a certain Canadian flavor to this issue, as she deals with the interest and involvement in country music of Canadian poet Bronwen Wallace. A further international tinge comes with Andrew Smith's essay on yodeling cowgirls and women in Australian country music. One need not be smitten only by ingenue Kasey Chambers to find Australian country music of interest.

Other essays in this collection run from the alpha to the omega, from the beginning to the very current. Charles Wolfe takes the reader back to the first woman soloist to record country music with his piece on the little-known Roba Stanley. Wayne Daniel's analysis of Polly Jenkins offers insight into the complex interplay among country music and other stage and musical traditions. Kristine McCusker chronicles the Rose Lee Maphis saga from 1930 to 1960, and Tracey Laird opens new doors to us in the person of Margaret Lewis Warwick and her pivotal role in the radio show *Louisiana Hayride.* Radio is also central to Michael Ann Williams's account of John Lair's role in making women visible at the Renfro Valley Barn Dance. Roni Stoneman participated in a virtual chronology of country music, as documented through the work of Ellen Wright.

The study of contemporary country music could be no more current than the career of Faith Hill, so ably documented and analyzed by musicologist Jocelyn Neal. Kathleen Hudson provides first-hand perceptions in her oral history of the Texana Dames. James Akenson takes a classroom-oriented perspective in which he sets forth a variety of ways in which country music might be used in teaching, from kindergarten to the university.

All in all, editors Wolfe and Akenson feel that this new thematic reader should engage the wide variety of American music fans and encourage scholars from diverse fields to further explore this complex and fascinating subject. Anyone wanting to communicate with editors Wolfe (CWolfe@mtsu.edu) and Akenson (JAkenson@tntech.edu) about other thematic collections should feel free to do so.

POLLY JENKINS AND HER MUSICAL PLOWBOYS

A VAUDEVILLE VALEDICTORY

Wayne W. Daniel

Vaudeville was America's most popular form of entertainment for some fifty years following the 1881 debut of the first variety show suitable for a "double audience" (suitable for both men and women) at Tony Pastor's Fourteenth Street house in Tammany Hall, New York.[1] By the early 1930s, the end was in sight for this American institution, as show-business moguls began lamenting its untimely death. For vaudeville's demise, they blamed not so much the Great Depression, as one might expect, but rather the competing entertainment media, specifically radio and motion pictures.[2] As movies and radio became the favorite sources of entertainment for most Americans, hordes of vaudeville performers, presumably seeking higher salaries and better working conditions, began to adapt their shticks to the requirements of the camera and the microphone.[3] Nevertheless,

Polly Jenkins

like all Americans, vaudeville performers were also affected by the economic and social forces of the Great Depression. Droves of jobless entertainers found it necessary to take advantage of the various relief organizations made available by the federal government.[4]

It was into this show-business environment, with all of its uncertainties, that Polly Jenkins, a native New Yorker, chose to launch her career as a vaudeville country-music artist. She was not the first performer of this genre with vaudeville ties. Well-known country-music acts with road-weary vaudeville experience include Lew Childre, Uncle Dave Macon, Jimmie Rodgers, and Otto Gray and His Oklahoma Cowboys. Polly Jenkins, however, may be the first—and possibly the only—woman to headline a country-music act on the vaudeville circuit. Her female contemporaries in the country-music field, among them Patsy Montana, Texas Ruby, the Girls of the Golden West, and Lulu Belle Wiseman, chose radio as the medium they hoped would lead them to fame and fortune. In deciding to pursue a career in vaudeville, Polly may have hoped to avoid certain aspects of regular radio work that she found unattractive and inconvenient, such as the rush back to the station from show dates in order to make early morning or weekend program commitments and the periodic need to relocate to new stations when the demand for personal appearances in a given territory had been exhausted.[5]

Polly Jenkins was born Mary Zoller on May 6, 1903, in the upstate New York town of Mohawk.[6] She was educated in the Mohawk schools, but during her professional career she made her home in Ilion, a town just two miles west of Mohawk. Polly once explained how she came to be a musician: "My parents, both loved music, but had never had a chance to make it their life's work," she says. But they were "determined, from the day I arrived, that I should have a piano, just taking it for granted that I could and would become a musician. When I was about nine, I started taking piano lessons, doing my practicing at home on an old organ we had on the farm."[7] Eventually, the organ was replaced by the long-anticipated new piano, and Polly continued taking lessons. She made her first public appearance while still a child, playing piano in a theater to which she was driven in a farm wagon. Her pay for this performance was $1.50.[8]

When she was in her teens, Polly began playing piano accompaniment to silent movies at the Bates Theater in Ilion. After adding the xylophone to what would eventually become an arsenal of instruments, she worked the RKO and Pantages vaudeville circuits, traveling from coast to coast. At first she performed in what was called a "dressed up" musical act. "Then, the novelty, rural musical acts were coming into their own," she once explained, "so we changed over and emphasized the novelty instrument angle."[9]

Along the way Polly formed a partnership with another musician, Erlau Wilcox, also of Ilion. By the time Wilcox, who was born in 1887, joined forces with Polly he had behind him an impressive show-business career. A music conservatory graduate, he had played piano in several silent movie houses in New York, toured the country with a minstrel show, promoted musical events in his hometown, and formed his own stock company, which played from Maine to Florida and in the Bahama Islands.[10] It was at this time that Mary Zoller became known as Polly Jenkins. Billed as Polly and Uncle Dan, the two began broadcasting a morning program over WIBX in Utica, New York. Among the novelty instruments featured on this show were alarm clocks, tuned to the musical scale and used to ring out tunes to awaken radio audiences. During a later radio stint at Philadelphia's WCAU, the act became known as Polly Jenkins and Her Plowboys. Polly's first documented vaudeville performance under that billing is a notice in the October 6, 1934, issue of *Billboard* magazine, announcing the appearance, during the week of September 29 through October 5, of Polly Jenkins & Her Ploughboys at the Colonial Theater in Dayton, Ohio.[11] The spelling of Polly's act appears in print variously as Plowboys, Ploughboys, and Plow Boys. Her group later performed under the names Polly Jenkins and Her Pals and Polly Jenkins and Her Musical Pals.

In addition to traveling just with her own band, Polly worked with other acts during the 1930s. Among these was Otto Gray and His Oklahoma Cowboys, one of the most widely known western acts of the 1920s and 1930s. Traveling with Gray at the same time was Benjamin Francis "Whitey" Ford, who later became famous to radio audiences as the Duke of Paducah. During the 1935–36 season, Polly, Uncle Dan, and Sterling Simonds, who was billed as "Buster," worked out of Chicago with various WLS road shows. A number of WLS *National Barn Dance* artists such as the Arkansas Woodchopper, Red Foley, and George Goebel appeared with Polly's act on personal appearances throughout the Midwest. During this time Polly and her group worked with Gene Autry, who arrived in Chicago in late December 1935 to play a series of show dates in the area. Autry, a former WLS and *National Barn Dance* star, had just finished making his fifth feature film in Hollywood.[12]

By this time, Polly and Uncle Dan had assembled a veritable orchestra of novelty instruments that the two played as part of their stage show.

Polly Jenkins and Her Plowboys, circa 1940. Left to right: Walter Lewis, Jimmy "Deacon" Ames, Polly Jenkins, Cliff Japhet, Erlau "Uncle Dan" Wilcox.

Among this musical miscellany were the hay rake, the musical hat rack, the musical wheelbarrow, musical coins, cowbells, sleigh bells, sheep bells, and musical funnels. Many of these instruments were invented and constructed by Uncle Dan. Cliff Japhet, a popular country music performer, recording artist, and songwriter who worked as one of Polly Jenkins's Plowboys for several months on two different occasions, described some of these unconventional instruments:

> The hay rake was made of a series of copper tubes of different lengths. They were hung lengthwise, by a small wire on each tube, from a moveable rack. The tubes were played by drawing one's hands, covered with light-weight cotton gloves, dusted with powdered resin, down the length of the tube. Each tube was a different note of the scale of C. It was a very shrill sound which resulted from this technique and could not be used on the radio, as we found out the hard way by using it once on the air in Erie, Pennsylvania. The shrillness of the sound forced the volume so high that it put the station off the air.
>
> The wheelbarrow was a xylophone made to resemble a wheelbarrow and was wheeled into place when its turn appeared in the show. Both Polly

and Uncle Dan played it, and also played duets upon it by using mallets in the usual manner.

The musical coins were different-sized brass discs which were spun on a marble-topped portable ironing board. Each coin gave a different note of the scale as it was spun.

The musical cowbells were composed of about sixty different-sized real cowbells hung on a moveable rack made of regular three-quarter-inch water pipe in an upright position. These, too, were played by using xylophone mallets.

Sleigh bells were straps of sleigh bells that were formerly worn by horses during the winter months while pulling sleighs. They were hung from one end of the straps to a moveable rack and were played by drawing the fingers of one's hands down across the face of them.

Sheep bells were stood on a small stand and were played simply by picking them up by their straps and shaking them individually for whatever note of the scale you needed. Each bell [produced] a different note of the scale. The musical funnels were just regular-sized funnels that had different sound reeds—which were taken from an old-fashioned foot pump organ—soldered into their slender outlet necks. A rubber bulb was then fitted over these necks. They were clamped to a small light-weight rack and were activated by squeezing each one as needed, in the same manner as one would squeeze a small bicycle horn.[13]

Polly was always on the lookout for other novelty instruments to add to her collection. In an ad in *Billboard* in 1946, she announced that she would pay cash for "sleigh bells, piccolo bells, theremin, solovox and any other novelty."[14] After her retirement from the vaudeville circuit, Polly stated that "we were recognized as the leading novelty musical offering."[15] In addition to the novelty instruments and piano, Polly also played more traditional instruments like organ, accordion, xylophone, marimbaphone, and vibraphone.[16] Although she was known for the novelty instruments featured on her shows, Polly's repertoire and style were strictly within what was then called the hillbilly genre. "Hillbilly music was in demand," Polly's niece, Mary LaPoint, recalled, "so that's what they played."[17]

During her pre– and post–World War II career as a vaudeville artist, Polly and her troupe performed in theaters, large and small; nightclubs; fairs; and other places that showed promise of drawing an audience. From October 1940 through November 1941, for example, Polly and Her Plowboys played more than fifty mostly two-day weekend engagements in theaters and other venues up and down the East Coast, from Maine to Georgia with a brief detour into Ohio and West Virginia. (See Table 1 and Figure 1.) When the group appeared at the East Point Theater in East Point, Georgia, on March 16, 1941, their performance was sandwiched between showings of the movie *True Confessions,* starring Carole Lombard and Fred MacMurray. Such was most likely the arrangement followed at theaters in the other cities on their itinerary. The average size of the towns where Polly and her group performed on this 1940-41 tour was 12,409, and they were located 113 miles apart, on average. Typically there were five days between engagements. Cliff Japhet, who worked with Polly from August 6, 1939, through March 23, 1940, remembers what a typical Polly Jenkins and Her Plowboys show of that time period was like: "We'd bring the novelty instruments out on stage covered with horse blankets so as not to reveal what they were," Cliff says. "We'd start off performing a conventional song, and then we'd alternate novelty numbers and standard songs."[18] Uncle Dan provided comedy. Dick Land, writing in *The Mountain Broadcast and Prairie Recorder,* declared that "Polly and her Pals is rated among the greatest laughing attractions in vaudeville. . . . It truly is a happy event for the entire family, as it is clean, wholesome comedy and entrancing music. It is a show that mother, father, sister, brother and even grandma will enjoy."[19] Cliff Japhet points out that, although "Vaude was on its last legs" when he was working with Polly and Dan, he remembers that they would sometimes be on the same bill, which would have five to seven acts featuring such vaudeville staples as magicians, jugglers, trained animals, and dancers. At the larger theaters they worked with some of the big names in the business, such as Hot Lips Paige and Louis Prima.[20]

In 1939, Polly Jenkins and Her Plowboys played a four-month engagement at New York City's Village Barn, a venue known for booking rural-oriented acts. Both *Billboard* and *Variety* reviewed the show, which also featured several other acts, including a "memory marvel," a trio of dancers, a female vocalist, and a male balladeer. The reviewer for *Billboard* stated that "Holding down the featured spot are Polly Jenkins and her Plowboys. Quartet sings and plays accordion, harmonica, bass fiddle and guitar, plus a variety of homemade instruments concocted of gadgets. Act is straight off the cob, but intentionally so, and it fits in perfectly with the barn's rustic décor."[21]

Coming down somewhat harder on the act, *Variety* reported that "Show goes really corny with entry of Polly Jenkins and her Plowboys. Three males play bass fiddle, guitar and harmonica while Polly handles an accordion and other instruments. Outfit is vet vaudeville turn and gradually is becoming acclimated to night club work. The panto stuff and instrumentalizing is forte, but there's too much blasting with the cowbells and xylophone."[22]

Figure 1. Polly Jenkins and Her Musical Plowboys Itinerary, 1940–41 Season

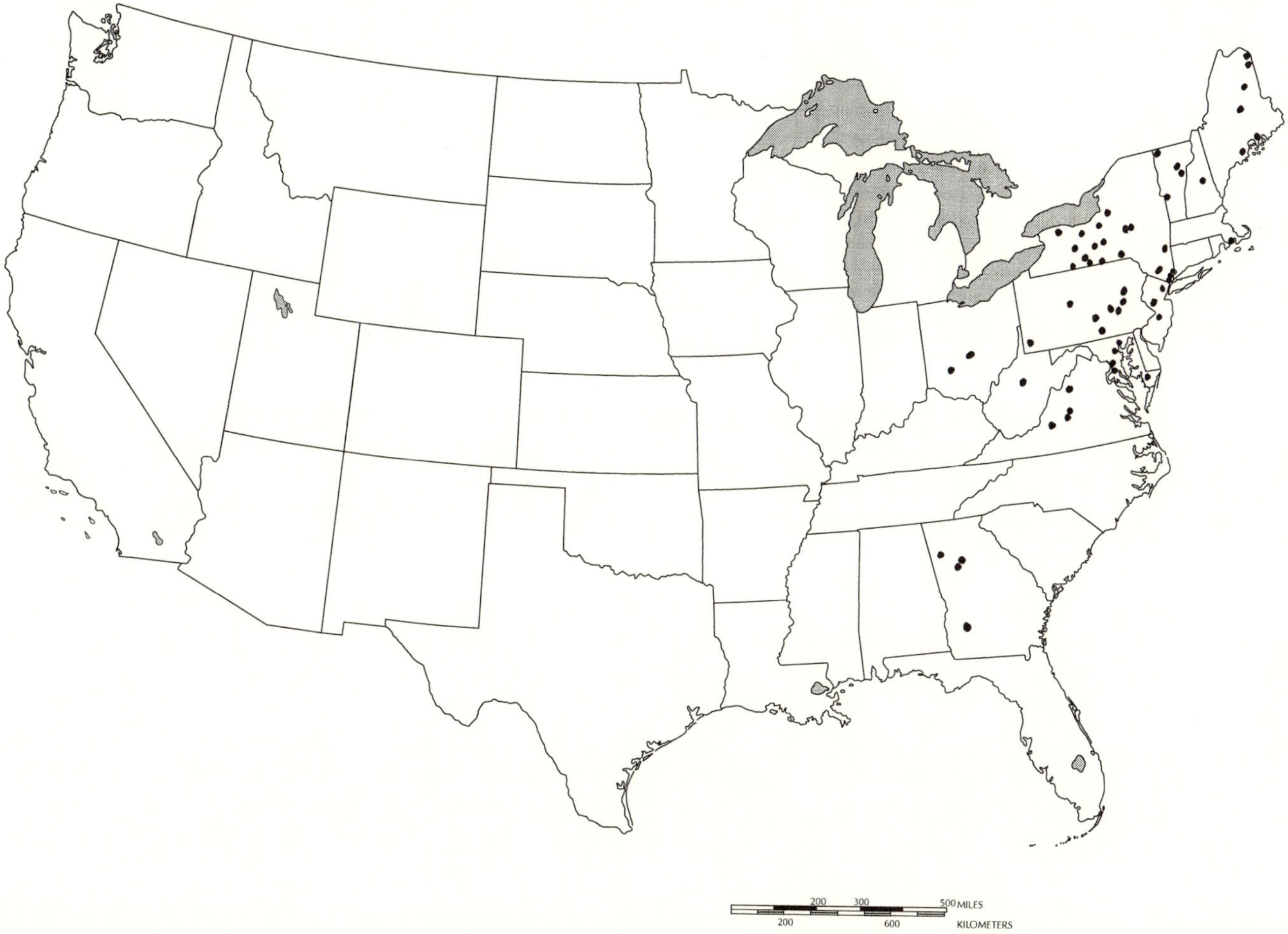

Table 1. Polly Jenkins and Her Musical Plowboys Itinerary, 1940–41 Season

Dates	City	Population	Venue	Between Dates Days	Between Dates Miles

Agent: John Singer, New York City

Dates	City	Population	Venue	Days	Miles
1940					
October 4–5	Trumansburg, NY	1,130	Care Fair		
October 11–12	Barre, VT	10,909	Opera House	5	244
October 18–19	Sherman Mills, ME	1,058	Opera House	5	241
October 25–26	Presque Isle, ME	7,939	State Theatre	5	45
November 1–2	Ft. Fairfield, ME	2,693	Theatre	5	10
November 8–9	Dexter, ME	3,714	Theatre	5	149
November 15–16	Ellsworth, ME	3,911	Grand Theatre	5	54
November 22–23	Rockland, ME	8,899	Theatre	5	55
November 28–30	Rutland, VT	17,082	Paramount Theatre	4	199
December 6–7	Ilion, NY	8,927	(Not available)	5	113
December 13–14	Ilion, NY	8,927	(Not available)	5	0
December 25–27	Pulaski, NY	1,895	Kallett Theatre	10	67
1941					
January 2–3	Ellenville, NY	4,000	Kallett Theatre	5	153
January 9–11	Baltimore, MD	859,100	State Theatre	5	202
January 16–18	Wilkes-Barre, PA	86,236	Irving Theatre	4	138
January 24–25	Salisbury, MD	13,313	Wicomico	5	198
Jan. 30–Feb. 1	Roanoke, VA	69,287	Roanoke Theatre	4	250
February 9–11	Washington, DC	663,091	Atlas Theatre	7	194
February 14–15	Lynchburg, VA	44,541	Academy Theatre	2	151
Feb. 28–March 1	Albany, GA	19,055	Ritz Theatre	12	494
March 7–8	Rome, GA	26,282	Gordon Theatre	5	195
March 15–16	East Point, GA	12,403	East Point Theatre	6	62
March 21–22	Decatur, GA	16,561	Decatur Theatre	4	11
March 28–29	Lynchburg, VA	44,541	Academy Theatre	5	395
April 4–5	Staunton, VA	13,337	Visullto Theatre	5	50
Week of April 6	Washington, DC	663,091	Atlas Theatre	0	120
April 18–19	Saugerties, NY	3,916	Orpheum Theatre	11	274
April 24–26	Binghampton, NY	78,309	Capitol Theatre	4	99
May 1–3	Hornell, NY	15,649	Majestic Theatre	4	113
May 9–10	Waverly, NY	5,450	Capitol Theatre	5	82
May 16–17	Baldwinsville, NY	3,840	Palace Theatre	5	82
May 23–24	Newark, NY	9,646	Schine Theatre	5	40
May 30–31	St. Albans, VT	8,037	Empire Theatre	5	231
June 6–7	St. Johnsbury, VT	7,437	Palace Theatre	5	60
June 12–14	Laconia, NH	13,484	Colonial Theatre	4	70
June 18–20	New Bedford, MA	110,341	New Bedford Theatre	3	134
June 26–28	Spencerport, NY	1,340	Volunteer Firemen	5	371
July 4–5	Bath, NY	4,696	Fairgrounds	5	62

Table 1. Polly Jenkins and Her Musical Plowboys Itinerary, 1940–41 Season

Dates	City	Population	Venue	Between Dates Days	Miles
July 11–12	Penn Yan, NY	5,308	Band Box Cottage	5	27
July 18–19	Reading, PA	110,568	Himmeireich's Grove	5	168
July 27	York, PA	56,712	Valley View Park	7	49
August 2–3*	Hummelstown, PA	3,264	Clown Park	5	21

Agent: Claude H. Long, Chicago

Dates	City	Population	Venue	Between Dates Days	Miles
August 9–10	Reading, PA	110,568	Himmeireich's Grove	5	41
August 15–16	Ithaca, NY	19,730	Fair	4	151
August 22–23	Corning, NY	16,212	Plaza Theatre	5	36
August 29–30	Washington, PA	26,166	Basie Theatre	5	213
September 5–6	Clearfield, PA	9,372	DeLuxe Rink	5	111
September 12–13	Grantsville, WV	1,052	Kanawha Theatre	5	203
September 19–20	Wilmington, OH	5,971	Murphy Theatre	5	150
September 26–27	Circleville, OH	7,982	Grand Theatre	5	48

Agent: Polly Jenkins

Dates	City	Population	Venue	Between Dates Days	Miles
October 6–8	Hazleton, PA	38,009	Theatre	8	375
October 10–13	Paterson, NJ	139,656	Majestic Theatre	1	95
October 17–18	Lambertville, NJ	4,447	Strand Theatre	3	56
October 23–25	Baltimore, MD	859,100	State Theatre	4	117
Oct. 31–Nov. 2	Camden, NJ	117,536	Tower Theatre	5	121
November 7–9	Astoria, NY (Not available)		Steinway Theatre	4	89
November 13–15	Glen Cove, NY	12,415	Cove Theatre	3	18
November 19–23	Jamaica, NY (Not available)		Jamaica Theatre	3	18**

*Assumed dates, actual dates not available. **Estimated distance.

Total engagements: 58
Average length of engagement: 2 days

Average number of days between engagements: 5

Total performance dates: 137
Average population of engagement city:
12,409
Average distance between engagements:
113 miles

Engagement dates, locations, and venues: *Billboard*

Population data: *Sixteenth Census of the United States: 1940 Population, Volume I, Number of Inhabitants* (Washington, D.C.: United States Government Printing Office, 1942)

Distance between engagements: Various highway maps. (Straight-line manual measurements between points.)

Polly Jenkins's cadre of musicians varied in size from a twenty-person unit touring with her in 1940 to a three-person act featured during the last few years of her vaudeville career. In addition to Uncle Dan, Buster Simonds, and Cliff Japhet, those who worked with her included Lee "Zeke" Allen, one-time performer with Otto Gray's Oklahoma Cowboys; guitarist Wallie Moore, who later worked with the WGAR Range Riders in Cleveland; George "Gib" Bourne; yodeler and bass player, Walter Lewis Rochet, whose stage name was Walter Lewis; Jimmy "Deacon" Ames, a fiddler who had worked with Doc Schneider's Yodeling Cowboys; and singer-guitarist Buzz Collins. According to Cliff Japhet, George Bourne also wrote western stories for pulp magazines. Humorous letters he wrote to *The Mountain Broadcast and Prairie Recorder* are reminiscent of the comical stories appearing in Western pulps of the 1930s and 1940s.[23]

Next to Uncle Dan, the musician who had the longest tenure with Polly Jenkins was Lucille Bonebreak, whose stage name was Texas Rose. Texas Rose was born in Texas, but at an early age she moved with her parents to Pennsylvania, where she grew up. Prior to joining Polly's show, she performed on the radio station WJEJ in Hagerstown, Maryland. When Polly played a theater there, Texas Rose successfully auditioned for the show, and spent the next eight years with the troupe. Cliff Japhet remembers her as "a terrific yodeler," vocal soloist, bass player, and guitarist. She had learned to yodel while tending to the animals on her father's farm, where she also helped out with other chores.[24]

Polly Jenkins's show-business career, following as it did the end of the golden age of vaudeville, spared her the travails of train travel that earlier vaudeville performers immortalized in their tales of long jumps between railroad towns, all-night jaunts in day coaches, and sleep-depriving train changes at three o'clock in the morning. Polly's era was that of the automobile, and that was her mode of transportation. When Cliff Japhet worked with Polly, she was traveling in two vehicles, each equipped with sound equipment. Polly and Uncle Dan rode in a 1935 Pontiac coupe, while the rest of the entertainers jockeyed for space among their instruments in a Chevrolet truck. Fortunately, the larger novelty instruments such as the hay rake and wheelbarrow could be collapsed to save space. In seeking entertainment venues, Polly sometimes used the services of a booking agent, while at other times she did her own booking. Even when she was filling dates arranged by her agent, she would use her own initiative to fill in gaps between the prearranged jobs. Cliff Japhet says that they tried to book "a small chain of theaters in towns close to each other, then stay in a hotel that was central to them all. Thus we'd be located in

Polly Jenkins and Her Plowboys making a guest appearance on radio station WLEU in Erie, Pennsylvania. Left to right: Cliff Japhet, Jim "Deacon" Ames, unidentified announcer, Uncle Dan at piano, Polly Jenkins, Walt Lewis.

one spot more or less for a few days. On dates that were quite a distance, we'd usually leave a date open for traveling, 'cause one-nighters is hard enough without stretching yourself too thin." Cliff says that their equipment included a portable typewriter, and hotel rooms served as temporary offices from which Polly and Uncle Dan sent out letters to venues ahead of their route seeking gigs for the open dates on their calendar.[25]

Lacking a powerful radio station to serve as home base from which to announce her personal appearances and keep her name in the public's mind, Polly Jenkins had to make maximum use of other promotional strategies. For one thing, she was diligent in seeing that her show dates were published in *Billboard* magazine. As soon as she arrived in a new town for a performance, Polly began making arrangements to appear on a local radio station. "We are always broadcasting locally wherever we are," she wrote *The Mountain Broadcast and Prairie Recorder* in 1940.[26] By 1946 Polly's act had been broadcast over more than 150 radio stations.[27] Cliff Japhet remembers advertising their shows using the sound devices with which their vehicles were equipped. "We had a sound system on the roof of the 1935 Pontiac coupe and one on the Chevy panel truck," he recalls. "Each vehicle carried a phonograph turntable. We'd get permission from the town to use it. It was called bally-hoo. If it was a big town, we'd often use one [of the vehicles] in one end of town and one at the other end, or sometimes in a neighboring town. Then [we'd] announce the [show] date in between the music."[28]

Polly Jenkins's musical activities were not limited to the vaudeville stage. She also wrote songs, made records, and appeared in a movie. Polly's original compositions include songs with such titles as "Little Captain"; "They Drafted Zeke from the Mountains," a World War II–era novelty song; "The Kid with the Guitar," a sentimental war song; and "Why Did We Say Goodbye?" and "Sealed with a Kiss," which were typical hillbilly love songs. Polly and former *National Barn Dance* performer Max Terhune collaborated on two songs, "Goodnight Texas" and "Fiddlin' Fuzzy." According to *Billboard* magazine, these songs were two of the more popular tunes in the Polly Jenkins show, and "Fiddlin' Fuzzy" featured "the versatility and skill of the unit's famed wizard of the fiddle and

Polly Jenkins, Erlau "Uncle Dan" Wilcox, and Texas Rose, most likely during the mid-1940s.

bow, Uncle Dan."[29] Polly promoted her songs aggressively. Ads in such publications as *Billboard* and *The Mountain Broadcast and Prairie Recorder* let readers know which artists were featuring her songs on the radio and invited performers to write her for complimentary professional copies. Subscribers to *The Mountain Broadcast and Prairie Recorder* found a copy of Polly's "The Kid with the Guitar" enclosed with the January 1944 issue of the magazine. During her career Polly published two song folios, *Songs of the Mountains and Prairies* (ca. 1940) and *Heart Throbs of the Hills* (1937).

In 1938 Polly Jenkins appeared with Gene Autry in the Republic Pictures film *The Man from Music Mountain*. Other performers in the movie include Smiley Burnette, Rudy Sooter, and Frankie Marvin. Polly recalled that "Gene saw and liked our musical novelties" when they worked together on the WLS road shows. "In 1938," she said, "we finally managed to cancel our eastern time and make the trip out [to Hollywood] for a picture with Gene, which was a happy experience." In the movie the novelty instruments are featured in the song "Long, Long Ago." In addition, Polly accompanies Gene on the accordion while he sings "Good Bye, Pinto." In its review of the film, *Variety* declared that "Polly Jenkins and her Plowboys are among the more entertaining features with their instrumental stuff. She plays bells effectively, also a squeeze box. It's all obviously vaude, but it breaks up the film well."[30]

Toward the end of her vaudeville career, Polly also found time to make a couple of records. In the spring of 1948 *Billboard* announced that "Cowboy platters soon will release a new band, Polly Jenkins and Her Musical Pals, spotting Texas Rose, yodeler."[31] The two records were released later in the year as Cowboy 801 and Cowboy 802. Cowboy 801 featured "I'm Gonna Straddle My Saddle," with Texas Rose as vocalist. The flip side was a Polly Jenkins/Texas Rose duet, "Sealed with a Kiss." The two sides of Cowboy 802 were "In My Shanty Down in Ypsilanti" and "Let's Stop Feudin', Sarah Jane."

One of the highlights of Polly Jenkins's career was her long-running association, during World War II, with the United Service Organizations for National Defense, Inc. (USO), a private, nonprofit social-service agency chartered on February 4, 1941, to provide social, welfare, and recreational services for members of the United States armed forces and their families.[32] In 1942 Polly Jenkins's act became one of thousands of USO entertainment units that toured the continental United States "performing on makeshift stages, barren ground, especially designed touring trucks, and in military base theatres."[33] During this time, Polly's act usually con-

Polly Jenkins on the set of the movie *The Man from Music Mountain.* Left to right: Sterling "Buster" Simonds, Polly Jenkins, Gene Autry, Erlau "Uncle Dan" Wilcox.

sisted only of Uncle Dan, Texas Rose, and herself, and was billed as Polly Jenkins and Her Pals. With so many young men serving their country as doughboys, male entertainers to fill the bill of Plowboys were hard to come by, hence the act's name change. "I think we were the only tabloid troupe who were allowed to keep their own transportation as the novelties were in demand and enabled us to give the boys something a little different," Polly said after the war.[34] The term tabloid (or tab) show was used in vaudeville circles to refer to a shortened version of a full-length show, as the name implies. In 1943 *Billboard* stated that Polly Jenkins's act was "one of the most popular outfits entertaining servicemen. Now in their second year with USO, they have appeared at more than 300 camps in all parts of the country."[35] When the war came to an end, so did the USO phase of Polly's career. She and her Pals played their last USO engagement in Eureka, California. They had entertained servicemen at more than 900 different military establishments and, according to Uncle Dan, had performed in every state of the union.[36]

After their stint with the USO, Polly, Uncle Dan, and Texas Rose resumed their travels as a vaudeville act, performing again at fairs, theaters, and other venues until Uncle Dan's death on May 4, 1949. Uncle Dan was on tour with Polly in Springfield, Massachusetts, when he suffered a stroke that caused his death at the age of sixty-two.

The death of Uncle Dan brought to an end the career of Polly Jenkins and Her Pals, but it did not end Polly's career as an individual performer. She returned home to Ilion, New York, where she continued to be active in the music business. "Till the day she died," recalls her niece Mary LaPoint, "she'd play for the folks at her apartment housing and anyone else that asked her to play. She'd play the piano and talk about her theater days."[37] In a 1978 letter to Cliff Japhet, written just five years before her death, Polly talked about her post-vaudeville life. "I taught piano and accordion for thirteen years," she wrote. "I have developed a combination country-western, honky-tonk style which seems to appeal to audiences. Not working in clubs or other similar entertainment centers. There is an ex-professional banjoist in a neighboring town, who I work with at different local spots, mostly senior citizen projects, hospitals, etc., gratis. We work up a storm, standard tunes, honky-tonk, mixing in requests from audiences, whatever type they ask for. I am amazed that I remember so many songs and tunes, but the years of entertaining do a lot for us, don't they?"[38]

Mary Zoller, more widely known as Polly Jenkins, died on October 17, 1983, in the Mohawk Valley General Hospital, in the state of New York. She was eighty years old. At the time of Polly's death, vaudeville was a relatively unfamiliar word to a generation that found its entertainment on radio and television, and in the movie house. It had been thirty years since *Billboard* discontinued its vaudeville section, which at one time had been a widely read source of information about troupers like Polly Jenkins, who trekked from small town to small town and from big city to big city performing live from the stages of theaters, fairgrounds, and nightclubs across the country.

Notes

1. See Douglas Gilbert, *American Vaudeville: Its Life and Times* (New York: Dover Publications, Inc., 1963), 10, and John E. DiMeglio, *Vaudeville U.S.A.* (Bowling Green, Ohio: Bowling Green University Popular Press, 1973), 4.

2. "The History and Evolution of Vaudeville," *The Billboard,* 29 December 1934, 65, 81.

3. See "Vaudeville's Contributions to Other Branches of Show Business," *The Billboard,* 29 December 1934, 66, and Hal Halperin, "What's Become of the Vaude People?" *Variety,* 8 January 1941, 146.

4. See Hallie Flanagan, *Arena* (New York: Duell, Sloan and Pearce, 1940), 14–15; "CWA Actor Relief in Sight?" *The Billboard,* 17 February 1934, 1, 53; "Three Cities Arranging Aid for Unemployed Performers," *The Billboard,* 4 August 1934, 18; and "CWA Vaude Relief Nearer; Appropriation Is Passed," *The Billboard,* 25 August 1934, 15.

5. Ronnie Pugh, "From Schoolhouses to Arenas: A History of Country Music Touring," in *The Encyclopedia of Country Music,* ed. Paul Kingsbury (New York: Oxford University Press, 1998), 556–59.

6. Mary Zoller obituary, Herkimer (New York) *Evening Telegram,* 18 October 1983.

7. "Polly Jenkins (Our Star of the Month)," undated, uncredited magazine article.

8. Dick C. Land, "Polly Jenkins and Her Pals," *The Mountain Broadcast and Prairie Recorder,* June 1947, 18, 29.

9. Ibid.

10. Ibid.

11. *The Billboard,* 6 October 1934, 34.

12. *Standby,* 7 December 1935, 15.

13. Cliff Japhet, telephone conversation with the author, 27 July 2000. Additional undated written description provided by Cliff Japhet.

14. *The Billboard,* 8 June 1946, 41.

15. "Polly Jenkins (Our Star of the Month)," op cit.

16. Dick C. Land, "Polly Jenkins and Her Pals," op cit.

17. Mary LaPoint, letter to the author, 5 September 2000.

18. Cliff Japhet, telephone conversation with the author, 27 July 2000.

19. Dick C. Land, "Polly Jenkins and Her Pals," op cit.

20. Cliff Japhet, telephone conversation with the author, 27 July 2000; e-mail to the author, 21 October 2000.

21. *The Billboard,* 1 April 1939, 19.

22. *Variety,* 22 March 1939, 55.

23. *The Mountain Broadcast and Prairie Recorder,* December 1944, 6, and September 1945, 7.

24. Dick C. Land, "Polly Jenkins and Her Pals," op cit.

25. Cliff Japhet, e-mail to the author, 14 July 2001.

26. Polly Jenkins, letter to *The Mountain Broadcast and Prairie Recorder,* September 1940, 11.

27. Dick C. Land, "Polly Jenkins and Her Pals," op cit.

28. Cliff Japhet, e-mail to the author, 14 July 2001.

29. *The Billboard,* 18 August 1945, 67.

30. *Variety,* 17 August 1938, 23.

31. *The Billboard,* 22 May 1948, 37.

32. Dick C. Land, "Polly Jenkins and Her Pals," op cit.

33. Lynn O'Neal Heberling, "Soldiers in Greasepaint: USO–Camp Shows, Inc., During World War II" (Ph.D. diss., Kent State University, 1989), 1.

34. "Polly Jenkins (Our Star of the Month)," op cit.

35. *The Billboard,* 4 September 1943, 64.
36. *The Mountain Broadcast and Prairie Recorder,* December 1945, 28.
37. Mary LaPoint, letter to the author, 5 September 2000.
38. Polly Jenkins to Cliff Japhet, 18 November 1978.

"AND NO MAN SHALL CONTROL ME"

THE STRANGE CASE OF ROBA STANLEY, COUNTRY'S FIRST WOMAN RECORDING STAR

Charles Wolfe

They came into the jury-rigged temporary studio one hot morning in Atlanta. It was August 26, 1924, barely a year after Fiddlin' John Carson had in the same studio recorded "The Little Old Log Cabin in the Lane," the record historians now acclaim as the "first" country record. It was also three years before Sara and Maybelle Carter would stand before the microphone in the famed Bristol sessions; nine years before Patsy Montana would join forces with the Prairie Ramblers to become the country's first million-selling female singer; twenty-eight years away from the day Kitty Wells would change the face of The Grand Ole Opry with "It Wasn't God Who Made Honky Tonk Angels"; and sixty-nine years from Martina McBride's own statement of triumph over abuse in "Independence Day."

But today the first shot in that long struggle would be fired, not by a well-coiffed, nattily dressed, strong-willed diva, but by a nervous, fifteen-year-old Georgia farm girl with a strong alto voice and a headful of good songs. Her name was Roba Stanley.

Her music was good: strong, appealing, winsome, and popular. The saga of women in country music should have started with her—but it didn't. After a career that lasted only nine or ten months, she suddenly turned her back on the music and the recordings. She quickly dropped into obscurity—an obscurity so deep that when historians and folklorists like D.K. Wilgus began researching the early days of the music, they were told, and so reported, that she was long since dead. Thus she never made it into the history books, the museum exhibits, the record reissues; only

Roba Stanley, a superb singer from Georgia, who was the first woman soloist to record country music when she recorded "Single Life" back in 1924. Until the author discovered her living in Florida, she was unaware of her pioneering role in music history.

the handful of record collectors who happened to be lucky enough to have some of her old Okeh 78s recognized her name. Fewer knew anything about her, or why she suddenly abandoned her career.

Finally the singers ahead of the Stanleys, a couple of local evangelists named Mr. and Mrs. J. Douglas Swagerty, had finished their pious mewlings, and Roba's group began to unpack their instruments. It was really her father's string band, which would be billed as the Stanley Trio, headed by her father, sixty-six-year-old Rob Stanley, a familiar figure in local fiddling contests. Also present was a family friend, William Patterson, to play second guitar and harmonica. It would be another three years before the record companies began using electric condenser microphones, and on this day the Okeh Company was still using the old acoustic horn method that had been in operation almost since the days of Edison. Years later, Roba recalled the studio vividly: "There was one big old room, high upstairs in this building. We sang into a big horn, and they had this big old piece of wax turning, just like a record, cutting grooves into the wax. I remember that we had to get pretty close to the horn. It was pretty hard work." The band started off with the sentimental standard "Nellie Gray" and then rocked into the familar comic song "Whoa Mule," with Roba singing. While the standard verses of the song were included, Roba merged them with a strange, surreal set of words about a victim of mistaken identity. Her first verses began:

> The saddest time I wonder,
> My heart is filled with woe,
> With all my grief I ponder,
> What I do and do not know.
>
> Cruel fate is on me bound,
> Trouble I seem to be,
> There's another feller in this town,
> Just the image of me.
>
> Whoa mule, I tell you,
> Whoa mule, I say,
> Keep your seat Miss Liza Jane,
> And hold on to the sleigh.

The song continues, alternating mule misfortunes with "the feller that looked like me"; it is an odd mixture of the new and the old. And as such, it set the stage for a method Roba seemed to be developing, one in which she tried to "personalize" older traditional songs. It was a brilliant strategy for an artist on the very cusp between traditional and the new commercial music; in an age before country commercial songwriting had even been defined, what better way to put your stamp on a song than to make the old new?

After the two sides with the Stanley Trio, the recording manager (Ralph Peer, the same man who would discover the Carter Family and Jimmie Rodgers three years later) asked Roba to do two sides on her own, and it was these sides that became the first solo recordings by a female country singer. They were "Devilish Mary" and "Mister Chicken." The first was another very old traditional ballad from Ireland, originally called "The Wearing of the Britches" and collected by master songcatcher Cecil Sharp in eastern Kentucky in 1917. It was remarkably modern in tone—especially from a rural fifteen-year-old Georgia girl in 1924—since it dealt with spousal abuse and eventual divorce. The last stanzas of the Stanley version went:

> We hadn't been married but about six months,
> She decided we better be parted,
> She up with her little duds,
> And down the road she started.
>
> A rink tum, dink tum, dearie,
> Prettiest gal that I ever saw,
> Her name was Devilish Mary,
>
> If ever I marry the second time,
> Won't be for the love nor riches,
> It'll be a little girl about two feet high,
> So she can't wear my britches.
>
> A rink tum, dink tum, dearie,
> Prettiest girl I ever saw,
> Her name was Devilish Mary.

The flip side to this record was a old vaudevillian "coon song" called "Mister Chicken," which was probably a favorite at the Georgia fiddling contests the group haunted. The record, Okeh 40213, was released in January 1925; the artist was listed as "Roba Stanley and William Patterson."

To fully understand Roba Stanley's love for the music she helped define, we have to know something about her father and the musical climate of which he was a part. Robert Morland Stanley was born in 1858, three years before the Civil War, in Dacula, Gwinnet County, about forty miles northeast of Atlanta. He was one of a number of fine fiddlers from the area, all of whom were overshadowed by the spectacular commercial success of its most famous son, Gid Tanner, leader of the Skillet Lickers. The entire Stanley clan was musical and long-lived. Roba laughed, "My father lived to be 90. My grandfather lived to be 100. My great-great-grandfather never did die, that anybody ever heard tell of." Most of these venerable peers lived in the Gwinnet County area for most of their tenure, and the family can trace its ancestory here from the time the country was settled. So Roba's musical traditions were honestly come by.

The front porch of the old Stanley house was a gathering place for all manner of local music-makers during the 1910s and 1920s. Rob had a brother, Early, who played a lot, and the children in both families played. Roba had three brothers who helped teach her and encouraged her to perform. The region was rich in musicians who later won fame on radio and records, and many of them attended the Stanleys' front-porch jam sessions: Gid Tanner, his son Gordon and younger brother Arthus, Fiddlin' John Carson, the blind guitar player and singer Riley Puckett, Earl Johnson, L.D. Snipes, and others. They would help establish Atlanta as the first center for country music, with recording best-sellers like the gospel-singing Jenkins Family (Okeh), Carson (Okeh), banjoist-singer Land Norris (Okeh), and Gid Tanner and Riley Pickett (Columbia)—all of whom recorded before 1925. Many of them also appeared on WSB radio, which took to the air in 1922.

However, even before the advent of Atlanta's mass media, it had emerged as a center for old-time music through its hosting of one of the South's largest fiddling contests. The modern incarnation of the contest, hosted and organized by a group called the Old Time Fiddlers' Association of Georgia, dated from 1913, and was regularly held in the huge Municipal Auditorium in downtown Atlanta. For years Rob Stanley was a regular at these festivals; a 1914 newspaper account mentions him as "one of the leading contenders." In 1920 Rob actually won first place in the contest, and was described as "one of the oldest of the fiddlers attending the annual convention" (he was actually only sixty-two). The news account of his prize-winning performance is touching and curious: "Mr. Stanley, white-haired and wrinkled, played 'We Will Follow Jesus,' when his turn came to take the chair. Fiddlin' John Carson, presiding, stated that after the death of one of his sons in the World War, Mr. Stanley played nothing but sacred music. He was awarded the championship by unanimous vote." The Stanleys did indeed have a son killed in the war, but Rob obviously overcame this vow of grief and in later years played favorite traditional fiddle tunes like "Bile Them Cabbage Down," "Whoa Mule," and "Alabama Gals." By a curious coincidence, one of his favorites was the topical ballad "Little Mary Phagan." That song was about the

1913 murder of a young girl in an Atlanta pencil factory—a girl that was only fourteen when she died, about the same age as Roba herself.

By the years 1923 and 1924, as Carson began to make his first records for Okeh—many of which sold very well—Rob began inviting Roba to come along with him as he played various dances, contests, and show dates. Roba had begun to play by picking up her brother's guitar—itself a relatively new instrument in the South, definitely a young person's instrument. "My brother would be down in the field at work," she recalled. "And I'd take the guitar—I couldn't tune them for the longest time—and I'd go down to the field and get him to tune it for me." She was soon doing a creditable second to her father's fiddling as he played at square dances, both in private homes and in local legion halls. It tickled her father, who by this time was old enough to be her grandfather, to have her playing with him, and she soon became his favorite partner. Was it unusual to see a teenaged girl playing at rural Georgia dances in the early 1920s? "Yes, I guess so," Roba reflected. "I know I was the only girl playing—at least I don't remember seeing any more girls."

About this time, two other events would point Roba and her father in the direction of the recording studio. The first was Rob's decision to help with the political campaign of a man named Sam Brown, who was running for the U.S. Congress from Georgia's Ninth District. Gid Tanner played for him during this campaign as well. Roba recalled touring widely around the district trying to drum up support for Brown, and feels it was during one of these tours that she was heard by a Mr. Polk, who owned a number of furniture stores in Atlanta and was a major sponsor for the fledgling radio station WSB. Polk was so impressed with what he heard that he asked Roba and her father to play on his show. They accepted. As it turned out, it was probably the best thing to come out of the Brown campaign; the politician lost the election and in despair took his own life.The second event was an outgrowth of the first—in early 1924 Rob and Roba made their radio debut on WSB. Polk's furniture store was the sponsor and Mr. Polk himself did the announcing. "We got telegrams," recalled Roba. "Lots of them. Some from other states." WSB was then the most powerful station in the South and could easily be heard throughout the eastern United States. Back home in the Dacula area, their appearance generated quite a stir. One of the Stanleys recalled: "There was only one radio in the area, and that was in nearby Lawrenceburg. The sheriff had it in the jailhouse. Everybody from miles around here went. The yard was full; they couldn't get in the house. The man would use earphones to get it when it was coming in; and when it was time he would get it the best he could, he'd switch it on to speakers so folks out in the yard could get it." Roba and her father went on to make several more appearances on the station, but in the meantime Mr. Polk—not to be confused with Polk Brockman, who had set up John Carson's first recording—contacted the General Phonograph Company, maker of the Victrola records put out by the Okeh label. In those days, records were all sold in furniture stores, since the Victrola machines that played them were considered rather expensive pieces of furniture. When a major dealer in the South's largest city wanted the company to record somebody, the studios paid attention. Okeh engineers had visited Atlanta in July 1923—at which time they recorded John Carson, among others—and had returned for a second session in March 1924. Now they were scheduling a third session, for August, and the Stanleys and her father were added to the list of artists to be recorded. When the day came, they drove down to Atlanta, and made the four songs described above.

Roba remembered that they got a lump-sum payment for the sides they made, and that when the records came out in January and February 1925, they sold well locally. Though no royalty sheets have survived, Roba felt that "Devilish Mary" was probably the best-selling record from the session—a feeling validated by the frequency with which collectors turn up the disc to this day.

But even before the first records were released, Okeh's A & R Director Ralph Peer was impressed enough to get the trio and Roba back into the studio for more recordings only four months later, on December 1. Listening to the test pressings from the first session, Peer noticed that Roba had potential; even at the tender age of fifteen, her voice was strong and clear, deeper than the handful of other singers he had heard, such as Connie Sides. It was ideally suited to the limitations of the acoustic sound of the time, and she had a pronounced North Georgia accent that no city singer could fake. Solidly rooted in a rich and largely untapped North Georgia singing tradition, Roba had access to a great trove of regional songs.

She recorded three more songs that December. The first was a fine version of the American classic "Frankie and Johnnie" she called "Little Frankie." Her version of a woman done wrong who seeks revenge on her lover Alvin starts with an unusual stanza:

> Frankie woke up one morning,
> She heard old Rover bark,

> I bet you half a hundred,
> Poor Alvin's in the dark.

After the murder—described in vivid and bloody detail—Frankie is tried but found not guilty.

> And when they tried little Frankie,
> They placed her on the stand,
> Says "Frankie, you're a free woman,
> Go kill you another man."

The second was an old blues song called "All Night Long," which was somewhat bowdlerized but nevertheless interesting in that it switches point of view from male to female about halfway through. "Railroad Bill," another regional favorite, was one Roba personalized and localized by stitching into it a number of references to local places and people:

> Railroad Bill, ought to be killed,
> Got my home in Lawrenceville,
> Oh, drive on you Railroad Bill.

> Went to Dacula to get some meat,
> Stanley Brothers sell 'em cheap,
> Oh, drive on you Railroad Bill.

> Went to Dacula to get me some flour,
> Pool and Pounds, they sell' em higher,
> Oh, drive on you Railroad Bill.

> Went to the mountain to get me a load,
> Met Sheriff Garner in the middle of the road,
> Oh, ride, ride, ride.

By the middle of 1925 it seems apparent that Roba, even at her young age, was on the threshold of becoming the first woman solo-singing star of the new country-music genre. Okeh was using her photo in their ads and catalogues, and her records were widely played. She also attracted the attention of one of the major singers of the time, Henry Whitter, a Virginia millhand who had talked Okeh into giving him a tryout as early as 1922. Whitter was a popular singer who had recorded the first authentic version of the classic "Wreck of the Old 97," as well as a number of other sides. At an Okeh studio in Winston-Salem, Whitter had seen publicity pictures of Roba and had heard her records, and he was impressed. He wrote her father and asked if he could come down and perform with the Stanley Trio on occasion. Always willing to have another guitar player and singer in the group, Rob readily agreed, and Whitter soon arrived in Dacula.

Whitter's motives for doing this are obscure. One possible reason would be that he was smitten with the attractive teenager who could sing so well, but Roba denied that he ever made any attempt to court her. "He was a handsome young man," she remembered, "but he also explained right away that he was married at the time and was trying to make a living with his music." It might have been that Whitter was thinking of using the Stanley Trio as the core of a new string band he was thinking of forming; there had been a band from the Galax area that had made several records, but it was now broken up. There is some indication that, as one of Okeh's stars, he was working together with the company to help develop and promote talent. Whatever the case, he did perform with the Trio, and remained impressed. In later years, when Whitter designed a promotional flyer listing all the famous musicians he had played with, Roba's name was prominently featured. (A reproduction of this poster can be found in *JEMF Quarterly* 38.)

Whitter also accompanied Roba on what would be her last recording session, in July 1925, also in Atlanta. She did a piece called "Old Maid Blues" and then the song that would become her masterpiece, a largely original lament called "Single Life." The complete words, as transcribed and verified by Roba herself, read as follows:

> Do not care for pretty little things,
> Always felt like dancing,
> Streets all lined with one dollar bills,
> Girls all sweet and dainty.
>
> Single life is a happy life,
> Single life is lovely,
> I am single and no man's wife,
> And no man shall control me.
>
> Some will come on Saturday nights,
> Some will come on Sunday,
> And if you give them half a chance,
> They will stay till Monday.
>
> Single life is a happy life, etc.
>
> Cupid came last Saturday night,
> Took him in the parlor,

Every time he'd hug my neck,
He'd say now don't you holler.

Single life is a happy life, etc.

Boy fell in love with a pretty little girl,
He'll talk as gentle as a dove,
He'll call her his honey and spend all his money,
And show 'er he's solid on his love.

Single life is a happy life, etc.

Would not marry a red-headed boy,
Would not marry for money,
All I want is a brown-eyed boy,
To kiss and call me honey.

Single life is a happy life, etc.

Boys keep away from the girls I say,
And give 'em plenty of room,
For when you're wed they'll bang you til you're dead,
With the bald-headed end of the broom.

Single life is a happy life, etc.

This was an amazing song, especially for 1924, and the only recording of it made in the annals of early country music. (It should not be confused with Sara Carter's masterpiece done at the Bristol sessions in 1927, "Single Girl.") By the time she recorded it, young Roba was getting good at customizing old songs, but there is some evidence that, aside from a few commonplace stanzas like the one ending "the bald-headed end of the broom," Roba wrote most of this herself. Its imagery and rhythm and scansion suggest that Roba was a natural-born songwriter, as well as an early defender of women's rights. In an age and society where women were expected to marry and find happiness only as wives and mothers, to assert that freedom and independence are good was a remarkable statement. Bob Oermann and Mary Bufwack, writing years later in their classic study *Finding Her Voice: The Saga of Women in Country Music*, concluded about "Single Life": "It was strongly feminist stuff, even by today's standards" (68).

"Single Life" was released just three months later, in October 1925. Ironically, however, by then the bravado that Roba had so strikingly demonstrated had been seriously challenged. In the fall of 1925 she met a young man from Miami and abruptly decided to get married. "It was love at first sight," she recalled. "I just quit everything and got married. My parents were a little concerned about how young I was, but then they liked Mr. Baldwin a lot." After her marriage, she moved with her husband to Miami. And gave up her music. She explained: "My husband didn't like for me to play out in public much. There was no way to keep recording—they were up there in Georgia and I was in Miami, and lucky to get home once a year. They kept playing, but when I left, it almost broke things up. I carried my guitar with me, but I played very, very little, and in just three or four months I wasn't playing at all." Roba started her own family—she would eventually have three children—and eventually gave her guitar away to some nephews who showed an interest in music. Then she settled into obscurity.

In 1977 I was preparing, with Patty Hall, an anthology of early women in country music that was eventually released as *Banjo Pickin' Girl.* I had heard Roba Stanley's records and was determined to include a couple of them in the set. However, there was virtually no information about Roba, except for persistent rumors that she had died many years earlier. By coincidence, my colleague Gene Wiggins was at the same time researching his biography of Fiddlin' John Carson, which was eventually issued as *Fiddlin' Georgia Crazy* by the University of Illinois Press. He had stumbled onto relatives of Rob Stanley's family—Rob had been a crony of Carson's—and found out that Rob's daughter Roba was still alive. We searched the telephone books in Miami, but we had no luck. Then another old fiddler mentioned that he thought Roba had moved to Gainesville. We tried again, and soon I was talking to a friendly, chipper lady who was absolutely amazed that anybody remembered her old records—and was still interested in them. A number of telephone interviews followed, and I found Roba did not have any of her old records. I compiled a cassette tape and sent it to her, and memories of the songs and the sessions began to come back to her. She carefully transcribed all the lyrics and had them typed out and sent to me—a considerable boon since some of them were hard to decipher. Later I asked another colleague, Peggy Bulger, who worked nearby, to visit Roba and talk more. She did, taped the interview, and shared it with me. This and my own phone interviews and correspondence are the source for this article.

There is a coda to the story. Newspapers got hold of the story about Roba and had a field day. She was interviewed numerous times, but the pinnacle came in the late 1970s, when she travelled to Nashville. She was given a special tour of the Country Music Hall of Fame, and was saluted from the stage of the Grand Ole Opry. Roba passed away in 1986, still bemused at her pioneer status in what had become a million-dollar industry, and occasionally wondering what might have been if she had followed her music.

"DO YOU WANT MUSTARD?"
"YUP!"

FIRST LADY OF BANJO RONI STONEMAN

Ellen Wright

On her birth certificate, dated May 5, 1938, she is identified only as a female and the seventeenth Stoneman child. It would be a few months before her harassed parents decided what to call her. But the reticent birth certificate actually turns out to indicate quite a lot about the future direction of the life and personality of Veronica Loretta "Roni" Stoneman. As a Stoneman, she would be part of an important musical tradition. As the seventeenth child, she would benefit from the expert instruction of her older siblings and eventually come to be known as the "First Lady of Banjo." And as a female, she would live the hardships that enabled her to create a comic masterpiece, Ida Lee Nagger, the feisty *Hee Haw* woman at the ironing board, beloved by millions of Americans across the nation.

Understanding Roni Stoneman's achievements requires some insight into both her environment and the way she reacted to it, so in addition to recapping the basic milestones of Roni's life, this essay will focus on a few revealing incidents, presenting her recollections of them in her own words. These passages come from interviews recently conducted in preparation for a book-length treatment of Roni's life.[1]

First, a little history. In the late 1920s, ten years before Roni was born, the Stonemans had prospered, and they had done so via their music. The ambitious Ernest V. "Pop" Stoneman and his spirited, encouraging wife, Hattie Frost Stoneman, were two of the first country musicians ever recorded. He played the autoharp, guitar, and harmonica, she the fiddle. Whether they performed together or he with other musicians, the songs

Roni flaunts her famous and genuine gap-toothed grin. No blackening was used.

found an audience and sold well. A few of them (for example, "The Titanic") would become classics of the country repertoire. The 1930s, however, were a devastating time for the recording industry and the Stoneman fortunes in particular. By the time Roni was growing up, the family had moved from Galax, Virginia, to the D.C. area, where Ernest could scrounge together a number of jobs (mostly in carpentry), supplementing them with occasional musical gigs. It didn't add up to much. The Stonemans were living, twelve of them, in a one-room shack.[2] The furniture consisted of a table, some chairs, and a few beds. Food was mainly beans, cornbread, biscuits and gravy, canned goods brought back from summers spent in Galax, and, from time to time, mackerel rolled in cornmeal. Clothes either came from charity donations or were handsewn, often from flour sacks. The roof was covered with a tarpaulin. There was no running water. It was, says Roni, "poorism":

> Daddy bought that piece of land and built that house with whatever he had. When he would do work for churches, they would give him the lumber from an old church they was tearin' down. And he'd bring some of the lumber and he'd put it on the walls, and fix it up the best he could. There was no closets. There was no dresser drawers. There was a pan of water setting on a stand in the middle of the floor for washing and shaving. You talk about poorism, we had it. Poverty-stricken? That's average. Anybody can be poverty-stricken. I'm talking about poorism. Like get-down dirt poor.

There were few toys, of course. But what they did have was music. Pop used psychology. He would make instruments, put them on the bed, tell the children not to touch them, and leave the house. The results were predictable: most of the children quickly became accomplished musicians. This would lead to the first substantial improvement in their finances. Here's how Roni recalls what happened:

> I remember so well. I was standing right beside Mommy by the table, the old eatin' table as they'd call it, and there was some beans on the stove, and some cornbread Momma had made. And Daddy came in and he set down right at the head of the table and he said, "Hattie, there's a contest to be goin' on at Constitution Hall." And he said, "I would like to get in that contest. The winner would get twenty-six weeks on television." And my momma said, "Well, Ernest, go ask the boys." My brother Eddie lived across the creek. Daddy made a little bridge, just made it out of plank. And she said, "Well go ask the boys if they would pick with ya." Eddie was "the boys," I guess, and the rest of 'em. I mean, he was the older one. And he went across the creek and came back, poor Daddy limpin' across the creek, he came back and set down, and Mommy said, "What's the matter, Ernest?" He said, "Well, Hattie, they don't want to play with me. The boys are not going to play with me." And Momma said, "Why not?"—Momma had a lot of spark in her. "Because," he said, "they got electrical instruments now, and they say I play too old timey for 'em."
>
> And Momma said, "Well, I'll tell you what, Ernest. How long do you have before the contest?" And Daddy said, "Oh, we got about three months, I guess." And she said, "That gives you time to start makin' the instruments for the little ones. We'll take the little ones, and we'll beat 'em." Honest to God. I remember saying, "Wow, do I get to go?" And Daddy started comin' in every night or so, carved out a neck of an instrument. And fixin' up things. On Saturday, we'd go downtown, and get things like brackets and stuff, go up to the hardware store. Daddy would even make his clamps to make the instruments. And he had pieces of glue that was thin as 'bout two or three pieces of paper, and it was yellow, and it come in sheets, just pieces of it. And he had a can, and he'd put it on that old oil stove. That big tank was clear, and you could see the oil, you could see the oil in it. It would go "burgle, burgle, burgle," and you would turn it and you would light the match. He had put that can with that piece of solid plastic in and it would turn into glue. And that's what he glued with. And then how he would hold the neck good? He would take a drill, and take a wooden peg up into that neck, and support it and make it extra solid, and it made the neck not come off.
>
> So he started makin' the instruments, and so we all got in that old truck. I'd give anything to have that. . . . You know, if I had that truck today, I'd think I was rich. I'd be the richest person in the world. But it was a rumble seat truck, you know, and Daddy made a tool chest side, and bent iron bars, and then put canvas for us kids to ride in, and that's how

we rode around. Didn't have any heat in there—you could freeze your butt off. When we went over a bump, you'd hurt your fingers—I can't tell you how many times we got our fingers mashed. And Daddy said, "Dad-blame it, didn't I tell y'all to watch your fingers?" "Waaaaaaaa." "Dad-blame it, don't you know to watch your fingers? You're gonna need 'em for pickin'. Now dad-blame it, watch 'em fingers!" Every time we'd get in to go to play music, we'd go "aaagh." The boards would come down real hard, and if your fingers were underneath it, your fingers were mashed. You learn not to do that. And Momma would say, "Lord God, don't let your fingers get caught in that door now." Or, "Oh honey, you can't play that baseball because you'll get your fingers jabbed." Or, "Don't do that—you're gonna ruin your fingers." That was Momma. "Oh Lord a mercy, don't you do that with your hands. Don't you know that you're gonna hafta use those hands someday? You never know where that music's gonna take you. You gotta be careful about them fingers. Oh, Lord a mercy, Ernest." That was the way it was always at our house. But when Daddy told Momma that the boys wouldn't go, she got very uptight. She told him, "Make the instruments, and we'll go and beat 'em. Ernest Stoneman, we'll beat 'em. Just get my fiddle fixed up and I'll go and fiddle for you."

So, off we went. We opened up the doors at the big ol' Constitution Hall, and it was nothin' but marble floors. And I'd never seen a hallway. The house wasn't hardly that big. And they opened up them doors, and I went flyin', you know, like the Gravy Train dog, slidin'. And I thought, hey, this is really cool. And I went running straight back. Momma said, "Lord God, in the name of Jesus, come back here. Lord God, come back here. Where in the world are my younguns goin'? Oh, where is Roni?" And Roni was a hyper little nut, me. I went straight down, and on my left there was a dressing room. This guy was puttin' on his eyebrows, and puttin' on his moustache. And I climbed up his dressing table, there was lights everywhere, and I'd never seen nothin' like that, and I stared him right in the face, like why is he doin' that? He had, it was like Maybelline, in a little red thing, and he would make his eyebrows white and his moustache whiter, and he glued his moustache on. Well, I noticed his boots, came way up, and I never paid much attention to that kind of thing, but I did like his boots. And I thought, well, they're too big for him, so he's like us. Because, you see, we always had hand-me-down shoes. The school used to bring us down boxes of clothes and boxes of shoes that whatever came nearest to fittin' us, we took.

So Momma said, "Lord have mercy, in the name of Jesus, get outta there and quit botherin' that poor old man." And it was Grandpa Jones![3] And I kept starin' at him, wonderin' why. He was a young man then, but he was makin' hisself look old. And Momma says, "That poor old man." And he said, "She's not botherin' me, Mrs. Stoneman." And so Momma went on, and she says, "Well, I'm gonna git my fiddle," and Grandpa said, "I'll watch out for her. You just go get your fiddle." And here come Daddy, hobblin', limpin' down, and he got his guitar, and all the kids got their little instruments. I kept starin' Grandpa right in the face. I could get under your skin, just like the itch. Like the seven-year itch, or somethin'. I was like the little parasite, or whatever, that gets under the skin. And I'm lookin' at him, and lookin' at him, and he said, "Would you like to have a hot dog?" Well, I had never had a hot dog! I mean, we had beans, and cornbread, and peas, and vegetables or somethin'. Never had a hot dog. And I said, "Yup." He said, "Do you want a coke?" "Yeah." And I went walkin' with him.

All right, here I am walkin'. And you know I've seen this in my dreams and in my thoughts. I'm walking along beside Grandpa Jones, and I just come practically to his boot, just a little bit above it, and I'm walking along, staring at his boots, because they were too big, and he was okay with me, because he was like us. But I had my first pair of patent leather slippers, cause my brother was in the Pacific, in the war, or something. Billy—Billy was in the service at that time. He sent Momma some money to buy me and Donna a pair of patent leather slippers. She made our little dresses out of feed sacks, and there was flowers, a little floweredy pattern—and I'm walking along proud and lookin' at my shoes, and I'd look over at Grandpa's shoes. I can just *feel* myself there; you know, just now, the joy, of knowing that man. And then he said, "Okay, come on." So I went down all this big ol' hallway toward this concession stand. I didn't know it, but it was a concession stand. And I couldn't reach it. And he said, "She wants a hot dog." And he said, "Do you want mustard?" What did I know about mustard? I said, "Yup!" I was walking back carrying my hotdog and my coke, and I'm spilling my coke as I go, and he went, "Oops, you got it on your foot." I stopped and put my coke down on the floor and took my napkin and wiped it off my new shoes. And I kept looking at his boots.

My brothers went on first. The Stoneman Brothers, okay, the older brothers. They went out there first, and Momma just glared at 'em, cause she could really give 'em that look. They had another buddy with 'em and they played. Electric stuff. And the audience was clapping along. And I'm standin' out in the wings, just watchin'—"Oh, there's Eddie and 'em goin' now," and I was standin' there and I heard the audience applaud. And I thought, "Well, they didn't do as good as the other bunch did." There was about three hundred bands in that contest, it seemed like to me. It was a big thing! It was a big, big night, you know, getting in that contest and winnin'. You got twenty-six weeks on television with Connie B. Gay. And it would be a time for Daddy to make extra money to help put the roof on our house. Before that, we just had a canvas. We had a tarpaulin on the roof of the house. It was just one room. And when it rained, and the wind blew. . . .

But I remember the boys goin' out there and they got their time on stage. Now this was a big place, and the place was packed. They had been advertising on radio for many months and weeks. And when we got out there, they said, "And ladies and gentlemen, the Stoneman Family." They put us in a U. Daddy had us settin' down, because there was only, I think, two microphones. And Daddy had lectured all of us children, that when you sing, "Somebody's Waitin' for Me" at the chorus, "open your mouth and sing it as clear and loud as you could, because they only have but two microphones out there." And we had to be heard. So you had to get right in the mike, and you had to sing and that's what I did, I mean, that's what we all did.

And I was standin' there, and I remember singin', and Momma, she got the fiddle right down in that microphone. She was mad at my brothers, she saw them comin' off, and she was ready for bear! And she got out there, and she started fiddlin' and bringin' that bow down, and Daddy playin' as hard as he could, his guitar, right in that microphone. Mommy goes *da da dee dee da da*—that was her bow lick. And she was trying to be as loud as she could. Some man out in the audience yelled, "Swing her, Ma, swing her!" And here was all these little kids up there, okay? It must have been a sight. Daddy was playin' one of his old songs, and we sang the chorus. "Somebody's Waitin' for Me."

And you ought to seen all them people screamin' for us. We came off and they got us in this room and then they said, "Well, you're the winners." Connie B. Gay came in and said, "The winners are—the Stoneman Family!" And my brothers came out there and joined in, and we tore the house down. While we were playin', they came in and they was peekin' around by the stage, and Momma says, "Come on." They got in with us. And I thought, "That ain't fair," and I just looked at 'em as they come by me. But I stayed in the front. I wouldn't let anybody get in front of me.

The Connie B. Gay gig, shared by the whole family, meant more money, but it still wasn't much. The Stonemans still lived in the sparsely furnished one-room shack. They still lacked adequate food and clothes. This situation did, however, lead to the children exercising their creativity, both in the games they devised and in their obsessions with the instruments. A memorable incident for Roni, both in its short- and long-term consequences, was one of the times they played Russian roulette:

We'd get to running. The worst licking I think I got from Daddy. We'd be running around in circles cause we had no walls in our house.

Chun, chun, chun, diggety, diggety, diggety, dig. Over here to the left was a table that Great-grandpa had made. And Daddy had a bench on one side and some old chairs on the other. On this side was a little bed. A little bed or cot. Twin beds or a big bed—it all depended on what neighbor gave Mommy a mattress. Scott said, "Hey Roni, let's play Russian roulette." And I said, "Uh, okay. What do we do?" And he said, "Well, you know Daddy's setting over there reading his paper." Daddy would lean up against the wall to read his paper. Daddy was an avid reader. Read all the time. Read, read, read, always reading.⁴ When he was able to relax, that's what he did. And Scott said, "Let's run around near Daddy." Cause Daddy would go "uhuagh, uhhum," clearing his throat. "A little less noise, please," he'd say. Cause we'd all be in one house making the worst noise, a lot of racket. And Jimmy, Donna, me, Van, and I think Dean was in on it too, we decided we was gonna run around in a circle by Pop's chair. We'd go *diggety, diggety,*

diggety, yerrrr. Go as close to him as we could possibly get. Without him reaching out and grabbing us and killing us. That's Russian roulette.

And Scott would say, "All right, Roni, here we go. Now we're gonna run real fast, as fast as we can go, and get as close to Daddy as you can get. And then twirl out so he won't catch ya!" "Okay." *Diggety, diggety, diggety.* And Daddy'd go "uhuagh, uhhum." He'd clear his throat and he'd shake his paper a little bit. And he said, "A little less noise, please."

We'd stop right there by the door to prevent Daddy coming after us. He wouldn't get bothered getting up out of the chair and coming after us. He had a broken hip, and he worked all the time.

All right, and so here we go again. *Diggety, diggety, diggety, diggety, diggety.* And Daddy got louder—"A little less noise, please." And Scott said, "Now the next time he's gonna grab somebody. It's gonna be the end." 'Cause that's the way Daddy was. He'd give ya two warnings and then it was Katy bar the door! And Scott said, "Are you ready to make the next run?" "Yeah, I'm ready. Yeah, let's go for it!" All right, *diggety, diggety, diggety.* And then we got real close to Daddy, and Daddy shook his paper real hard. He didn't say anything. We stop and go up there and regroup. And then Scott said, "Let's go again." So here we go. *Yerrrrrrr,* around in a circle. And Daddy shook that paper. He reached out and guess who he grabbed? Didn't matter if I was at the end or not. I was the one that got caught. He knew Scott was the ringleader. Didn't matter. Scott was his fiddle player. One time I said, "Momma, how come Daddy whupped me so much? It wasn't my fault." And she says, "Well, honey, if you learned to play an instrument, and played with your father, you won't get whipped 'cause he'll need you to take you to play." And I was walking aside of her and I got to thinking. I remember doing this: "Yeah, he wouldn't whip me so much and whip me so hard if I played music with him and I played really good." And I thought, "Well, that's a reason to go out there and work in the woods." I'd have to go out in the woods 'cause Momma couldn't stand the racket 'cause five, six playing the same time, different instruments, playing different tunes. In that one-room shack, you know. I got to thinking if I was to play good, then Daddy wouldn't beat me anymore. And you know what? He never did.

Scott was not only the prime ringleader of the mischief, he was also, as he got older, the younger children's prime music teacher. Again, in Roni's words:

When I would start practicing the banjo, Momma would say, "Roni, we got to have the dishes done. Roni, Roni, we got to sweep the floor." I'd say, "Mommy, I never get to practice. I gotta practice, Mom, I gotta learn." She says, "Well, daggone it, honey, you gotta learn to sweep the floor too." So I would sneak out in the back, in the woods—we called it the ballpark. I'd go out there and practice on a stump because the stump would hold the banjo. Because the banjo was pretty heavy for my little skinny legs, and I couldn't hold it normally, so I'd put my legs out apart and put the banjo on the stump. I'd reach around it and pick and pick, and Scott would come out there. He would come out there and he'd say, "Did you get it right yet?" And I'd say, "Scott, I will if you just. . . ." He'd say, "Well, this is the way to do it." He'd show me and show me. "And just get that roll and keep it goin'. And don't stop and don't make it sound like a gallop—this is bad, don't do it like a gallop. Do it smoothly, and take your thumb and come down." A gallop is like usin' your fourth finger and your middle finger at the same time. It's not separating them. You're blurring it. Each string has a personality, Scott used to say. Each string has got its own sound, and that means it's got its own personality and its own character. It sounds so you hear it. So whenever you go down, you don't gallop. "Keep them strings a ringin'. Don't stop, don't let that string stop ringin'." He would beat that into my head. And you know, when you're learning it, it's hard, it's so hard. I'd say, "All right, don't teach me any more, Scott." Then I'd start cryin'.

And Scott used to fuss and say, "Now don't play like a girl! I don't want to hear you play like a girl!" And I thought, well how does a girl play? I didn't know the difference. And he would always fuss if I muffled a note on the banjo. He would always fuss at me. "You're sounding like a girl." Or "Mash that string right. Make sure it's clear. Make them notes clear." And he'd mash my fingers really hard on it. Why I wanted to play so bad, I do not know. And why I wanted to play like Scott wanted me to play, I don't know, other than I loved him so much. It must have been that, or I wouldn't have done everything. I thought he was the king.

As the younger children grew, so did their musical abilities. Donna became a superb mandolinist (at one point called the best in the country by Jethro Burns)[5] and Van, the youngest Stoneman, a strong guitarist and vocalist. Meanwhile Jimmy became proficient at a slap bass technique. Roni's banjo practicing paid off, and Pop was soon taking her to perform with him, most regularly as part of the group Pop Stoneman and His Little Pebbles. While she was still in her teens, Roni ripped into "Lonesome Road Blues" on Mike Seeger's pioneering album *American Banjo Scruggs Style* and thus became the first woman recorded playing the banjo three-finger-style, a performance that earned her the sobriquet "First Lady of Banjo." She also began to exhibit a quick wit and a real flair for unpredictable humor onstage. In 1955 Scott, who had become a virtuoso fiddler, got together with guitarist Jimmy Case and started assembling the Blue Grass Champs, which within a few years would include Jimmy Stoneman, Donna, Van, Roni, and Pop, and eventually be known as The Stonemans.[6]

The Stonemans began performing more and more around the D.C. area and then later in Nashville. In the early sixties the band finally obtained the country musician's holy grail, a guest spot on the Grand Ole

Opry. Right before they were to go on, they were told that if they ever wanted a return engagement, they had to play less well than they normally did, in order not to upstage the star performers. They looked at each other, wondering how this could be done, and then they turned to their ringleader. "Scott, what are we gonna do? What are we gonna do?" asked Roni. "We're gonna play better than we ever did in our lives," said Scott angrily. "We're gonna leave our blood on the floor." Their renditions of "Orange Blossom Special" and "White Lightning #2" led to an extended ovation, an encore, and a furious Hank Snow, whose half hour allotted time had been all but used up. They were not invited back.

By 1966, however, they had their own nationally syndicated television program, which would be popular for several years. The Country Music Association nominated the Stonemans for both Instrumental Group of the Year and Vocal Group of the Year five times running. They won Vocal Group of the Year in 1967.

The makeup of the band was not static: Roni would take brief leaves for maternity, Scott would be fired periodically because of his excessive drinking,[7] Hattie and the older siblings would make guest appearances, Patsy would join the group after Pop died in 1968, and non-Stonemans would occasionally fill in, sometimes for an extended time—though venues often stipulated that there had to be a certain number of Stonemans on stage.

The Stonemans recorded and toured extensively, two activities about which Roni now feels ambivalent. She's disappointed in the legacy left by the recording. The record companies maintained artistic control of their albums, and the Stonemans were steered away from the traditional songs they had been performing toward a Nashville sound and novelty numbers that did not represent their heritage or capitalize on their strengths. But Roni realizes that there may have been some commercial justification for that decision, given the musical tastes of the time. She also realizes that faithfully capturing the Stonemans on records was next to impossible: they prided themselves on showmanship, and their visual impact was a powerful part of their shows. As for the touring, although it was educational—for example, there were some amusing encounters with hippies out in California—it was also arduous. The band's managers had them going all over North America in what seemed like a scattershot way. No matter how much the family was performing, the take-home pay seemed small.

And Roni needed the money. She had married at sixteen, had four children in the next few years—Eugene, Becky, Barbara, and Bobby—

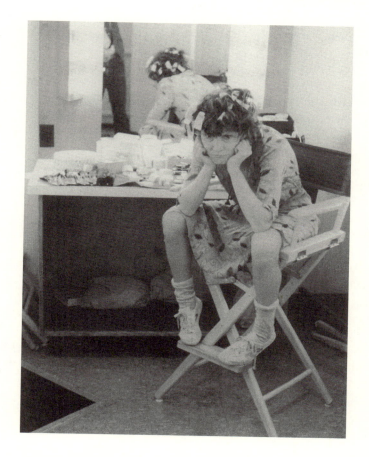

Roni as Ida Lee Nagger in her first and only dress. For years
Ida Lee had appeared in a ragged pink bathrobe.

and then later married again and had another child, Georgia. Both husbands had problems, the first a near-pathological aversion to work, the second substance abuse. Roni supported herself, the children, the husbands, and, for a time, two stepsons. At one point, before she began performing with the Blue Grass Champs, she was playing honky tonk six hours a night six nights a week (for $56 a week), dragging the banjo and herself home by bus through slums at 3 or 4 in the morning, then washing baskets of laundry during the day (by hand, for $1 a basket), and taking care of her young children. She credits her strong religious faith with getting her through that and other difficult times in her life.

Things got better when she started to perform with the Blue Grass Champs—a position that had to be earned ("They weren't going to let you in just 'cause you were family and had kids to feed"). But Roni hated the long road trips that took her away from the children, and, in spite of the CMA award, the recording, and the many bookings, she was still not making enough to support them. After a number of years, she decided to go out on her own. This of course presented its own difficulties, and her situation became desperate, aggravated by the fact that her second husband was physically and mentally abusing her. At one point she had to pawn her beloved Gibson Mastertone for money to feed the children.

Then, partly through the intercession of Tom T. Hall, she got the part of Ida Lee Nagger on *Hee Haw*.[8] The role was a natural for her. Like Ida Lee, she herself had spent a fair amount of time at the ironing board, undoubtedly wanting to scream at her husbands—whether she actually did or not. She had helpful (though to her, distressing) physical features—a walleye and a large gap in her teeth (real, not a tooth blacked out by a makeup artist)—features that lent themselves to comic mugging. And, most important, she had the experience of growing up among mountain women while possessing a lively interest in people and a natural gift for mimicry. She describes visiting the house of a neighbor as a child because she liked to watch the woman's outlandish behavior—the way she screamed at her sons, threatening them with a gun, or the way she rubbed her arm across her mouth to wipe away the dribbling snuff. Roni ran home imitating this gesture, which would become a hallmark of her portrayal of Ida Lee. The voice of Ida Lee came partly from this woman, partly from Roni's admiration of Marjorie Main as Ma Kettle. Through the years Ida Lee's part on the show grew, and Roni also developed other comic characters. Although appreciated by millions of viewers, Roni's acting has never had the critical acclaim it deserves. Her performances bring to mind such actresses as Carol Burnett, Lucille Ball, and Imogene Coca, comediennes who act with every muscle of their bodies and project an endearing mixture of common-sense intelligence and wild zaniness.

Though she was first hired for the Ida Lee role, Roni also became part of the *Hee Haw* Banjo Band, which played regularly on the show. Stringbean was her advocate, but Roni's new role seems to have been largely a result of the show's desire to spice its old-time country format with a dash of trendy feminism: Stringbean introduced her as "my little friend from women's lib." The emphasis on Roni's musicianship only went so far, however, because of cast rivalries. In one notable instance, Roni was dueling banjos with, and "outrunning," *Hee Haw* star Roy Clark in a

Roni, a haystack, and her Gibson Mastertone. In addition to comic roles on *Hee Haw,* she played regularly in the show's Banjo Band.

pre-taping warmup. Roni didn't realize that the camera was on them, and to her horror, the episode was aired. She was disciplined for this in a peculiarly humiliating way. For a time she was not allowed to play with the Banjo Band; she was exiled to a bale of hay, her banjo strings taped mute.

Despite such problems, Roni's basic experience of *Hee Haw* was extremely positive. The cast members were highly professional and they respected each other's talents.[9] The showgirls were not just beautiful girls, Roni notes, they were also superb actresses. And the sense of fun and hilarity that marked the broadcasts reflected genuine offstage camaraderie. "We always seemed like we were family," says Roni.[10]

It was therefore a great emotional loss when, after almost twenty years, she was part of the general purge of the show's cast. It was also a great financial loss. The program had provided a steady income, and Roni had been able to supplement that income with earnings from a heavy schedule of show dates—state fairs, conventions, and so on. These performances were necessary because Roni's next three husbands were no better providers than the first two, and Roni remained the major source of support of her five children. Getting show dates was largely a product of the *Hee Haw* name recognition, and when the program ended, so did Roni's market value, at least in the eyes of some promoters. More damaging may have been the Nashville rumor mill. There seems to have been a perceived—if not actual—prohibition against making use of the *Hee Haw* characters, a prohibition that could in practice have extended to the mere hiring of the actors and thus amounted to a *de facto* blacklist. At least, such was the situation as one booking agent explained it to Roni.

Whatever the reason, Roni had great difficulty getting jobs for several years, although she did become involved in some interesting projects, most notably a short-lived experiment with an all-girl band, the Daisy Maes, and a kind of musical ambassadorship tour of Belgium, during which she barely managed to head off a war developing between two of the participating groups, the Sardinians and the Kentuckians:

> I walked in the door and everybody turned and looked toward me, the Kentuckians, the Sardinians. All right, all the Kentuckians on this side and all the Sardinians set on this bench. And they're just setting there staring. They're mad at the Americans. So I just headed for the best looking Sardinian there. And this is the way I did. As I went, I grabbed a flower off the table and put it in my teeth. Like Rosa Lee. Like I'm dancing like the Spanish dancers with the rose in my mouth. And I went *du da rum,* and I went real fast and I grabbed him up and me and him went across that floor, like a hillbilly version of the tango. The ice was broken. Everybody started having a good time.

These days Roni has become something of a Nashville fixture, playing occasional formal gigs in town; she is informally called on to entertain when she happens to be in the bars and nightclubs. The resurgence of interest in roots music has led to an increasing number of out-of-town appearances. Her performance skills are as finely tuned as ever. The banjo playing is still extraordinary—marked by speed, drive, and intensity. When she launches into "Lonesome Road Blues," "Foggy Mountain Breakdown," "Cripple Creek," or "Rocky Top," the music is electrifying. Her singing is equally effective. Her voice has an almost bell-like clarity,

A recent photograph of Roni
taken for a show at the
Nashville Nightlife.

but there are undertones suggesting dimensions of vulnerability and resilience. And her onstage comic patter—a combination of down-home set
pieces and sophisticated ad-libs—still delights her audiences with its off-
beat wackiness. The total package still elicits standing ovations.

For those who seek symbolism in Roni Stoneman's life, the incident
at Constitution Hall is a good place to start. The intelligence, the spunk,
the interest in people, the unpredictability, the persistence, the curiosity
about life and impulsive willingness to fling herself into it—those qualities that led her to attach herself to Grandpa Jones and to try the hot dog
and mustard—are essential qualities of her personality. They are the same
qualities that also led her to join in the Russian roulette, to work at practicing the banjo, and to be curious about the women around her and
thus create Ida Lee.

Moreover, the strong attention to other people that is evident in the
vivid way she remembers the details of the Constitution Hall contest reflects what is perhaps her most striking personality trait, her spontane-
ous warmth toward others. It is unclear where this warmth comes
from—from the early experience of performing in a band that always con-
centrated on pleasing audiences, from having a compassionate mother
who lived her Christianity, from growing up in a large family and thus
never having enough attention as a child, from her closeness to her own

children, from a lack of love in adult relationships that led to a feeding off the love of audiences, or, almost certainly, from a combination of all of these factors. At any rate, this warmth, which often involves an uncritical acceptance of people, has had a strange mix of good and bad effects. It produced a difficult group of husbands, men who were not good partners for her, but it also produced five devoted children, a performer who charms by radiating love and humanity onstage, and a woman who goes out of her way to help others offstage. For three years, Roni was the chairperson of Tennessee's Association of Retarded Children and Young Adults, giving many performances for those whom she describes as "special." At festivals and shows, after entertaining, she actively seeks out people who she feels need extra encouragement. She'll hug a "special" woman who clapped inappropriately during the show, sing with a child who has a speech impediment, and spend extra time talking with a young wife who she suspects is being abused.

Roni Stoneman's life, though not easy, has had the richness of a juicy hot dog and a decidedly mustardy tang. Her success as a performer seems to be a product of her ability to communicate fully and directly the kind of person she is and to imply that her listeners share her high-energy, exuberant love of life. She's called the "First Lady of Banjo," but in the eyes of many of her devoted fans, she also has a strong claim to the title "First Lady of Country Entertainment."

Notes

1. For more on the family, see Ivan M. Tribe's excellent *The Stonemans: An Appalachian Family and the Music That Shaped Their Lives* (Urbana and Chicago: University of Illinois Press, 1993). Wayne W. Daniel's stellar "The Serious Side of Roni Stoneman," *Bluegrass Unlimited* 24 (June 1990) also focuses specifically on Roni.

2. The number of children varied, depending on how many of the older children were living at home.

3. Years later, of course, Grandpa Jones would become Roni's good friend and colleague on *Hee Haw*.

4. The reading paid off. In 1956, Pop Stoneman won $20,000 on a quiz show called "The Big Surprise" by answering questions about geography.

5. This occurred on national television. Apparently the talk show host said to Jethro, "Well, you must be the best mandolin player in the country." "No," Jethro said. "The best mandolin player is a woman, Donna Stoneman." Donna is uncomfortable with this praise, particularly when it's used to advertise or introduce her, in effect to brag about her. She is uncomfortable not only because such singling out goes against her strong evangelical Christian beliefs, but also on

professional grounds: she feels that such opinions are ephemeral, that on another occasion Jethro probably would have named someone else, and that at any rate, "There's nobody greater than everybody. Everybody has their own style." (Telephone interview, 18 September 2002.)

6. In 1956 the Blue Grass Champs, which then consisted of Jimmy Case, Scott, Jimmy Stoneman, Donna, and Porter Church, won on the "Arthur Godfrey Talent Scouts" show. Case left the group in 1958 to start his own band. The siblings Roni was closest to, after Scott, were Blue Grass Champs Jimmy and Donna. Of Jimmy, she says, "He would slap that bass. Everybody in the bluegrass world tried to mock Jimmy on that." Of Donna she says, "She is great. She is the true-blue most professional female or male, other than Scott, that I ever saw."

7. Scott's death from alcoholism in 1973 at the age of forty-one was a tragic loss for the family and for all lovers of fiddle music. Roni is currently overseeing production of a CD of his work.

8. Hall practically had to drag her over to meet Sam Lovullo, the producer of *Hee Haw,* at a big reception. That introduction facilitated her subsequent audition. (Hall also insisted that she take extra food home from the reception.)

9. It is not clear if Clark instigated or was even cognizant of the reasons for Roni's punishment. The whole episode seems something of a mystery.

10. In late May 2002, in Nashville, Roni and I ran into a former soundman for the show. "We were like a family," he said nostalgically.

GETTING THE WORD OUT

THE COUNTRY OF BRONWEN WALLACE AND EMMYLOU HARRIS

Gloria Nixon-John

First off, let me admit that I am not a country music aficionado. My early exposure to country music was limited to songs that my Italian father played on his mandolin, songs that he learned from friends he made while working in the coalmines of West Virginia in the early 1930s. (My father's renditions of "You Are My Sunshine" or "Your Cheatin' Heart" in his thick Italian accent indeed constituted a genre unto itself.) The only other country songs I heard while growing up were the songs that made their way onto the pop charts. It was the poetry of Bronwen Wallace that really led me to country music, and specifically to the work of Emmylou Harris.

In 1993 I walked into a small bookstore in Windsor, Ontario, where I found three collections of poetry by the Canadian poet Bronwen Wallace. The name caught my attention because Professor Anita Skeen at Michigan State University had suggested I read Wallace. The way she put it was, "I think Wallace has a voice that would mean something special to you." She was certainly correct about that. I remember sitting on the floor of that bookstore for hours that day, reading those poems as if my life depended on it. I read until the concerned shop owner asked me if I wanted to purchase the collections. So I bought *Signs of the Former Tenant* (1983), *Common Magic* (1985), and *The Stubborn Particulars of Grace* (1987). I also ordered Wallace's other collections, *Marrying Into the Family* (1980) and *Keep That Candle Burning Bright & Other Poems: Poems for Emmylou Harris* (1991, published posthumously).

It was later, after I had read the poems over several times, that I began to understand why I was so drawn to the poetry. It was as if I had finally found a poetic territory in which I could place the life and values of my working-class parents, a voice that included the voice of my mother. I had certainly not heard their voices and concerns in the poetry I had studied in high school or even college. And most of the poets I had studied were somehow expressing experiences and territories so foreign to my own experience that they were always the poetry of "the other," other century, other class, other geography, other life experiences, and usually other gender. What struck me first was that stylistically Wallace's poems were comfortable to read, as comfortable as my favorite pair of jeans, yet the lines also clearly carried the ethereal sense one gets while reading good poetry. And while I noticed that the lines and images were carefully crafted and unique, they were also filled with the structures and rhythms of working-class speech, and they told working-class stories, particularly the stories of women in the way that women tell their stories. Perhaps the connection I immediately felt to Wallace and to Harris is the result of the shared history we have. If one were to examine Wallace's life, Harris's life and my own life for some common thread, one would find that while education or circumstance has plunked us each down squarely into the middle class, our concerns, values, and sense of justice are still very clearly rooted in the struggles of the working class and that each of us has faced struggles common to women of the working class. Stylistically, Wallace and Harris have both worked hard to avoid any movement forward that involves forsaking the past. They both help us guard against forgetting the struggles of the working class, and they are both careful not to render the ordinary experiences and style of expressing these experiences invisible or, worse yet, obsolete.

The artistic efforts of both Wallace and Harris seem to be that of resistance. Both resists limiting themselves to their comfortable middle-class venue, and both resist the pressure of joining the trends of the larger, more validated artistic community. Both are true to their roots, and both illuminate those roots. Both have become an important platform for the concerns of women, and the style in which they express those concerns are rooted in authentic means of expression.

In Wallace's dedication in *Keep That Candle Burning Bright & Other Poems: Poems for Emmylou Harris,* she writes: "These poems are for Emmylou Harris, sparked by a song called 'Burn That Candle' which Winfield Scott wrote and [Harris] sings on an album called 'Quarter Moon

Bronwen Wallace.

in a Ten Cent Town' . . . [These poems] are homely like that and corny and clicked. . . . They burn from what is strong in me, as each of us, in our best moments, tries to love the noisy, untidy selves we've lost out there somewhere" (9–10).

When we look at the life of Bronwen Wallace, it is clear that her life choices and her artistic choices reflect her deep concerns for the plight of the working class, particularly working-class women. Her childhood experiences on her family's farm in rural Ontario kept her close to the land, where she gained an appreciation for the ways in which we are all tied to the land. And in the 1970s Wallace traveled to Windsor, where she became active in the labor movement. While there she helped to organize the Labor Center Organization—a group of some thirty people who infiltrated the factory to report about conditions to the Labor Commission (U.I.C.). Later, in Kingston, Ontario, Wallace helped to organize and run a shelter for abused women and children. These experiences helped to make her more aware of the particular concerns of working-class women, to notice the structures and rhythms of their discourse, and to use these concerns, structures, and rhythms in her poetry.

According to Bufwack and Oermann, Emmylou's choices led her to her own struggles as a working-class woman. The local music industry took little notice of Harris in the 1970s. Her marriage to Tom Slocum disintegrated, so as a single mother she tried to earn a living as a waitress with the help of food stamps and other governmental programs. These struggles led her to the need for consciousness-raising about women's issues (Bufwack and Oermann, 424). At this point, under the influence of her recent life experiences as well as of Gram Parsons, Emmylou made her move from folk to country. And if you listen to "Pieces of the Sky," you will hear Harris enter squarely into the mind and heart of the working class. As Harris put it, "There is the pulse of the people and what they want. I trust the people" (Bufwack and Oermann, 426).

In the winter of 1991, *The Open Letter—A Canadian Journal of Writing and Theory* dedicated a whole issue to the memory of Bronwen Wallace. In the introduction written by Susan Rudy Dorscht and Eric Savoy, we are informed that the prominent members of the contemporary poetry scene in Canada spoke highly of Wallace, but we are told that Gary Geddes "had to argue with little support from other academics or writers, for the inclusion of Bronwen Wallace in *15 Canadian Poets,* 1988" (Geddes, quoted in *Open Letter,* 5). Many of the articles in this issue of *The Open Letter* discuss why Wallace cannot be pigeonholed into any particular trend in contemporary poetry. Geddes also tells us that Wallace was "skeptical about recent developments in critical inquiry," but nonetheless the academics were intrigued by the "affinities between her innovative poetics and the tenets of feminist and post structural theories" (Geddes, quoted in *Open Letter,* 6).

And this situation is not unlike the situation Harris finds herself in. Harris has always been skeptical about the direction of country music. In the 1970s she became an uncompromising traditionalist. While her songs often deal with contemporary scenarios, she continues to remind us of her deep appreciation and understanding of the roots of that music.

In the introduction to *Feminine Endings: Music, Gender, and Sexuality,* Susan McClary tells us, "Like any social discourse, music is meaningful precisely in as far as at least some people believe that it is an act in accordance with that belief. Meaning is not inherent in music, but neither is it in language. Both are activists that are kept afloat only because communities of people invest in them, agree collectively that their signs serve as valid currency." Furthermore, she tells us, "Most members of a

Emmylou Harris. Courtesy of Vector Management. Photo by Michael Wilson.

given social group succeed in internalizing the norms of the chosen music and are quite sophisticated in their ability to respond appropriately" (McClary, 21). Clearly both Wallace and Harris have decided to deal in this " valid currency."

When Bronwen Wallace made clear her affection for country music, she was also making clear her affiliation with a particular social group, gender, and class. Because she was clearly "of the academy" and moving in literary circles, this was a telling move. R.W. Hodge says that country music signals the psychological and entertainment needs of a primarily "blue collar working class audience" (Hodge in Seeger and Reiser, 353). Further, Charles Gritzner adds: "It is this class of Americans which has given birth to the art form (country music), established its commercial popularity, and continues to derive the greatest satisfaction from its 'down to earth' mode of communication" (Gritzner, 857). In addition, "mundane themes result from the fact that the modern world is sadly lacking in proletarian heroes" (Landy, 68). Clearly, country music has often been cited as the folk music of the working class. It is a product of this class and a form of reality-based communication. It is the literature of this class set to music, a kind of subversive way to get the word out about the lived reality of an entire class. It does so because it provides a very reveal-ing self-portrait of the blue-collar working class, and the voice of that class is often female. What is even more significant to mention here is the fact that most country performers have lived the life of which they speak in their "country narratives." That is, "most performers, it would appear, have 'paid their dues.' With but a few exceptions, the majority of tradi-tional artists either write their own material, or adopt material authored by others within their relatively small, closely knit, professional commu-nity. . . . This appears to be an extremely important link in the folk chain; the message emanates from within the tradition itself" (Gritzner, 859). But it is even more than all this. The fact that country music has a female musical tradition is of importance to our connection with Wallace and to the social and political waves she was making when she chose the work of Harris as the focus inspiration for her last collection:

> We find women's voices ringing loudly in our folk culture. There was a female musical tradition in America long before the advent of entertain-ment industries. Women's activities as collectors of songs and as singers reflected their central family role as provider and mother. As music, work and leisure intermingled, women also had an important community role as bearers of tradition. And because women were so central as teachers, and keepers [of country music], a distinct female point of view was passed through the generations. (Bufwack and Oermann, x)

When Kitty Wells and Patsy Cline became extremely popular in the 1950s and 1960s, they opened a post–World War II door. At this time, men were writing sagas and songs about their travels and women were writing about a "bigger" world too, a world of cheatin', alcohol, abuse, and divorce (Oermann, 315).

In the 1970s, most male country singers were still writing about mothers in the home, rambling men, prison, hard work, disappointed love, and traditional religion. Similar to what was happening in poetry in the 1960s and 1970s, there was an elitist attitude toward country music while there was also a push in the university to study country music.

It is obvious that saga and narrative are both a part of the country music tradition, from "The Wreck of the Old 97" to the 1960s "The Ballad of Patty Hearst," both recorded by Red River Dave McEnery.

When Bob Dylan walked onto the stage with an electric guitar, many in the folk community felt very betrayed. He did not reaffirm what his followers had expected. Therefore, his statement was a political one (McClary, 27). He created a rupture of sorts. His followers also responded politically. He was believed to have made a mistake, believed to have breached the expectations of some social groups, the groups in which the established community placed him. Wallace did the same with her style and focus in poetry as well, and while she was writing in a "high art form," her public affection for country music was a symbol of that "breach." She was also pointing to the nature of her decisions with regard to the style her poetry took.

When Bronwen Wallace wrote the poems in her collection *Keep That Candle Burning Bright & Other Poems* prior to her death in 1989 and dedicated the collection to Emmylou Harris, her move was intentionally political. She said that she hoped the poems conveyed the voice of the ordinary, as the songs of Harris did, with their dropped g's; she also hoped the poems caught the pedal-steel sounds of that music and the spaces between longing and what is. Poet and critic Erin Claire Moure believes that the poems in this, Wallace's last collection, are "resisting the urge to compress further into 'the word.' Resisting at the same time the urge to expand the connection between individuals into 'characters' . . . a melody linked her to the most ordinary" (Moure, 40). This resistance, of course, is an expression of Wallace's insistence on the reality of her writing, a need to keep the political function clear and pure in that poetry. It denies the spin the capitalist, patriarchs, or the academy would put on it.

And "just as women have repeatedly refused to split their lives, to separate hand and heart, private and public, feeling and action in their struggles, so it is with their songs. . . . A political song doesn't have to be explicitly militant to be a song of resistance" (Henderson and Armstrong, 12). Wallace knew that, and Emmylou Harris knows that as well. That Wallace saw the need to affiliate herself with this musical form and more specifically with Harris, is significant, to say the least. In her "Songbirds and Hurtin' Songs," Wallace writes:

> Of course, when I'm listening to Emmylou Harris
> I'm listening to a whole lot of other people at the
> same time, like Gram Parsons, Rodney Crowell,
> Kitty Wells, Chuck Berry, Merle Haggard,
> Dolly Parton, and at least two busloads of
> church choirs. All that proves is that nobody
> sings alone, though it's equally true that nobody,
> not even Emmylou Harris, will ever sing
> "Sweet Dream of You" the way Patsy Cline
> did and that Jesse Winchester's rendition of
> "Songbird" can't hold a candle to Emmylou's.

> This is what I mean when I say that all lives
> weave that way, in and out, between all that we
> share and all that we don't, manners and mystery.
> History and the moment I get called on, as you do,
> to be nobody but me.
> (*Keep That Candle Burning Bright,* 17)

If we look at music history/theory (classical or otherwise) more closely, there are obvious differences between what are considered to be masculine and feminine narratives in most musical traditions. Not just in style but in placement as well. Of course the masculine narratives and characters are portrayed as active and are principal to the work. The feminine is contained, just like an easy obstacle.[1] This is not the case in country music. While this realm is thought to be geographically limited, the voice, the protagonist, and "the diva" are clearly female. Its history is female as well. This is strange when one considers that the territory south of the Mason-Dixon line has been, on the surface, slower to embrace feminism, slower to replace the skirt with trousers. (Did they have to sing longer and harder to be heard? Did they have to be more plaintive?) The rupture here comes from within, within one woman's story, one woman's family, one woman's town, and it is found where you least expected it. Wallace would say:

> I say there's nothing like country
> For a hurtin' song, something to do with steel strings,
> I think, and the way a country voice isn't afraid to let
> You hear the places where it breaks . . .[2]
> (*Keep That Candle Burning Bright,* 17)

Like Wallace's poetry, country music is direct, honest, and close to home. In a November 1996 interview that I conducted with Canadian poet Carolyn Smart, a close friend of Wallace's, she told me that Wallace was concerned that the debate about narrative and narrative structure might move those who create literature toward an established status quo and that for the most part this would erase women's voices again, particularly the voices of working women. Perhaps Wallace turned to country music for an example of where working-class reality was. I think Wallace knew that country music would not forsake this narrative bent.

According to a September 11, 2000, article in *Newsweek,* what makes Harris's solo album "Red Dirt Girl" so powerful is "the pairing of Emmylou's already emotive voice with her own heartfelt and poignant lyrics. The title track is her lovingly sad tale about the downward spiral of a childhood

Bronwen Wallace (right) and Canadian poet Carolyn Smart (left).

friend ('One thing they don't tell you 'bout the blues when you got 'em, you keep on fallin' 'cause there ain't no bottom'), while 'Bang the Drum Slowly' is an exploration of the void created by her father's death. Like any good country song, her subjects are derived from hardship and pain, but Harris's voice has a mystical quality, turning torment into dreamy escapism and hard-won redemption" (78).

Aware of this mystical quality, Wallace breaks open the more ordinary tropes of Harris's song "White Shoes," telling us that it is, in fact, a religious parable, that the ordinary is spiritual, and that it can take us somewhere. That is, the ordinary transforms us in extraordinary ways:

> I know I'll feel better, when I slide down into
> the leather sings Emmylou, when she sings "White Shoes,"
> a song in which she wakes up from a dream and
> sees them in a magazine and goes out to get them
> and wears them out on the town that night and
> meets The Guy. A song that I now understand to
> be a religious parable, just like "Wheels" or any

of those other songs she sings about truckers,
heading home.
(*Keep That Candle Burning Bright,* 14)

And these "religious parables" sung by Harris (or written by Wallace) are about the working class or the artifacts of this class, about a tow-truck driver, billboards, truck stops, T-shirts, bourbon, or good corn whiskey. Or they are about the laundromat and folding underwear, and Jesus can appear matter-of-factly rolling a cigarette in the old familiar dirt and sky (*Keep That Candle Burning Bright,* 34).

There is also a hopeful quality in both Wallace and Harris and a pride about what the working class can do, as well as a sorrow about what the women in particular must do to survive, and how it is that they are still held down by a structure that places man and machine above them. The folk wisdom of grandmother's grey sampler that appears in Wallace's "The Kingdom of the Father" would be at home in an Emmylou Harris song. The old photographs, the bad times Grandma and Grandpa Wagar had in 1927, the mending, the recipes, the brown hay, all possibilities grist for Harris—or for Wallace. There is most clearly, however, more to this connection then meets the ear. Just as Wallace was asking the question, "What is poetry?" with her work in the early 1980s, so music historians and popular culture theorists have been asking, "What is country music?" This new look at country music history and its roots beyond Nashville, beyond contemporary hit records, and beyond male superstars was an "attempt to place music in its social context and to explain why songs happen to do what they do. And [it was] an attempt to preserve and appreciate the music of the disenfranchised, the overlooked, and the ignored. Most important, this look is a document of women's lives . . . the backbone and lifeblood of America" (Bufwack and Oermann, ix). When we take the time to look at the story of women in country music, we have a look at the lives of the majority of American women. More specifically, we can look to country music of this time as a kind of music that gives us information and a story about the working-class and a rich, often matriarchal tradition:

> It stands as one of the only documents of working-class women's
> thoughts created by working class women for working-class women. . . . It
> describes poverty, hardship, economic exploitation, sexual subjugation,
> and limited opportunity. Sometimes it is self-defeating and reactionary,
> painful and despairing. But it also contains outspoken protest and joyful

rebellion, shouts of exaltation and bugle calls of freedom. There is human victory as well as sadness here, victory as well as heartache. The history of country music reveals a rich vein of positive images, self-assertive lyrics, and strong female performers. . . . There was a female tradition in America long before the advent of the entertainment industry. (Bufwack and Oermann, xi)

The connection here is obvious but still exciting to contemplate. The working of patriarchy evident in this music—long before the advent of entertainment as an *industry*—is well documented. That this form of music is dependent on the stories in the ordinary style of discourse is important to our connection between Wallace and Harris or Wallace and country music. What is also clear in the work of Bufwack and Oermann is that country music was the *voice of alienation and loss of community in industrial mass society*. Richard Peterson also tells us: "Among the recurrent elements of country songs is the strong sense of the narrative. For this reason, country music has often been called a storytellers' medium" (Peterson, 2).

What is also true is that the chord structures are also kept relatively simple in country music. George Hay of the Grand Ole Opry used to tell his musicians before they came in: "Keep it close to the ground tonight boys" (Hay, 12). Also, the penchant for stories in country music is not as prevalent in other forms of contemporary music. In jazz, the story is de-emphasized. Bluegrass, which evolved out of country, has more complex musical structures. Rock tends to focus more on a particular moment. Rap is a commentary that really features the artist rather than the story (Peterson, 2–3).

What is clear, particularly if we look at 1980, for example, is that men were still writing hell-raising redneck songs and women were exploring human relationships. Country music was and still is addressed to an adult working-class audience from both rural and urban backgrounds (Peterson, 8). Peterson believes that country music speaks mostly for the working-class but does so in terms that do *little* to bolster the appeal of Marxist ideology because country music represents a part of the continuing cultural heritage of the field hand and the factory worker—both of whom are linked to the past. This, it is clear, was the appeal of country music to Harris and Wallace. In "Bellyful of Bluebird Wine," Wallace places Emmylou into a setting:

> the table is covered with arborite . . . smeared with cigarette ashes,
> chip crumbs, squashy bits of pickled egg. The band is
> playing "The Last Cheater's Waltz," someone's done

you wrong, the bottle's let you down and there's
nothing but Sunday between you and the rest of the
week . . .
(*Keep That Candle Burning Bright,* 29)

It's also interesting that when we look at postwar music by men,
women are in part blamed for most of their problems. However, women
answered this charge loud and clear. One of those women is Emmylou
Harris. Harris, of course, was following the likes of Linda Hargrove and
Dolly Parton when she sang "Making Believe" (1977), and women like
Hargrove, Parton, and Harris moved country music into the mainstream.
Music that before was considered "hillbilly" suddenly became "folk" and
then "country-rock." Like Wallace's poems, these women moved country
into a bigger arena.

But why did Wallace focus on Emmylou Harris in her last collection
Keep That Candle Burning Bright & Other Poems? Why not some other
country diva? This was a nagging question until I found out more about
Harris's life.

Harris was not a coal miner's daughter or a country waif. She was a
middle-class music enthusiast who found purpose and meaning in country
music. Born in 1947 to a middle-class family in Birmingham, Alabama,
she moved frequently because her father was in the Marine Corps. Like
Wallace, she left college, in her case to pursue her music. She went from
small club to small club in New York City, but the music industry took
little notice of her. In an article published in *Nashville Magazine* Harris
says about her life: "My life, I suppose, has been a feminist one. I've dealt
with problems that the movement dealt with. . . . Like in my early days I
was a working single mother and found that two girls, each with a child,
couldn't share a house and each get food stamps at the same address.
There needed to be and still needs to be a lot of consciousness raising"
(quoted in McLaurin, 9).

The review Harris received in 1975 for her rendition of the classic "If
I Could Only Win Your Love" calls this single "a splash of mountain spring
water on the Pan-Cake-makeup face of Music City" ("Back to Country,"
in Bufwack and Oermann). That the maternal roots of country music
were of concern to Harris is clear. As she said: "I don't see why on the
Country Music Association awards show we can't see people like Kitty
Wells performing. . . . I think country music should take pride in its
roots." Her return to her roots was met with the same skepticism that
Wallace faced with her poetry. Harris said she trusted this form rooted in

the history of country because "I trust the people; I really do. . . . I believe there will always be an audience for pure country music. Uh, even if there isn't I'll still be singing it." And after she won awards in the early 1980s, she brought back some of the oldies—men and women both—like Buck Owens, George Jones, and Patsy Cline. When they expected her to go pop she gave the critics "Blue Kentucky Girl" and this, too, was an enormous success (Harris in Bufwack and Oermann, 426–27). The following Harris quotation is so similar to something Wallace would say that I must share it. When asked why she didn't go pop she said, "You can probably find all I like in even the smallest town. To me, there's just so much . . . in country music" (quoted in Bufwack and Oermann, 427).

In Wallace's 1991 collection, she talks of the death of Gram Parsons. She talks of Harris's voice blooming from death of Parsons. Most telling in this poem is Wallace's description of how Harris's singing affected her:

> Hearing her sing like that, my chest tightens, thick
> with all those voices I cannot name and never
> acknowledge. How I take whole lives in an afternoon,
> sitting around listening, drinking coffee, watching the
> light drift from pine tree to the garden, touching each
> thing it rests on freely, as we, sometimes are able to touch.
> How it was wanting brought me to those poems.
> (*Keep That Candle Burning Bright,* 42–43)

And in "Rhythm and Genes" in the same collection, Wallace writes:

> We all hear—though we may not be conscious of—the beat
> that strums through every human conversation. Rhythmic
> synchrony it's called, our sync sense, which like the other
> five, conducts us through the worlds we make of each
> others stops and starts, digression, turns and leaps of
> thought, hyperbole, lies, warnings, lover's cries—we move
> to music...you could say that the music we use to heal
> ourselves or bury ourselves, send someone off to war or
> marriage is actually composed of tears of adrenaline or
> those gushy swooshes of the heart that push us into each
> Other's arms.
> (*Keep That Candle Burning Bright,* 41–42).

Conclusion

I am listening to Harris as I write this (which is a sort of metaphor for the way this article lopes along, turns and changes direction), and it occurs to me that her songs move along (like the two-step, a slow lope, a train pulling out, a hammer on a nail). There is no disguise in Harris. She is clearly country, not "new country," not ashamed of the nasal voice, surrounded by honky-tonk rifts and slides.

I am looking at the poem "Great Aunt" when it occurs to me that perhaps I should try to sing a Wallace poem. And it is with this thought that the little clefts or spaces in the Wallace poems are so clearly like a deep breath that Harris might take or like the hesitation in the two-step before the dancer moves forward (or backward) again:

> Everyone says she's remarkable
> For 93 her mind so clear . . .
> and again
> Uncle Bill can remember her
> doing up tomatoes more jars
> than he could count as a boy...
> (*Marrying Into the Family*, 13)

When Bronwen Wallace was on her deathbed in 1989, she requested that an Emmylou Harris song be played at her funeral. It was fitting, I think, that Harris's song "Boulder to Birmingham" from her album *Pieces of the Sky* was used to conclude the memorial service. In this most somber, most traditional and formal of occasions, Wallace's last intent was for her mourners to hear the twang of guitars and the long vowels of Harris, joined by voices of a country choir singing a story about love and despair:

> I don't want to hear a love song
> I got on this airplane just to fly
> And I know there's nothing for me
> but all that you can show me
> is a prairie and a sky.
> And I don't want to hear a sad story
> full of heartbreak and desire
> last time I felt like this
> I was in the wilderness and
> the canyon was on fire.
> And I stood on the mountain
> in a meadow watched a bird
> watched a bird . . .

Notes

1. See Teresa DeLauretis, "Desire in Narrative," or, for a more in-depth discussion specific to music, James Webster's "Sonata Farm," *New Grave* 17.

2. Much like the breaks that occur in the capitalistic patriarchal structure.

Works Cited

Bufwack, Mary, and Robert K. Oermann. *Finding Her Voice: The Saga of Women in Country Music.* New York: Crown Publishers, 1993.

DeLauritis, Teresa. "Desire in Narrative," *New Grave,* 17:498.

Geddes, Gary, and Phyllis Bruce, eds. *15 Canadian Poets.* Toronto: Oxford Press, 1970.

Gritzner, C.F. "Country Music: A Reflection of Popular Culture," *Journal of Popular Culture* 11 (1978): 857.

Henderson, Kathie, and Frankie Armstrong. *My Song is My Own.* London: Pluto Press, 1979.

Landy, "Country Music: The Melody of Dislocation." *New South: A History* 26 (Winter 1971): 67.

McClary, Susan. *Feminine Endings: Music, Gender, and Sexuality.* Minneapolis: University of Minneapolis Press, 1991.

McLaurin, Melton A. *You Wrote My Life: Lyrical Themes in Country Music.* Philadelphia: Gordon and Beach, 1992.

Moure, Erin Claire. "Her Voice a Candle: A Review." *Books in Canada* (1989): 40–41.

Oermann, Robert K. "Honky-Tonk Angels: Kitty Wells and Patsy Cline." In *Country: The Music and the Musicians,* edited by Paul Kingsbury. New York: Abbeville Press, 1988.

Peterson, Richard A. *You Wrote My Life: Lyrical Themes in Country Music.* Philadelphia: Gordon and Beach, 1992.

Seeger, Pete, and Bob Reiser. *Carry It On! The Story of America's Working People in Song and Picture.* New York: Simon and Schuster, 1991.

Wallace, Bronwen. *Arguments with the World.* Edited by Joanne Page. Kingston: Querry Press, 1992.

———. *Common Magic.* Toronto: Oberon Press, 1985.

———. *Keep That Candle Burning Bright & Other Poems: Poems for Emmylou Harris.* Toronto: Coach House Press, 1991.

———. *Marrying into the Family.* Canada: Oberon Press, 1980.

———. *Signs of the Former Tenant.* Toronto: Oberon Press, 1983.

———. *The Stubborn Particulars of Grace.* Toronto: McClellan & Stewart Inc., 1987.

Webster, James. "Sonata Farm." *New Grave,* 17:990

ROSE LEE MAPHIS AND WORKING ON BARN DANCE RADIO, 1930–1960

Kristine McCusker

Doris Schetrompf was fifteen years old in 1939 when she appeared for the first time on a barn dance radio program, an urban-based radio genre that featured rural music. She remembered, "Just about every station had their own hillbillies," citing the four such stations in hometown Hagerstown, Maryland, alone. At her first performance, she remembered that the producer asked her, "What are you going to use for your name and I said I don't know. So can't you just see Doris Schetrompf?" The producer named her "Rose of the Mountains" for the rose she wore in her hair, and her theme song played that night was, "Oh Carry Me Back to the Mountains."[1]

Little did Doris Schetrompf, later Rose Lee Maphis, know that that performance would be the start of an almost fifty-year career in which her job evolved from laboring as, first, a Southern mountain girl, then cowgirl and, finally, hillbilly wife. Maphis carved out a long-term, though not spectacular, career because she implicitly recognized a fundamental truth of being a performing woman: as imagery in the country music industry changed, so too would definitions of skill and labor. Indeed, as the genre transformed itself in the mid- to late-1930s from a bastion of Southern images to one that incorporated both the South and West on stage as a means of reinvigorating the nation's self-image during moments of extreme crisis, what it meant to work on a country music stage changed, too.[2]

Historians have yet to examine stage performance systematically as work or assess how stage labor redefines central tenets of labor history, namely the meaning of skill and labor and the evolution of those terms over time. This essay does just that by marrying the literature on cultural production (the creation and sale of characters on stage) with labor history in order to understand the experiences of "girl singers" such as Rose Lee Maphis. To do so, I first describe how and in what ways performance was work, potentially lucrative employment that promised wealth and fame to a select few such as Lula Belle Wiseman and Minnie Pearl. That promise beckoned thousands of women who, like Rose, never amounted to more than opening acts on radio programs or stage shows. Second, I examine the ways Maphis as well as others confronted evolutions in their stage images and the attendant transformations in what it meant to work and be a skilled laborer. While the focus is on Maphis, she serves more as an example of the general experiences of women (and men) in the industry, and the narrative moves between her experiences and those of other performers.

The commercial country music industry emerged when rural Southerners moved to the big city in the 1920s, but its growth as a viable industry able to employ thousands occurred in the early 1930s, with the expansion of radio programming and the addition of sponsors willing to pay performers a living wage.[3] As the Great Depression cut into corporate profits, companies turned to new sources, attempting to find some mechanism to keep sales up. Radio seemed to be the key, or so the National Broadcasting Corporation (NBC) claimed. As companies cut advertising budgets by 25 percent, NBC reported, they increased their radio advertising by 416 percent. While NBC certainly exaggerated, some companies did find that radio helped keep them solvent. Miles Laboratories, for example, discovered it sold more than one million dollars' worth of Alka Seltzer in 1933 after the company advertised it on Chicago WLS's *National Barn Dance.* The rise in profits induced Miles to expand its barn-dance budget from approximately $120,000 in 1933 to $766,000 in 1936, which in turn allowed broadcasters to hire and pay an expanded cast of performers. Most programs did not expand quite so dramatically, but the relatively stable sponsor base did prove a catalyst to a general expansion in barn dance programs, which numbered some 500 by 1939.[4]

Perhaps what enticed companies most, beyond its ability to publicize specific products, was the genre's constructed image of sincerity. Performers sold themselves, the relationships they built with fellow musicians and fans, and the string band music they played as genuine, authentic, and traditional. Broadcasters imagined programs to be as traditional as the Southern mother who crooned to her babes as she wove homespun, a constructed image rooted in the Appalachian mountains that lauded women's preservation of the South's oral culture. These images reassured audiences that modern values, although seemingly responsible for the Great Depression, had not destroyed America's promise since incorruptible mountain women kept the South's oral culture free from the taint of the modern age. That supposed sincerity further reassured consumers that the products advertised on the shows were as genuine as the performers, not an attempt to profit from the crass commercialism that had caused the Great Depression.[5]

Contrary to country music historians' assertions that few women performed on a country music stage in these early years, it was women such as Linda Parker, Lula Belle Wiseman, Patsy Montana, and many others to whom broadcasters turned in order to make the industry's gendered foundation a living reality. After all, the Southern mother (and her Western counterpart, the cowgirl) was tradition embodied, not a commercial construction. Thus not only were women hired to perform, they played a critical role in defining what barn dance work would be. The industry's development included delineating what kinds of work one did, creating a work culture that both supported and undermined a sense of community among performers, and ascribing industry-specific definition of the terms *professional, skill,* and *labor.*[6]

Rose Lee Maphis's background suggests that there were consistent elements in a future "girl singer's" choice of performance work. She grew up in a musical family and listened to barn dance shows such as the *Grand Ole Opry,* eschewing popular fare such as Bing Crosby and Frank Sinatra. "That was not my appeal. I was just listening to any hillbilly music," she recalled. Rose learned to play string band instruments—the harmonica and then the guitar—using music books produced by favorite barn dance performers, for example, an Asher and Little Jimmie Sizemore book. Maphis discovered that she could sing, but found her vocal range limited. "The first song I learned was 'The Royal Telephone.' It was in the key of D. I remember that so well. . . . When I got my first guitar it was too high for me to sing but that's where I had to sing it because that's where the chords were for it." This meant she could fit the genre's standardized vocal range by straining her voice, but she was not a brilliant singer whose skill might push her to stardom.[7]

Once a woman—or, for that matter, a man—decided to work on stage, there were two kinds of performance work. The first kind was as a "wild-catter," typically the first jobs most worked, where hillbilly singers worked for free in exchange for the experience or for advertising a local concert. That experience was crucial because as radio professionalized and managers demanded that performers adhere to a professional ethic, few stations wanted an amateur on their stages. For the many workers on the wildcat circuit, radio work was haphazard and hard; low wages were paid, if any, and performers typically combined radio work with other jobs. Rose Maphis worked as a telephone operator, for example. Other women combined radio work with more traditional labor as well. Judy Perkins, a future performer on the *Renfro Valley Barn Dance,* ran an elevator for eleven dollars a week while working her first job in Findley, Ohio, and future star Kitty Wells ironed shirts for nine dollars a week as she broke into radio.[8]

Wildcatting was notorious for being an arrangement whereby performers were underrewarded. But another element of wildcatting—control over one's career—opened the possibility for a few to be remarkably successful. Cynthia May Carver, a tough and astute businesswoman who billed herself as "Cousin Emmy," was a rare example of a successful wildcatter. On the air, Emmy was everyone's cousin and had "a voice like a locomotive whistle and a heart of gold." Because she was a wildcatter, Emmy was able to control all components of her radio work, including where she performed, what songs she sang, even the kind of candy she sold at personal appearances, making in some cases $300 per week during the Depression. More importantly, wildcatting equaled independence for Emmy, who made contracts with managers and stations only when it suited her. She contracted with *National Barn Dance* and *Renfro Valley Barn Dance* broadcaster John Lair when he offered her profitable work, but avoided other broadcasters whom she felt exploited her. She wrote Lair in 1941 about one broadcaster, saying, "I don't get any brakes [*sic*] from the program directorial can tell he had ruther [*sic*] not have me here. But he can't very well fire me without a reason."[9]

The second kind of work was waged work on large urban stations, which had a substantial, reasonably secure sponsor base. Rose Lee Maphis found radio work in Baltimore after World War II ended. Those stations guaranteed a weekly salary paid by a sponsor and stable work for an extended period of time. Although they could not guarantee that advertisers would sponsor a program indefinitely (mercurial advertisers tended to pull out of programs at a moment's notice), WLS Chicago, for example, set a base pay for all musicians at thirty-five dollars a week in 1930; by 1936, it had risen to sixty dollars. Musicians also supplemented their salaries with "personals," extra concerts they performed regularly. This was a substantial shift from the early days of the country music industry, during which performers made their money primarily from personals, not from appearances on the radio.[10]

Rose does not remember how much money she earned, but according to other sources, salaries seemed to have been higher in part because, at least at Chicago stations, musicians' unions set a base pay and in part because performers bore the brunt of the costs associated with radio work. One had to join the Chicago Musicians' Union, for example, in order to play on the *National Barn Dance,* and artists paid $105 plus monthly dues. No musician could play on the radio without a union card, although singers could. Expensive instruments, managerial fees, and room and board on the road were other expenses. Some could become rich and famous, as in the case of WLS star Lula Belle who earned $200 a week plus more for personals. Jobs like Lula Belle's were examples of radio's promise, but few women reached this upper echelon.[11]

It is difficult to determine whether gender circumscribed salaries because only one broadcaster, John Lair, systematically saved figures. In some cases, the evidence suggests that women could transcend some assumptions concerning women's work and its devaluation in the general society because popularity with listeners, not gender, determined a higher-than-average salary. Moreover, unions seem to have set a standard for musicians that did not differentiate between male and female musicians, although this is impossible to confirm. There were two factors, however, that did affect a woman's ability to earn a significant wage. First, producers hired more men than women. Cast photos of the *National Barn Dance* and the *Grand Ole Opry,* for example, do feature women but they are outnumbered by men. Other shows had more egalitarian hiring practices; in one cast photo, the *Renfro Valley Barn Dance* showcased a nearly equal number of women and men. Second, broadcasters and musicians gendered most string band instruments as masculine. In the world of barn dance radio, men played fiddles, bass, banjo, and later, electric guitar and drums, although an exceptional woman, such as fiddle and banjo player Lily May Ledford, could appear on stage playing those instruments.[12]

For wildcatters or well-paid employees, personals were another common experience for barn dance performers. They "booked out" when not appearing on the air at schools, fairgrounds, or movie theaters, for audiences who heard about them via radio advertisements. Listeners flocked to performances to see their favorite musicians, in many cases to see if the performers were truly the good, honest people listeners had heard on the radio. "I have met some of the Barn Dance gang in person and find them as common and friendly as anybody could be," one listener, George Biggs, reported to *Stand By!*, WLS's fan magazine.[13]

Personals were time-consuming and exhausting because the time spent on the road was usually extensive, so extensive, in fact, that many performers kept tour diaries in order to track where they had been. Performer Jennie Bowman, for example, traveled every day from January to May, and then from August to December in 1931, when she wildcatted for a hillbilly promoter in the northeast. Working conditions were consistently bad because personals demanded monotonous travel, greasy diners, and un–air-conditioned cars, which meant night driving to avoid the summer heat.[14] Maphis remembered the grind of a daily program and personals, saying, "It became hard work like when you did an early morning program, you did an afternoon program and you go out [perform personals] that night and you do a show and you don't get back from that until [the] wee hours of the morning. And then you gotta go do that early morning program again. Now then's when it was work."[15]

Because of barn dance radio's unique contradictions, a continuous pattern of moving typified most careers, and it was the rare performer who stayed at one station for her entire career. Rose Lee Maphis was typical of this pattern of movement, working four radio stations in five years. Listeners wanted exciting new entertainers along with the familiarity of a routine. Broadcasters thus tried to balance listeners' daily exposure to established acts by constantly searching for "fresh" talent. This meant that performers parted ways with a station once an area had been "worked out," or overplayed. A bored listener, after all, would tune into other stations looking for new performers. These contradictions were not the only reasons performers left stations. Disagreements with management also caused performers to leave, especially when the musicians could receive better offers from other stations. The loss of a sponsor could throw still others out of work.

Women left because of management problems, but pregnancy and, to a lesser extent, marriage also caused some to leave, although some, including Rose, married musicians and stayed on stage. For example, one of *Renfro Valley Barn Dance*'s Coon Creek Girls was always pregnant or sick, and other women worked to fill in her space. Former Coon Creek Girl fill-in Betty Callahan said, "I swear everybody in Renfro Valley has been a Coon Creek Girl, I reckon. Even the boys."[17]

However, women could combine radio work with their families with little censure from the audience. Because they represented tradition on stage, being a mother was beneficial to one's career, since marriage and children fulfilled the genre's prophecy. Lula Belle Wiseman thought, for example, that it was the birth of her daughter that caused her to win *Radio Digest*'s much-coveted title "Radio Queen of 1936." Performers' mothering responsibilities thus did not necessarily hamper their career; they could also help it.[18]

Because of the lucrative possibilities of barn dance radio, management exploitation was egregious. Some managers, for example, dangled promises of a well-paying job in front of a performer in order to make her behave. Broadcaster John Lair wrote a colleague about Granny Harper in 1941 that "Granny, the old jitterbug, don't seem to want to come. I'll let her drop off here a little and she'll be anxious later on if we still want her." Management also kept lucrative offers from performers if it was not in the station's best interest. A Hollywood movie studio offered to pay Lula Belle Wiseman $20,000 to star in a film, but management never told her about it. The exploitation was enough for Lula Belle to comment that WLS management was "mean as ratdirt."[19]

A vibrant and powerful work culture muted broadcasters' exploitation, a work culture that included a substantial grapevine. Performers kept their friends informed about management practices, whether it be their respective salaries or a station's financial viability. A performer's popularity with listeners—known as her "drawing" power—was another factor that tempered management exploitation. If a performer was popular, management wanted to retain her services by increasing her salary or promising her perks.[20]

A code of silence formed a core part of that work culture; tradition, after all, could only become absolute if performers behaved in a publicly professional manner and kept silent about offstage antics—particularly with the genre's double standard. Men drank, smoked, and had illicit sex—and management tended to ignore their improprieties. Lula Belle recalled that performing men were "always trying to get around you. You know, young girl, free, trying to get you somewhere in a bed." Rose remembered that marriage "really wasn't all that important. . . . We were a little skeptical" after seeing the amorous behavior of male performers.[21]

While managers tended to turn a blind eye to men's antics, it was a different matter altogether when women drank, smoked, or even hinted at sexual promiscuity. The definitions of tradition, with their intricate ties to female virtue, precipitated this. If women proved to be immoral, the music they preserved could be called corrupt and the authenticity of the programs could be called into question. Thus, when agents wrote broadcasters to sell them on a new performer, women's ability to behave was a critical requirement. Talent agent William Ellsworth, for example, wrote John Lair about one woman, saying, "Christine Campbell may be the gal you want. She never takes a drink or smokes and attends strictly to her own business." Maphis changed her behavior to fit the industry's pristine image of moral motherhood, recalling, "I guess we all smoked but you didn't smoke in public. Didn't want people to see you smoke. It wasn't a very nice thing for a girl to do." She also remembered that she was not a drinker, and when she appeared in public she and other women "would all go together." The double standard ceased to be a problem once Rose Lee married her husband, Joe Maphis. She said, "Because I was married to Joe, I was not a threat."[22]

Finally, there were standards embedded in the industry's work culture for behavior toward fellow performers, especially on stage. Maphis remembered, "On the Old Dominion Barn Dance that's when [I] really learned the thing [being professional]. I really remember about working there whoever is working at the microphone to the audience you supported them with your attention. They had your attention. You didn't jabber, jabber. Talk to whoever you were sitting by or standing by. You reacted to the person at the microphone. . . . You didn't do your number and go sit down."[23] The point of appearing supportive on stage was to impress the audience that the musicians had constructed an old-time community based on faith and support.

To hire talented women such as Rose Maphis, employers turned to industry-specific definitions of skill that were multifaceted, complex, and in constant flux because of the evolution of characters, in particular the addition of Western imagery on stage in the mid- to late 1930s. First, skill meant being a talented instrumentalist who could play and sing string band music. Rose Maphis was an adequate guitar player, but others were truly talented musicians. Cousin Emmy, for example, played fifteen instruments, traditional and otherwise, including the banjo, fiddle, guitar, hand saw, rubber gloves, and "a tune I makes by just slopping against my cheeks with my hands," according to a 1943 interview.[24]

Broadcasters and booking agents also considered a skillful performer one who could become a "hillbilly" or cowgirl singer, as opposed to an opera or "pop" singer who could sing either Bizet's *Carmen* or croon the latest Bing Crosby tune. Skill, in this case, was a woman's ability to act a part and be believable to her audience. Thus, women who were not born in the South or West had to manufacture a background, a drawl (the appropriate singing style), and then be convincing on stage. An agent, for example, wrote one broadcaster about Michigan native Audrey Homberg, who had "an acquired hill-billy dialect and comedy style" and could perform multiple roles, including "do a dance step, and claims to be able to get a lot of laughs clowning. She reads music and has a large library of western, and hill-billy songs." The exceptional skilled worker could perform multiple roles, not all of them musical, but all were roles deemed appropriate for women in the larger society. At a station in Blytheville, Arkansas, for example, Rose Maphis worked not only as a musician, but was the station's secretary as well.[25]

It was not just the addition of new characters that caused evolutions in what it meant to be a skilled worker; evolutions in character also occurred when solo performers joined troupes. During World War II, Maphis, for example, joined with three other women and transformed herself into a cowgirl. "I was always fascinated with a cowboy," she remembered: "I always loved the Western dress. I loved the reading, the Western novels. The cowboy life just fascinated me. . . . It was the fascination of the cowboy in love with the girl and I always like to see the Western movies." The cowgirl captured fan desire for simplicity and plain living with her songs of open ranges, horse rides, and solid, independent folk during the Great Depression, another set of images that would serve to authenticate America.[26]

The women first chose a name, the Saddle Sweethearts. Names, after all, were critical since they identified the act and cued the audience in what to expect from them. Clothing was the next step—in this case, vests with fringe, hats, and cowgirl boots. The final component of the Sweethearts' new act was the addition of a male group that served as stage chaperones—in this case, a group called Bud and the Saddle Pals. "Girl" singers had to worry about "carrying a bad name," as one performer remembered, and used these chaperones to preserve their wholesome image when performing in public venues. At the same time, because their sexuality was a commodity on stage, they provided that critical element for Bud and the Saddle Pals. Indeed, the industry standard was, according to Rose Lee, "you just didn't want a show with just guys."[27]

Critical to making this new package of characters work was rehearsal time. Practice, after all, made a band perfect, or at least, seem natural, unrehearsed, and comfortable with the repertoire and image it had constructed for itself. Called "seasoning an act," rehearsals allowed performers to assess which woman's voice fit a given song, especially how to phrase and pronounce words similarly, and to work a harmonic blend between various voices. Rose remembered, "I think Betty was the one who mainly sang the lead and Mary did the tenor and I did the baritone. We would do a song three different ways. We'd do it with the lead in the middle, with the lead on top and that would put the tenor on the bottom and then also the lead on the bottom and the two above."[28]

Rose faced one more evolution in character when she married her husband, Joe, in 1951; at the same time, barn dance music was evolving into country-and-western music in the 1950s. Rose incorporated her husband into her act, indicated by another name change (now Rose Lee Maphis), and the two evolved into critical characters of this new country-and-western music: the hillbilly couple who embrace plain, simple values. The Maphises made dramatic changes in their repertoire and stage act when they embraced in particular the California Sound, the electrified country-and-western music associated with Southern migrants to California. It was the new music and performance venues that caused the greatest transitions for Rose Lee. She remembered, "Those days [on the East Coast] you didn't work in clubs. . . . You weren't a very good person if you did. . . . It just wasn't respectable." The same restrictions did not exist in California, however, and the Maphises did personals in bars and honky tonks exclusively.[29]

Musical instrumentation evolved with her character, which caused her to learn a new skill, playing the electric guitar. There was now a new beat to the music and the music's electrification gave it a harsher, harder sound. The instrumental changes caused an attendant transformation in their musical repertoire as well. Rose Lee said, "When you worked the clubs that's where the people . . . that's where you had your heartache and that's where you're smoking and you're drinking." Songs that referred to that lifestyle were thus appropriate to these venues, since they spoke directly to the audience's experiences, as in the Maphises' most famous song, "Dim Lights, Thick Smoke (and Loud, Loud Music)." Finally, the audience's behavior changed as well. Instead of family groups that picnicked while performers played, Maphis found that "out there [in California] they're dancing . . . people gettin' up and dancing."[30]

In conclusion, performing women such as Rose Maphis could carve out long-term careers by recognizing that the production of cultural imagery required a skilled labor force. To sustain her career, she understood the fluidity of those images as well as the constant state of flux of the stage. Indeed, it was Rose's ability to evolve from mountain girl to cowgirl to hillbilly wife that allowed her to build a long and substantial career as a "girl singer" on barn dance radio.

Notes

1. Rose Lee Maphis, interview with author, 19 May 1998, hereafter cited as Maphis Interview 1; D.K. Wilgus, "County-Western Music and the Urban Hillbilly," *Journal of American Folklore* 83 (April 1970), 162. Maphis's name changed legally to Rose in the 1950s when she began recording. Maphis is her married name; Maphis Interview 1. Stations such as WJEJ were important to the small towns they served because they helped banish cultural isolation, especially for rural folk. See George O. Carney, "Country Music and the Radio: A Historical Geographic Assessment," *Rocky Mountain Social Studies Journal* 11:2 (April 1974), 19–32, especially 29.

2. The exception to this is Tracy C. Davis, *Actresses as Working Women: Their Social Identity in Victorian Culture* (New York: Routledge, 1991). Historian Patricia Cooper has written an article on women and radio work, but she focused on women's building of radios during the Great Depression. Patricia Cooper, "The Faces of Gender: Sex Segregation and Work Relations at Philco, 1928–1938," in Ava Baron, ed. *Work Engendered: Toward a New History of American Labor* (Ithaca: Cornell University Press, 1991), 320–50.

3. See comments in Bill C. Malone, *Don't Get Above Your Raisin* (Urbana, Ill.: University of Illinois Press, 2002).

4. James N. Gregory, *American Exodus: The Dust Bowl Migration and Okie Culture in California* (New York: Oxford University Press, 1989); Jack Temple Kirby, "The Southern Exodus, 1910–1960," *Journal of Southern History* 49 (November 1983), 28; M. Killian Lewis, *White Southerners* (Amherst: University of Massachusetts Press, 1985), 91–119; Bill C. Malone, *Singing Cowboys and Musical Mountaineers: Southern Culture and the Roots of Country Music* (Athens: The University of Georgia Press, 1993), 114; Jack Temple Kirby, *Rural Worlds Lost: The American South, 1920–1960* (Baton Rouge: Louisiana State University Press, 1987), chapter 8; Chad Berry, *Southern Migrants, Northern Exiles* (Urbana, Ill.: University of Illinois Press, 2000); Susan Smulyan, *Selling Radio: The Commercialization of American Broadcasting, 1920–1934* (Washington, D.C.: Smithsonian Institute Press, 1995), 40; "Radio Advertising," *Broadcast News* 2:4 (25 June 1932), 3; Jack Hurst, "Barn Dance Days," *Chicago Tribune Magazine* (5 August 1984), 8–13, 15, clipping, WLS folder, Country Music Foundation, Nashville, Tenn.; Miles Laboratories' Annual Report, 1934, n.p. Annual Report, 1936, Bayer-Corporate Papers, Elkhart, Ind.

5. Kristine M. McCusker, "Bury Me Beneath the Willow: Linda Parker and Definitions of Tradition on the *National Barn Dance*," *Southern Folklore* 56:3 (1999), 223–44.

6. Margery W. Davies, *A Woman's Place Is at the Typewriter: Office Work and Office Workers, 1870–1939* (Philadelphia: Temple University Press, 1982); Ruther Milkman, *Gender at Work: The Dynamics of Job Segregation by Sex During World War II* (Urbana: University of Illinois Press, 1987); Patricia A. Cooper, *Once a Cigar Maker: Men, Women, and Work Culture in American Cigar Factories, 1900–1919* (Urbana: University of Illinois Press, 1987); Susan Porter Benson, *Counter Cultures: Saleswomen, Manager, and Customers in American Department Stores, 1890–1940* (Urbana: University of Illinois Press, 1986); Dorothy Sue Cobble, *Dish-*

ing It Out: Waitresses and Their Unions in the Twentieth Century (Urbana: University of Illinois Press, 1991); Wendy Gamber, *The Female Economy: The Millinery and Dressmaking Trades, 1860-1930* (Urbana: University of Illinois Press, 1997).

7. Rose Lee Maphis, oral interview with author, 24 March 1999, hereafter cited as Maphis Interview 2.

8. Judy Perkins to Harry Rice, 10 September 1996, Southern Appalachian Collection; Maphis Interview 1; Charles Wolfe, "We Play to Suit Ourselves: The Perry County Music Makers," *Old Time Music* 14 (Autumn 1974); Douglas B. Green, "Kitty Wells: The Queen Still Reigns," *Country Music* 8:9 (June 1980), 41–44; Betty Callahan Baker oral interview with Harry Rice, March 27, 1995, Southern Appalachian Collection. The term "wildcatting" comes from, but does not originate with, Lily May Ledford, unpublished autobiography [ca. mid-1970s], Southern Appalachian Archives and Minnie Pearl to Susan G., published as "In the Good Days (When Times Were Bad)," *Journal of Country Music* 13:3 (1990), 4–6.

9. Maphis Interview 1; "Cousin Emmy," *Time* 42:23 (6 December 1943), 62; Cousin Emmy, Wheeling W.V., to Mr. Lair, August 1937; Cousin Emmy to Mr. Lair, 11 February 1941, Lair Papers; Cousin Emmy Song Book, no publisher listed, probably self-published, 1939; Lair to Freeman Keyes, 21 June 1938; "Rural Radio Round-Up," *Rural Radio* 1:10 (November 1938), 16, Country Music Foundation; "Rural Radio Round-Up," *Rural Radio* 1:8 (September 1938), 14, Country Music Foundation.

10. Salary figures from 1930 are from John Lair to Ernest Hodge, 20 October 1930, Lair Papers; for the fifty dollar per week figure, see Lair to Earl W. Kurtz, 29 December 1949, Lair Papers; Cobb to Lair, 2 November 1943, Lair Papers; Lair to Si and Fanny Otis, 7 February 1940, for Girls of the Golden West, Lair Papers; Russel M. Seeds Company, Inc., invoice for the Girls of the Golden West, 6 March 1941, Lair Papers; Lair to Margaret Lillie, 26 August 1937, Lair Papers; Maphis Interview 2; Ledford, unpublished autobiography.

11. Maphis Interviews 1 and 2; Ledford, unpublished autobiography; Perkins to Rice, 10 September 1996; George C. Biggar, "The WLS National Barn Dance Story: The Early Years," *JEMF* 7:3 (autumn 1971), 105–12; managerial contracts for Linda Parker, Hugh Cross and others in the John Lair Papers. Unions were a part of Chicago radio from at least 1930. See John Lair to Ernest Hodge, 20 October 1930, Lair Papers, in which Lair tells Hodges that "Chicago is a union town." See also Lair to Leonard, 3 April 1941; Lair to Leonard, 16 April 1941; Ricca to Mr. Lair, 18 April 1941; and Lair to Ricca, 16 April 1941, all Lair Papers; Russell M. Seeds Company, invoice to John Lair for Girls of the Golden West for "sixteen appearances @ $50/each=$800.00," Lair Papers; Wayne W. Daniel, "Lulu Belle and Scotty: 'Have I Told You Lately That I Love You?'" *Bluegrass Unlimited* 20:9 (March 1986), 70–76; William E. Lightfoot, "From Radio Queen to Raleigh: Conversations with Lula Belle," *Old Time Country* 6:2 (1989), 4; salary listing, Bayer Corporate Archives.

12. Maphis Interview 2; Daniel, "Lulu Belle and Scotty," 70–76; Lightfoot, "From Radio Queen to Raleigh," 4; salary listing, Bayer Corporate Archives; Photo Collection, Country Music Foundation; Keystone Fence, "Meet the Radio Folks" [ca. early 1940s], Lair Papers; Ledford, unpublished autobiography. For histories

that describe the ways that gender determined salaries, see Davies, *A Woman's Place Is at the Typewriter,* and Milkman, *Gender at Work.*

13. George Biggs, *Stand By!* 3 (7 August 1937), 2; Kristine M. McCusker, "Dear Radio Friend: Listener Mail and the National Barn Dance, 1931–1941," *American Studies* 39: 2 (summer 1998), 184.

14. Maphis Interviews 1 and 2; Charles K. Wolfe, "Up North with the Blue Ridge Ramblers: Jennie Bowman's 1931 Tour Diary," *Journal of Country Music* 6:3 (fall 1975), 136–45; Patsy Montana, "Portraits from the Most Popular Country Show on Air," *Journal of Country Music* 10:3 (1985), 33–48; Emory and Linda Martin Log Book, microfilm copy, Country Music Foundation; Patty Flye Peavey Papers, microfilm copy, Country Music Foundation; Mary A. Bufwack and Robert K. Oermann, *Finding Her Voice: The Saga of Women in Country Music* (New York: Crown, 1993), 272–73; William Ellsworth to Lair, 13 March 1941 and 15 June 1942, both Lair Papers; C.J. "Red" Foley to PTA, Madison, Ind., 20 November 1939, Lair Papers.

15. Maphis Interview 1.

16. Maphis Interview 2; Robert K. Oermann, "Louisiana Lou," *Old Time Music* 34 (summer/autumn 1980), 14–15; Richard A. Peterson, *Creating Country Music: Fabricating Authenticity* (Chicago: University Press of Chicago, 1997), 111.

17. Ledford, unpublished autobiography; Charles E. Arnett to Mr. Lou Wolfson, Overseas Department, USO-Camps Shows, Inc., 15 December 1943, Lair Papers; Virginia Sutton Bray to Harry Rice, 29 September 1994, Southern Appalachian Archives; Baker to Rice.

18. Maphis Interview 2; Midkiff to Rice; Patty Piye Peavey, interview with John Rumble, 27 June 1986, Southern Appalachian Collection; Rosie Ledford Foley, Minnie Ledford, and Lily May Ledford Pennington to C. Faurot, September 1966, Southern Folklife Collection, Manuscripts Department, Wilson Library, The University of North Carolina, Chapel Hill, N.C.; Lightfoot, "From Radio Queen to Raleigh"; Ledford, autobiography; WLS *Family Album* (Chicago: Prairie Farmer Publishing, 1938), 20, Country Music Foundation; Lightfoot, "From Radio Queen to Raleigh."

19. Lair to Glenn Hughes, 2 Febraury 1941, Lair Papers; Lightfoot, "From Radio Queen to Raleigh."

20. Midkiff to Rice; John Lair to Leonard, 3 April 1941; Ricca to Mr. Lair, 18 April 1941, both Lair Papers.

21. Maphis Interviews 1 and 2; John Lair to Shorty Hobbs, 4 June 1942, Lair Papers; Beth Cremer to unknown interviewer, 16 January 1969, Southern Appalachian Collection; Lightfoot, "From Radio Queen to Raleigh," 10.

22. Maphis Interviews 1 and 2; "Women in Country Music," television special, CBS, January 1992; William Ellsworth to Lair, 15 June 1942, Lair Papers. It is unclear what kind of sexual liaisons women had while working as barn dance performers. Rose Maddox, for example, did have affairs with men, but because she worked in California, where the music and performances were less bound to definitions of tradition prevalent in stations east of Mississippi, she did not encounter much opposition. Sarah Cannon also dated fellow performers and went to parties when not on the road. Jonny Whiteside, *Ramblin' Rose: The Life and*

Career of Rose Maddox (Nashville: The Country Music Foundation Press and Vanderbilt University Press, 1997); Sarah Colley Cannon, interview tapes for autobiography, no date, Gand Ole Opry Museum Archives, Gaylord Entertainment, Nashville, Tenn.

23. Maphis Interviews 1 and 2.

24. Ibid.; "Cousin Emmy."

25. William M. Ellsworth to John Lair, 13 February 1941, Lair Papers; Maphis Interview 1.

26. Maphis Interviews 1 and 2; Comber, "Patsy Montana," 10–11; Montana, "Portraits from the Most Popular Country Show on Air," 33–48; Robert K. Oermann and Mary Bufwack, "Patsy Montana and the Development of the Cowgirl Image," *Journal of Country Music* 7:3 (1981), 18–33.

27. Maphis Interview 1; "Women in Country Music."

28. Maphis Interview 1; Minnie Pearl [Sarah Colley Cannon] with Joan Dew, *Minnie Pearl: An Autobiography* (New York: Simon and Schuster, 1980), 156.

29. Maphis Interview 2.

30. Maphis Interview 1.

"RECONSIDER ME"

MARGARET LEWIS WARWICK AND THE LOUISIANA HAYRIDE

Tracey E.W. Laird

No measure of time
Just the cradle then the blues
Just one second thought
And you win or you lose

Never had to give up so much
Never felt so helpless
Can't stand much more
No wonder it's short
From the cradle to the blues
It's a long lonely road to travel and lose. . . .
—"From the Cradle to the Blues," Mira Smith and
    Margaret Lewis, 1959

Hello baby, yes, it's really me.
After all the wrong I've done
I guess you're surprised to see me
Here at your door like a sparrow with a broken wing
Who's come back to beg you, Oh my baby, reconsider me
Oh pleeeeeease reconsider me
I can't make it, not without, oh you can't you see
So if you will let me I will love you eternally
Oh baby, baby, baby,
Reconsider me
—"Reconsider Me," Mira Lewis and Margaret Smith, 1969

Under the egg crates, two women write. In 1959, Margaret Lewis and Mira Smith composed "From the Cradle to the Blues" in Shreveport, Louisiana. Ten years later, in Nashville, the two women wrote "Reconsider Me." There are several different ways that these two songs might be used to tell stories about country music. One story might tell of an invisible drain that sucked talent from Shreveport to Nashville throughout the 1950s. Like many musicians and musical entrepreneurs before them, Lewis and Smith honed their skills in Shreveport and then migrated to the citadel of country music, where success was more likely.

Another story might describe the intersecting careers of two women writing songs from the depth of their experiences in a circumstance—both geographic and temporal—where blacks and whites regularly exchanged music and culture in live performance and over the radio. This story begins with an obscure song released only on the regional Ram (Royal Audio Music) label and culminates in the success of "Reconsider Me" on both the R&B and Country charts. ("Reconsider Me" was a hit for soul singer Johnny Adams in 1969 and for Narvel Felts in 1975.)[1]

Then, as with every tale, there is the unabridged version: it unravels both yarns and stretches them further across time in both directions, forward and back. It starts when *The Louisiana Hayride* was a radio barn dance, often called the "Cradle of the Stars." The success of the show inspired Mira Smith to build her own recording studio, Ram Records; it also drew Margaret Lewis to Shreveport to join the *Hayride* cast and pursue her aspirations as a performer. This story ends when Margaret Lewis returned to Shreveport after a seventeen-year stint as a Nashville songwriter and became chair of a local non-profit organization she founded with her husband, the Foundation for Arts, Music, and Entertainment (FAME). Two decades later, FAME still works to transform the art-deco Municipal Auditorium (from which *Hayride* first broadcast) and its blighted environs into a "historic music village" to commemorate and celebrate Shreveport's place in music history.[2]

Lewis grew up with her ear glued to the wireless and her eyes fixed to a Baptist hymnal in the dusty hinterlands of West Texas. From her early childhood, she soaked up radio sounds ranging from Bob Wills on the heels of the sunrise farm report to Peggy Lee in the evenings on stations out of Lubbock.[3] But KWKH was her doorway east to another world. Its AM signal reached from Shreveport to the dry West Texas farm where Lewis lived. She was nearly six years old when *The Louisiana Hayride* first broadcast on April 3, 1948. It soon became a family tradition for the Lewis family to gather around her grandparents' cabinet radio every week, catching the twangy strains of guitars plucked by Johnnie and Jack and the Tennessee Mountain Boys, featuring the sonorous, plaintive tones of

The cast of the Louisiana Hayride, 1958. Courtesy of Maggie and Alton Warwick.

Kitty Wells. The quality of reception depended on the weather, as the 50,000-watt AM signal bounced up and down like a stratosphere yo-yo to the California coast and beyond.

Along with her parents, grandparents, and three siblings, Lewis anticipated and savored the Saturday night mix of country music performers whose procession across the *Hayride* stage and over the airwaves earned the show its nickname, "Cradle of the Stars": string bands and duets, such as the Bailes Brothers and Johnny and Jack; honky-tonk innovators like Hank Williams, Webb Pierce, and George Jones; golden-throated crooners like Slim Whitman and Jim Reeves; comic or novelty singers such as Cousin Emmy, Cousin Wilbur, and Bill Carlisle; gospel groups like the Four Deacons, the Plainsmen Quartet and the Deep South Quartet; western swing bands like Paul Howard and His Cotton Pickers; bluegrass talent like Ralph and Carter Stanley, Mac Wiseman, Charlie Waller, Charlie Monroe, and Jimmy Martin;[4] spoken word performers like Red Sovine and T. Texas Tyler; Cajun country musicians like Jimmy C. Newman and Rusty and Doug (Kershaw); and performers who pushed the boundaries of country music like the raucous Maddox Brothers & Rose.[5]

Lewis's musical tastes broadened around the same time her family moved in 1952. Stations like KWKH still broadcast farm news and country music in the early morning hours and around noon. In the late morning and early afternoon, they played soap operas and variety programs that originated from the networks. But in the late 1940s and early 1950s—

during the era before format radio—KWKH added afternoon and late-night disc jockey shows of R&B and jive to the daily schedule. *Louisiana Hayride* announcers Ray Bartlett and Frank Page adopted the names "Groovie Boy" and "Gatemouth," respectively, attracting a generation of young listeners, many of whom, like Lewis, were drawn as much to *The Hayride*'s country music broadcasts as they were to the rhythm-and-blues shows.

Lewis formed a band, the Thunderbolts, in 1956. They performed country, R&B, and the style of music that came to be called rockabilly. "When we went to Levelland, then the early rhythm-and-blues had come on to the scene. And we had a little radio station there in Levelland that played that in the evening. . . . [The Thunderbolts] were like rockabilly and early rock-and-roll and early [rhythm-and-]blues and country. So we were kind of formatting just like the radio station. I even liked a lot of the Jo Stafford records . . . and early Peggy Lee, you remember the female singers like that. And especially Ruth Brown and LaVern Baker were real big influences." In Levelland in West Texas, Margaret Lewis and the Thunderbolts were a simulacrum of what was happening all over the South, as the musical and cultural exchange between black and white musicians accelerated, along with the rest of society during the decade after World War II.[6]

The apogee of the cultural dynamic that characterized Lewis's generation was the rock-and-roll moment—that span of five or six years when the long, troubled history of conflict and cultural exchange between whites and blacks in the South culminated in the music of Carl Perkins, Jerry Lee Lewis, Chuck Berry, and Little Richard. The dominant figure in the 1950s rise of youth culture was Elvis Presley, who gained his first widespread national exposure on *The Louisiana Hayride* in 1954. The Elvis juggernaut was, in fact, rock and roll inchoate. Furthermore, Presley's promulgation of rockabilly from the *Louisiana Hayride* stage in Shreveport exposed the critical (and sometimes overlooked) country roots of rock-and-roll. As a hybrid of elements from black and white Southern musical traditions, rockabilly had antecedents that extended to the spirituals and gospel songs of the South's more evangelical denominations, as well as to the music of Leadbelly, the Allen Brothers, Bob Wills, and the Maddox Brothers & Rose.

The story of Elvis most famously represents the same compelling cultural force that brought Margaret Lewis to rehearse with the Thunderbolts in West Texas. On the *Hayride,* Elvis Presley performed country songs like "Blue Moon of Kentucky" by Bill Monroe, "Just Because" by

The Municipal Auditorium in Shreveport, Louisiana, 1929. Courtesy of Maggie and Alton Warwick.

the Shelton Brothers (recorded by them as the Lone Star Cowboys in 1933), and "I'll Never Let You Go (Little Darlin')," a 1941 song by Jimmy Wakely. He also performed rhythm-and-blues songs like "That's All Right, Mama" by Arthur "Big Boy" Crudup, "Mystery Train" by Junior Parker, and "Good Rockin' Tonight" by Wynonnie Harris. Presley even performed "I Don't Care If the Sun Don't Shine" (a pop tune omitted from Disney's *Cinderella*), and the famous Rodgers and Hart song, "Blue Moon."[7]

Presley's music, along with that of Carl Perkins, Jerry Lee Lewis, Bill Haley, Chuck Berry, and Little Richard, flew in the face of the record industry's notions of racially segregated musical categories, first established with the "race" and "hillbilly" catalogs of Southern roots music created in the 1920s. Rock and roll and its country cousin equally undermined the industry's understanding of "popular music," as songs by Haley, Berry, Presley, and Fats Domino topped the popular charts in the mid-1950s.[8] Elvis Presley, the Everly Brothers, Jerry Lee Lewis, Johnny Horton—all white performers who originally performed within the context of country music—between 1956 and 1960 recorded songs that simultaneously scaled the country and western, rhythm-and-blues, and popular music charts.[9] Racial desegregation, which would take painful decades to progress, was significantly occurring with relative speed in the music dubbed rock and roll.

For his eclectic repertoire, distinctive rhythmic sensibility, and increasingly brazen but stunning showmanship, Presley found a receptive audience in Shreveport's Municipal Auditorium and on tour with *Hayride* package shows throughout the area. Presley's music made sense in Shreveport, which had long been a crossroads for a variety of musical styles and cultural impulses. Only in such a place could long-held notions of musical categories be slowly—if not quietly—undermined. Presley's music made sense to Lewis when she saw him perform on one of the *Hayride* touring shows, which were always met with enthusiasm in Texas venues.[10]

For ambitious young Margaret Lewis, hunkered at the radio to hear every song on the weekly barn dance, the *Hayride* was the doorway of promise to a career as a singer/songwriter of national renown. Hank Williams had set a mythical precedent when he joined the cast three months after it began broadcasting, only to blaze to stardom with vaudevillian Emmett Miller's old tune "Lovesick Blues." The radio barn dance had thus been the natural choice of venue for the nineteen-year-old "Hillbilly Cat" and his Blue Moon Boys, especially after being rejected by the Grand Ole Opry in Nashville. Soon after, Elvis blazed his own trail to fame. He departed the *Hayride,* buying out the remaining months of his *Louisiana Hayride* contract for $10,000 in order to record for RCA Records, at about the time Lewis and the Thunderbolts set their sights there.

In 1957, Margaret Lewis and the Thunderbolts won first runner-up in the Johnny Horton Talent Show sponsored by station KDAV in Lubbock, Texas. Horton, the *Louisiana Hayride*'s last big star, sponsored the competitions along with manager Tillman Franks in small cities across Texas. Their prize was a chance to appear on the *Hayride.* Within weeks, Lewis took a Trailways bus with her sister Rose to Shreveport, where she performed Buddy Holly's song "That'll Be the Day" and "some country songs." After returning home, her performance led to several guest appearances whenever the *Hayride* toured nearby. The following year, Lewis moved to Shreveport and joined the *Louisiana Hayride* cast, thereby coming to the attention of Mira Smith, who was bringing the *Hayride*'s most promising young musicians into her Ram Records studio on Lakeshore Drive for jam sessions and recordings.

Smith's musical tastes spanned the entire spectrum of regional sounds. She not only recorded younger Hayride musicians in Shreveport, she scoured north and south Louisiana and east Texas for talented black and white players. Since building her own studio with a Crown tape recorder, a Rok-U-Kut Acetate Disc Cutter in the control room, and

Margaret Lewis and Mira Smith on stage at the Louisiana Hayride, May 21, 1960. Courtesy of Maggie and Alton Warwick.

sound baffles made from egg cartons, Smith had recorded players ranging from rockabillies Roy "Boogie Boy" Perkins and The Lonesome Drifter (Thomas Johnson), rhythm-and-blues stylist TV Slim (Oscar Wills), and swamp-pop rocker Jimmy Bonin.[11] Margaret Lewis signed a Ram contract in 1959 at the age of seventeen, releasing her own tune, "Cheaters Never Win," that same year.

Smith was a songwriter as well as a record producer. Eighteen years her senior, she became a mentor to Lewis; it evolved into a partnership. The two women spent hours experimenting with sounds—Smith's guitar and Lewis's voice, both instruments containing all the impulse and energy wrought by decades of close and constant contact between white and black culture. Within a year of their recording "From the Cradle to the Blues" at the Shreveport studio, the "Cradle of the Stars" broadcast its last show on August 27, 1960.[12] *Hayride* management had struggled for several years with dwindling audiences in the wake of cultural phenomena beyond their control: rock and roll, television, and the hive-like centralization of music industry. In the black hole left after the *Hayride* ended, Shreveport was no longer a viable place for a professional musician to make a full-time living.

A generation of young musicians left Shreveport for the promise of being paid to play in Tennessee and California. Their sensibilities had been nurtured on the ubiquitous country and rhythm-and-blues shows heard on KWKH and in live local venues. They drew on instincts developed in Shreveport's musical milieu, and entered the music business in an era when the studio determined industry success, not the stage. Multi-instrumentalist Jerry Kennedy became a session musician and record producer in Nashville, producing Roger Miller, the Statler Brothers, Reba McEntire and others, while also playing bass on the Roy Orbison standard "Pretty Woman" and dobro on Jeannie C. Riley's crossover hit "Harper Valley P.T.A."[13] Bassist Joe Osborn became an influential session musician in Los Angeles during the 1960s and early 1970s, later in Nashville until 1989, when he retired to north Louisiana; over the years, he recorded with acts as divergent as The Mamas and the Papas, The 5th Dimension, Barbra Streisand, and Hank Williams Jr.[14] Guitarist James Burton first performed in Ricky Nelson's band, then became Elvis Presley's guitarist for the last eight years of his career; meanwhile, he recorded in the studio with Gram Parsons, Joni Mitchell, Emmylou Harris, and John Denver, with whom he also played for seven years.[15] Kennedy, Osborn, Burton, and others had grown up in Shreveport, played the *Hayride* stage, and made their earliest recordings in Mira Smith's studio.

Margaret Lewis and Mira Smith wound up in Nashville at the behest of Shelby Singleton, an old contact from Shreveport who had been A&R Director at Mercury Records and was starting his own publishing and record companies, SSS International and Plantation Records. Lewis and Smith joined his small cadre of songwriters, composing more than one hundred recorded songs, including "Country Girl" and "The Girl Most Likely," recorded by Jeannie C. Riley; "Mountain of Love," recorded by David Houston; "Wedding Cake," recorded by Connie Francis; and others.[16] Tunes like "Reconsider Me" and "Soul Shake" cut across soul and country sensibilities.

After seventeen years as a songwriter, Lewis left Nashville in 1981 and returned to Shreveport to marry. Alton Warwick had helped his cousin Mira build her homemade studio back in the mid-1950s, which was where he met Lewis; the two had always remained in contact. Warwick was an executive at the ARKLA Gas Company when he and Lewis decided to marry. Lewis originally planned to move to Shreveport and retire from the music profession, but the city where she began her career seemed to beckon a new vision. In part, this vision was borne of sorrow over the state of dilapidation that had befallen the historic Municipal Auditorium and the area around it, once known as "St. Paul's Bottoms"; the city council renamed the area "Ledbetter Heights" in 1982 in an effort to honor African-American folksinger Huddie "Leadbelly" Ledbetter and inspire community revitalization.[17]

In the mid-1980s, Lewis became the North Louisiana representative on the board of the newly formed Louisiana Music Commission, whose statewide mission was to promote music industry development.[18] From Lewis's perspective, restoration of the Municipal Auditorium was a vital first step: "It was so sad when I came back to Shreveport after all those years and saw the decline in the music industry here and the blighted state of the building where the *Hayride* began, the Municipal Auditorium. The roof was leaking and it was about to fall in and the city [which owns the building] was seriously talking about tearing it down. . . . When you begin at a place like that, it personally means something to you." The Warwicks had each maintained contacts from their previous occupations that proved helpful, Alton through his political relations work at ARKLA and Margaret through the music industry. At a luncheon with state representatives organized by her husband, Lewis presented her vision of a renovated Municipal as the locus of a Shreveport Historic Music District. They met with city officials, inviting notable figures in the entertainment industry like Joel Katz, the Atlanta-based lawyer and former chairman (currently general counsel) of The Recording Academy (NARAS), to speak about the feasibility of the project. Meanwhile, thanks to the completion of a decades-long lock and dam project by the Army Corps of Engineers, the riverboat gambling industry found a profitable home on Shreveport's Red River, making tourism a feasible industry in the area for the first time. For most of the twentieth century, oil and gas dominated the region's economy. City and state leaders were receptive to the merits of Lewis's vision of a Historic Music District with the Municipal at its center, but neither group was forthcoming with financial support.

Katz, whom Margaret had known from her days as a songwriter, suggested an alternative to the Warwicks. In 1997 they formed a nonprofit organization, FAME, whose goal was to raise funds independently, and then pursue the restoration of the historic district in partnership with the city council. They enlisted the support of local businesspeople, including volunteer assistance from a local architect to draw up preliminary blueprints. They began producing shows to raise funds for the project. "Our first show . . . was a fundraiser celebrating Governor Jimmie Davis's ninety-eighth birthday. . . . When we went to visit Governor Davis in Baton Rouge at his home, I wanted to do something real special for him. So I said, 'Governor, who is your favorite singer? Who would you like more than anybody to be on this show with you?' And he said, 'Well I doubt if he would come but I really like Merle Haggard.'" Through Shelby Singleton, Lewis arranged for the appearance of Haggard, who agreed to honor his long-time fan and raise funds for FAME; in exchange, Lewis arranged a paying gig for Merle Haggard at the local Horseshoe Casino.

Since this initial effort, FAME has produced other shows, including *Hayride* reunions and another birthday party for Davis before his death in 2000. With financial momentum behind them, FAME began acquiring state funds for the Municipal renovation. The organization no longer relies on volunteers; they have hired city planning consultant Hunter Morrison, who for over twenty years steered the revitalization efforts in Cleveland, Ohio, to fully flesh out the formal plan for Shreveport. FAME expanded its search for financial support to the federal level, with Washington lobbying efforts that coincided nicely with an invitation from the Smithsonian Folklife Festival for Margaret Lewis Warwick to bring her Louisiana Hayride Band to perform in Washington, D.C. FAME also hosted a Southern American Music Conference in May 2002, which was intended to expand the effort. The next phase of restoration for the Municipal Auditorium includes the construction of a Southern Music Museum inside the building.

Signs of success are already in place. The street in front of the Municipal now bears the name Elvis Presley Boulevard, and FAME is purchasing bronze statues of Hank Williams and Johnny Cash by sculptor Bill Rains, which will be the first in a series of Southern musical figures to line the street on either side. Rains has been commissioned to create others, including George Jones and Kitty Wells. As momentum continues to build, the Warwicks hope eventually to transform the abandoned nearby car lot they bought in 1994 into a *Hayride*-themed cafe, with live music. Lewis is ready to abdicate her chair of FAME and direct her energies toward more entertainment-oriented development work; to that end, she is searching for a new full-time director of FAME. Her initial moxie redirected, Warwick reflected on what gave her the gumption to pursue her vision: "I guess my tenacity comes from my pioneer heritage because . . . anybody that'll settle West Texas is too stubborn to give up on anything. So I guess that comes from my heritage because to me this is such a natural. It's something that should have been done years and years ago. The value of what Shreveport has is the missing piece of the American music landscape. We're the only city that has this kind of music heritage that has not done something to honor it or re-establish it or in some way do something." The FAME project began with a vision of the Municipal, whose physical structure had fallen into ruin since Hank Williams first yodeled his way through "Lovesick Blues" in the late 1940s, or since a tentative Elvis Presley performed both sides of his new Sun Records release, or even since a hopeful high school–aged Margaret Lewis covered a song by her fellow West Texan rockabilly, Buddy Holly. The catalytic, experimental energy of *The Louisiana Hayride* was suffused in the music performed on its stage, but was also realized in the pursuits of a generation of musicians who cut their teeth there and left to pursue their musical dreams.

In a similar way, FAME's vision has expanded to include the full richness and breadth of Shreveport's music history. The Southern Music Museum plans to honor the exclusively Anglo *Hayride* players alongside the African-American musical legends like Leadbelly, blues guitarist Jesse Thomas, and roots recording mavericks Oscar Woods and Ed Shaffer. The formal plans for the Historic Music Village include renovation of structures like the Star Theater, where Bessie Smith played regularly, and the Calanthean Temple, where swing blared from rooftop gardens. If there was promise and beauty in the energy of the rock-and-roll moment, it was the hint, the dream of community—of a space where blacks and whites come together to heal a troubled history and share the intersections of rich traditions of music and culture.

Margaret Lewis Warwick's vision of the Shreveport Historic Music District would be a memorial to the fertile stream of Southern music that flowed from the head of Texas Avenue down to the Red River; at the same time, if fully realized, it would be a space for new creative energies to build. In essence, Lewis has posed a query on behalf of the city of Shreveport: "Oh please, reconsider me . . . ?" She directs this question to the writers of the story of Southern American roots music who have left places like Shreveport largely on the periphery. Only time will provide an answer. Perhaps white and black civic leaders and citizens will begin to imagine new paradigms of community and new dreams of a shared future, as they revitalize the physical spaces where music first made those relationships seem possible. If reconsidering Shreveport's place in music history accomplishes this, then Lewis's question is well worth asking.

Notes

1. Both versions are available on commercial recordings. See, for example, Johnny Adams, *Reconsider Me: Golden Classics Edition,* Collectables, COL-5741, 1996; and Narvel Felts, *Drift Away: The Very Best of Narvel Felts, 1973-79,* Bear Family Records, BCD 15690, 1996. The original demo of the song, with Margaret Lewis singing lead vocals and Mira Smith on guitar, can be found on a re-release of Ram material. See *Shreveport Stomp,* vol. 1, *Ram Records "Master of the Trail" Series,* Ace, CDCHD 495, 1994. "From the Cradle to the Blues" is included on the follow-up to *Shreveport Stomp*: Margaret Lewis with Grace Tennessee and her Guitar, *Lonesome Bluebird,* vol. 2, *Ram Records "Master of the Trail" Series,* Ace, CDCHD 572, 1994. ("Grace Tennessee" is a pseudonym for Mira Smith.)

2. Margaret Lewis Warwick, telephone interview with the author, 19 September 2002. Tape recording and transcript in author's files. Quotations and biographical information about Lewis are from this interview.

3. KFYO was a 5,000-watt station that broadcast local programming as well as network programming. Under the leadership of "Pappy" Dave Stone, KDAV was an early prototype of format radio, programming exclusively country music from its first broadcast in 1953. Bud Andrews, General Manager of KDAV, telephone conversation, 2 October 2002.

4. Steven R. Tucker, "Louisiana Saturday Night: A History of Louisiana Country Music" (Ph.D. dissertation, Tulane University, 1995), 479. The Louisiana Hayride is placed in a social and cultural context that extends back to Shreveport's founding in 1836 as a port and point of division along the Red River in the author's dissertation, "Shreveport's KWKH: A City and Its Radio Station in the Evolution of Country Music and Rock-and-Roll" (Ph.D. dissertation, University of Michigan, 2000).

5. Tucker, 426, comments on the wide variety of musical styles that appeared on *The Lousisana Hayride*: "Hayride crowds came to expect a rich mixture of gospel music, sentimental or 'heart' songs, pop tunes, contemporary country hits, honky-tonk weepers, bluegrass tunes, comedy and novelty numbers, and folk music, a mixture that reflected the image and reality of Louisiana as a musical melting pot."

6. See W.T. Lhamon Jr., *Deliberate Speed: The Origins of a Cultural Style in the American 1950s* (Washington, D.C.: Smithsonian Institution Press, 1990), for an analysis of the "acceleration" of culture in the postwar era.

7. See Peter Guralnick, *Last Train to Memphis: The Rise of Elvis Presley* (Boston and New York: Little, Brown, and Company, 1994), 132. Elvis Presley, *Sunrise Elvis Presley,* CD 67675-2, RCA, 1999, contains five tracks of acetates recorded from *Louisiana Hayride* broadcasts; they are mainly of historic significance because the audio quality is so poor. Some of this material also appeared on a

recent release, Elvis Presley, *Good Rockin' Tonight: The Complete Louisiana Hayride Archives,* CD MME-72628-2, Music Mill Entertainment, 2000.

8. See Charles Hamm, *Yesterdays: Popular Song in America* (New York: Norton, 1979), 407.

9. Ibid.

10. Frank Page, interview by the author, 23 February 1996, tape recording in author's files. Page was chief announcer for the Hayride throughout most of the 1950s until 1957 when he took over as producer. Page also reflects on the particular fervor of Texas audiences in his spoken narration on Elvis Presley, *Good Rockin' Tonight: The Complete Louisiana Hayride Archives.*

11. Ray Topping, liner notes to *Shreveport Stomp.* These artists can be found on other Ace re-releases produced since the mid-1990s, including Roy Perkins, *Roy "Boogie Boy" Perkins with Bobby Page and the Riff Raffs,* vol. 3; *Ram Records "Master of the Trail" Series,* Ace CDCHD 619, 1995; and *Shreveport High Steppers: Rockabilly and Hillbilly,* Ace CDCHD 818, 2001.

12. Tucker, 516.

13. Jerry Kennedy, interview with the author, 7 March 1996, Nashville, Tenn., tape recording in author's files. For a lively account of Kennedy's early career, including substantial quotations, see John Grissim, *Country Music: White Man's Blues* (New York: Paperback Library, 1970), 27–34.

14. Joe Osborn, interview with the author, 2 August 1999, Shreveport, Louis., tape recording in author's files; also from an advertisement produced by Lakland Basses in Chicago (for the Joe Osborn signature bass) and from the Joe Osborn website.

15. See Steve Fishell, "James Burton: First Call for the Royalty of Rockabilly," Guitar Player 18 (June 1984): 88–101; and Rich Kienzle, "James Burton," in *Great Guitarists: The Most Influential Players in Blues, Country Music, Jazz and Rock* (New York: Facts on File, 1985): 192–97. Colin Escott writes about him in "James Burton: Play It James," in *Tattooed on Their Tongues* (New York: Schirmer, 1996), 163–75.

16. Topping, liner notes, *Lonesome Bluebird.* Ray Topping places Lewis and Smith in Las Vegas when the pair wrote "Mountain of Love" as well as "I Almost Called Your Name," recorded by Margaret Whiting; this would have occurred during a period between Shreveport and Nashville when Lewis sang in Las Vegas clubs and made a handful of recordings.

17. The area was also declared a National Historic District. On 22 October 1994, the Shreveport Regional Arts Council sponsored construction of a $25,000 bronze statue of Leadbelly pointing toward the district. Information about Shreveport's efforts to memorialize the singer can be found in numerous articles in the *Shreveport Times* and in *The Lead Belly Letter,* a quarterly publication devoted to the singer's life and music. See particularly Greg Gornamous and Chester Williams, "Lead Belly Memorialized," *Lead Belly Letter* 3:1/2 (winter/spring 1992), 1, 5; and Sean Killeen, "Shreveport Lauds Lead Belly," *Lead Belly Letter* 4: 4 (fall 1994), 1.

18. The Louisiana Music Commission was founded and directed by musician/businessman Lynn Orso.

HOME TO RENFRO VALLEY

JOHN LAIR AND THE WOMEN
OF THE BARN DANCE

Michael Ann Williams

John Lair's contributions to the development of country music are indisputable. In his role at the Chicago radio station WLS and later with his own *Renfro Valley Barn Dance,* Lair helped define the radio barn dances of the 1930s and 1940s. Lair transcended the aural nature of radio, constructing a mythical hometown not only on air, but also as a physical entity in Rockcastle County, Kentucky. As country music's first auto-tourism site, during its heyday *Renfro Valley* brought in larger live audiences than any other radio barn dance. Although never elected to the Country Music Hall of Fame himself, Lair played an important role in shaping and supporting the early careers of several inductees, including Red Foley, Merle Travis, and Homer and Jethro. However, Lair will perhaps be more remembered for creating the acts of three of the most popular female country performers of the 1930s: Linda Parker, Lulu Belle, and Lily May Ledford.

In accounts of his relationship with Lily May Ledford, a more negative aspect of Lair's legacy emerges. Years after her retirement from *Renfro Valley,* Lily May found a second career on the folk revival circuit. In these years, she expressed her decades of frustration under Lair's management, which she felt actively hindered the development of her career. In accounts by Ledford and others, Lair emerges as a control freak wedded to the almighty dollar, and as an "artificer" deliberately undermining the authentic performances of traditional musicians. As we now re-examine the careers of some of country music's pioneers, how should we view Lair's contribution to the role of women in country music? Was he an early supporter of women performers or did he simply find them an easier mark for manipulation than the male musicians he managed?

In his childhood, and throughout his life, John Lair was always surrounded by women. Lair had only one sibling, his doting older sister Virginia Clyde. In his childhood, Lair strongly attached himself to both his mother and his paternal grandmother. As the only grandson of his paternal grandparents, Lair received plenty of attention from them and his unmarried aunts. Lair's youngest daughter, Barbara, thinks perhaps this family influence shaped Lair's abiding interest in promoting female performers: "I think now there's a connection you might make from his childhood past, his enjoyment of the female companion in his elderly aunts and grandmothers."[1]

Lair's father and paternal grandfather did not approve of fiddle music or dancing, but there were several female ballad singers in his family, including his great-grandmother Matilda Dalton Coffey and his grandmother Ann French Lair. This legacy from his ancient great-grandmother sparked Lair's lifelong hobby, collecting old music manuscripts and sheet music. As he told a classroom of students:

> [She] sang and played a little concertina. And she scared the heck out of me. And I'd just stand rapt and afraid to move and she thought I was so taken with her music, you know. So when she died, she had one thing among her very few treasures, she had one thing she treasured most. She had an old handwritten copy of a song called "The Silk Merchant's Daughter" that her sweetheart had written down for her and gave it to her the night he left there to go down and join Andrew Jackson at the Battle of New Orleans. Well, he never came back, but she always kept that song and she told the folks before she died she wanted me to have it.[2]

During World War I, Lair left Rockcastle County, Kentucky, to serve in the entertainment forces, an experience that left Lair with a passion for theatrics. After returning home, Lair drifted through several careers before landing a job with the Liberty Mutual Insurance Company, which ultimately led him to Chicago. In 1924 he married Virginia Crawford, who had been a student of his during a brief stint teaching high school. Although much more shy than the outgoing Lair, Virginia would play an essential role behind the scenes at *Renfro Valley*. Despite his reputation for thriftiness, Lair was not especially good at accounting. As Barbara Lair Smith recalled: "Mother had a business head on her. Daddy prob-

ably couldn't have carried *Renfro Valley* as long as he did without Mother
. . . . Any profit or any money realized, Daddy put right back into the
business. Mother, pretty much, with her souvenir shop and frugalness or
whatever, put four girls through college and clothed them."[3] Although a
busy—even driven—man, by all accounts Lair found time to be an atten-
tive father to his four daughters. Lair brought his theatrical skills to father-
hood, and some of his daughters' most precious memories seem to be his
efforts to stage special events for them, such as smoking little pipes and
telling stories in the briar patch or cooking potatoes and apples in the
ashes of the fireplace. As Nancy Lair Griffin later recalled, "I think Daddy
always had in mind, even dealing with us, and with everybody, to make
something a memory, to build a memory. That this would be something
you would look back on and remember, and so let's make it special."[4]

Creating memories and enacting the past would become Lair's stock
in trade. Hearing Bradley Kincaid and others on WLS in Chicago, Lair
believed that he knew performers from home who could make it on the
radio. At first, Lair simply did that, bringing Karl Davis and Hartford
Connecticut Taylor up from Kentucky. With Karl and Harty, the Renfro
Valley Boys, and Kentuckian Doc Hopkins, Lair started the Cumberland
Ridge Runners. Soon Lair was looking further afield for musicians than
his home county and he began to concentrate more on theatrical presentation. Lair added fiddler Slim Miller to the act, largely because of Miller's
comical appearance. Lair's final two choices for the Ridge Runners emerged
as the most successful radio performers of the group. While Lair discovered Red Foley in Berea, Kentucky, just up the road from his boyhood
home, Lair took his greatest leap into artifice with his choice for the first
female performer for the Ridge Runners, a redheaded nightclub singer
named Jean Muench. Dressing her in gingham, Lair rechristened her
Linda Parker, the Sunbonnet Girl.

Although their time working together would be brief, John Lair always remained devoted to Linda Parker, or at least the idea of Linda
Parker. Even twenty years later, Lair was still searching for the next Parker
in his young female talent. Despite this devotion, Lair was not above
creating some competition for his female performers. He found some in a
teenage girl who aspired to be the next Linda Parker, even at the height of
Parker's career. As is typical of many of Lair's "discoveries," Lair saw
talent where the station managers could not. Years later Lair recalled of
the young Myrtle Cooper: "She'd been down there to audition three or
four times, trying to sing Linda Parker songs, they wouldn't pay any attention to her. And I heard about her, George Biggar and I talked about it,

I told him I thought I could do something for her. So I had her come down to the house and listened to her. I told her, I said, 'Now you, I can't do anything for you with the straight ballads because I've got Linda doing that.'" Instead Lair encouraged Cooper to study the comic act of vaudevillian Elviry Weaver and to develop a bold and sassy persona to contrast with Parker's sweet and demure one. Lulu Belle, as she was called, quickly developed a loyal fan base, and WLS soon promoted her as "the Radio Queen." Lair later admitted that Lulu Belle's quick rise in popularity caused hard feeling among his other performers: "The rest of my act, oh, they didn't like her at all. They were loyal to Linda, you know, and Lulu Belle just took the show away from her."[5]

Neither Linda Parker nor Lulu Belle stayed under Lair's management for long. Lair originally paired Red Foley with Lulu Belle, who played his girlfriend from back home. However, when Foley married Eva Overstake of the Three Little Maids, Lair matched Lulu Belle with newcomer Scott Wiseman. Lulu Belle and Scotty became partners offstage as well, marrying in December 1934 with Wiseman taking over management of the act. The following year Linda Parker died suddenly from appendicitis at the age of twenty-three. Parker's untimely passing brought a flood of letters to WLS from fans stricken with grief.

Despite his sadness at losing Parker, Lair quickly sought another female act and found it in a young girl "even more real than Lulu Belle." Lily May Ledford first auditioned with her group, the Red River Ramblers, at WLS in 1935. Once again, Lair found talent where the management saw none. Lair ultimately persuaded WLS to let Lily May perform, at the same time convincing her to sign a five-year contract with him as manager, rather than to sign up with the radio station. In 1936 Lily May performed as a solo act and soon gained popularity on WLS. However, by this time, Lair already had plans to jump ship, taking with him his popular performers.

Lily May Ledford, from the Red River Gorge of eastern Kentucky, bore a closer resemblance to the image Lair created for her than had Linda Parker or Lulu Belle in their respective stage personas. Although already a veteran performer, she really did hail from Appalachia, and she had learned her music largely through traditional means. Lily May got to keep her own name and, although she found her stage costume old-fashioned, Linda Parker had worn a cornier costume and Lulu Belle dressed in a far more outrageous outfit. However, possibly as a result of this, Ledford had a much harder time separating herself from her stage persona and, under the scrutiny of big city audiences, she found herself quite sensitive to

Lily May Ledford with Burl Ives. Ledford preferred a far more sophisticated image than the calico outfits Lair insisted she wear on stage. Photo courtesy of Southern Appalachian Archives, Berea College.

hillbilly stereotypes. Having moved to Chicago under the care of Lair, she longed for a more sophisticated image. The photo of Ledford in an issue of WLS's weekly magazine *Stand By,* looking "collegiate in a bright red sweater with a turn-over collar, worn with a gray tweed skirt," represented the image Lily May preferred, rather than the depiction of her as "Lily May, Mountain Gal," in the comic strip sponsored by Pinex Cough Syrup.[6]

Once again Lair encouraged competition among the female performers at WLS, urging Lily May to give Lulu Belle a run for her money. Although far too shy—not to mention in awe—to present much of a challenge, Lily May soon found her own fan base. While Lair continued to search for female performers, increasingly they were seeking him out. Uncharacteristically, there was one female performer who would become a country-music legend that Lair let slip through his fingers. Cynthia May Carver grew up near Glasgow in south central Kentucky. As a young girl, "Cousin

Emmy" toured with the Carver Family, one of the earliest professional hillbilly groups. Carver and the Log Cabin Boys, who performed at WWVA in Wheeling, West Virginia, arranged with Lair to have a music book published.[7] In August 1937, on the eve of his departure from Chicago, Lair wrote Emmy releasing her from any actual or potential agreement: "If you have a deal there that looks good to you go ahead and take it. I haven't done anything for you yet, so don't consider that I have any claim on you. If I had gone ahead and advertised you or started a campaign to boost you in any way I would expect you to go through with me, but since nothing has been done you are not obligated to me in any way, so go ahead with the deal and maybe we can get together some other time."[8]

Several years later, however, Cousin Emmy was still hoping to cut a deal with Lair. Now in Knoxville and unhappy with her treatment at WNOX, she wrote, "Mr. Lair, I will cut you in any way you see fit. Now is our chance to make some money." Lair replied that he could not afford to buy time, but that he could perhaps help with sponsors or a songbook deal.[9] Shortly thereafter, Cousin Emmy reached the height of her fame at KMOX in St. Louis and in 1947 crossed over into the folk world by recording "Kentucky Mountain Ballads" for Alan Lomax.

Another young woman was more successful in her pursuit of a contract with John Lair. In 1937 Ohio farm girl Evelyn Lange, two years younger than Lily May, won a spot on WLS in a talent contest. Lair indicated that he might be interested in working further with her. In August Lange impatiently wrote back to Lair, saying that she and her sister were improving their act and were "still craving a job." She added, "In this last issue of our Standby Magazine we read in the 'Listeners' Mike' article an item suggesting an all-girl program. If you take up this lady's nice idea we would like for you to stop and think about us, and please give us a break if you can."[10] When she found out that Lair had moved on to Cincinnati, she and her mother hopped on a bus to pursue Lair there. Perhaps Lair admired her spunk, or maybe, as Lange later suggested, he simply felt pressed for time and wanted to get rid of her; in any case, Lair suggested that she meet him on a certain date at his sister's home across the river in Covington, Kentucky.[11] Lange's moxie had paid off, and she won a place in Lair's new all-female band, the Coon Creek Girls.

The Coon Creeks combined the same elements of authenticity and artifice that Lair had already mixed in the Cumberland Ridge Runners. Lair always advertised his group as four girls from eastern Kentucky, although in fact that only applied to the Ledford sisters, Lily May and her sister Rosie. While no Coon Creek existed in their native Red River Gorge, there was, in fact, a "Pinch-Em-Tight Holler" near where they grew up, and this became their mythical hometown. Evelyn Lange, soon to be called "Daisy," an Ohio farm girl, had learned her repertoire largely from the radio. The fourth member of the group, mandolinist Esther Koehler, came from Milwaukee. During the outpouring of grief from fans at the death of Linda Parker in 1935, Koehler, a "true W.L.S. Friend," sent in the handwritten lyrics and music of a song, "Silent Singer," which she dedicated to Linda Parker. In the song, Koehler wrote of her hope to meet Parker in heaven one day.[12] The song apparently brought about an encounter less divine, if nonetheless still coveted. Two years later Koehler became "Violet" of the Coon Creek Girls.

Although the energy and spontaneity came from the girls themselves, Lair crafted their image. Although he bestowed on Evelyn and Esther flower names to fit with Lily May and Rosie, he rejected the girls' choice of name, Wildwood Flowers, in favor of the Coon Creek Girls. Lair had already used the place name "Coon Creek" in some of his *Renfro Valley*–themed programs on WLS and, according to Lange, he also wished to signal that the girls played "hillbilly"-styled music. Lair not only controlled the public image of the Coon Creeks, he also kept close watch over their private lives. With such young women, Lair felt an obligation to keep an eye on his charges. In retrospect, Lange later suggested, Lair's paternalism was not unwarranted. As she recalled, "Boss watched us carefully, we were all very young and very dumb."[13] Lair also invented a chaperone of sorts who toured with the group, a mythical aunt from Coon Creek, "A'nt Idy," played by Margaret Lillie.

Not all the performers who thought that Lair could give them a break were young. In January 1937, Margaret Lillie, a veteran vaudevillian who had toured with the Weavers, wrote to Lair that she would like to try radio. "I have a blue's voice also can sing hillbilly songs," she added. Lair, who had seen Lillie's act, responded that he might be able to use her in September or October. In August he wrote to tell her that he was moving on to Cincinnati, adding, "As I told you once before it is doubtful if I can get much money for you in the beginning but am certain that I can build you up in a 'Lum and Abner' type of show to the point where you can command a good price."[14] For Lillie, Lair constructed the persona of A'nt Idy Harper and paired her with his own large baby-faced nephew, Harry Mullins, who played her son, Little Clifford.

Although he had previously used the name "Renfro Valley" in his programming on WLS, Lair's move to Cincinnati allowed him to launch his own barn dance show.

Former vaudevillian Margaret Lillie as A'nt Idy. Photo courtesy of Southern Appalachian Archives, Berea College.

Renfro Valley Barn Dance began its life on superstation WLW, playing to live audiences in Cincinnati and later Dayton, before taking up residence, in 1939, in Rockcastle County, Kentucky. A'nt Idy and Little Clifford, not Lair's all-girl string band, emerged as the first hit act of the new show. Some fans wrote to Lair ahead of time to confirm that Idy would perform. "We will have to drive better than 300 miles so we want to be sure we could see Aunt Ida when we come," wrote a woman from Mattoon, Illinois.[15] A'nt Idy and Little Clifford typically toured with the Coon Creeks—and John Lair worked his performers hard. The exhausted Daisy Lange regarded the White House, where the Coon Creeks gave a legendary performance for the King and Queen of England in 1939, as "just another place to play." Although she found the pay "fairly decent," it didn't go far once they had covered their hotels, costumes, and other expenses. Finally the girls got up the nerve to ask for a raise. According to Lange, Lair gave "such a sad story" about his financial woes that Rosie Ledford offered to give up her salary.[16]

Certainly Lair took advantage of the naïveté of his young performers, but his financial difficulties during this period were not imaginary. Lair had little control over the purse strings of his operation and often pleaded with his partner, Freeman Keyes, for more money for his acts. In June 1938, Keyes, an advertising executive in Chicago who bore the responsibility for lining up sponsors as well as the overall financial management, wrote to Lair, "Now as for the talent situation and money, I am wholeheartedly in agreement with you that we should get money for our talent, and the Lord knows we are trying to get money for it, and are going to get good money for it this fall." Elsewhere in the same letter, Keyes insisted, "I have tried to take the financial end of the worries off your shoulders. I have tried to use my best judgment."[17]

During his two-year sojourn in Ohio, Lair gave his imaginary community a material form; by 1939 his complex at Renfro Valley, in Rockcastle County, Kentucky, was completed. Although Lair eagerly anticipated the move back to Kentucky, not all of his performers felt prepared to make the leap. If Lair had been under the illusion that his female performers would be more tractable, he soon learned otherwise. "Daisy" Lange and "Violet" Koehler left the Coon Creeks to work with the Callahan Brothers in Texas. The tough old veteran Margaret Lillie also balked, insisting on more money and the right to her stage name. Lair wrote to Keyes, "I can't see where we'd gain anything by that. She'd be here about five weeks, then walk out with the name and go back to WLS or WLW for spite. If she really wants to come back and do the right thing I want her and I believe the contract submitted is fair but I can't pay her fifty dollars for all dates and I don't feel like turning the act over to her."[18] Lair already had employed another performer, Ricca Hughes, to "pinch hit" for A'nt Idy, though audiences often complained if they did not get to see the original Idy perform as part of the *Renfro* cast. Lillie did eventually move to Renfro Valley, but the act was never as popular as it had been, and she died a few years after the move.

One of Lair's original partners in the *Renfro* business also jumped ship. Red Foley was no longer the shy, country boy Lair had discovered in Berea. As Lair wrote to Keyes, Red was "fully sold on the big white hat stuff and I don't believe we could tempt him to come down." However, part of the opposition came from Foley's wife. "Eva hit here proclaiming loud and long she'd never have any part of this damn country," Lair added.[19] With a few loyal performers, among them the Ledford sisters, Slim Miller, and his nephew Harry Mullins, Lair found himself forced to rebuild his barn dance with new talent. In constructing his new complex, Lair had something very different to offer his performers than he had in Chicago and Cincinnati. If *Renfro Valley* isolated the performers from the mainstream of the entertainment business, the "valley where time stands still" did offer a stable home life for the performers who wished to stay.

In September 1940, John Lair wrote to Freeman Keyes that he was looking for "new and better talent." He also complained that the Coon Creek Girls "seem to have gone to hell generally as far as their work goes."[20] In rebuilding the act, Lair retained the idea of the Coon Creeks, but the group tended to include a rotating roster of performers. The Ledford sisters, Lily May and Rosie, plus younger sister Minnie ("Black Eyed Susie") usually formed the core of the group, but at various times any number of other women joined the Coon Creeks whenever one or another of the Ledfords took time off for family responsibilities. The first *Keepsake* published at Renfro Valley pictured Lily May with the three Amburgey Sisters as the Coon Creek Girls. Lair seldom noted the changing line-up, although he always touted the Coon Creek's famous performance at the White House. Throughout the 1940s and 1950s, many of the young women who performed at *Renfro*—the comedic acts excepted—filled in as a transitory member of the Coon Creek Girls at some time. Even the rebellious "Violet" rejoined the act for a time after she married the Ledfords' brother, Custer.

The early years of *Renfro Valley* included a number of novelty acts, not all of them human, such as "Si, Fannie and Abner, two people and a trained mule," and Billy Sheets, the Singing Dog Trainer, with Rex, the Wonder Dog. Although the majority of his radio audience never saw the live show, Lair's comic acts, in particular, played on visual humor. With the success of "A'nt Idy," Lair added other female comedians and novelty acts. In 1940, the six-feet-plus "Little Eller" joined the cast, paired with the diminutive Shorty Hobbs. About the same time, and at the other end of the spectrum of female stature, the four-foot-nine, jig-dancing, pipe-smoking Granny Harper began to perform on the *Renfro Valley* stage. Although already close to sixty when she began, "Granny" would remain as part of the cast for another twenty-five years.

While Lair desperately sought new talent in his first years after moving back to Rockcastle County, his emphasis at *Renfro Valley* would always be more on developing the shows rather than individual acts. Unfortunately for the performers, Renfro's rural setting did not afford the show business connections and opportunities of a barn dance in a big city. Generally, the performers at *Renfro Valley* of the 1940s and 1950s could be divided into two groups: those, such as Homer and Jethro, who made a name for themselves and then moved on to greener pastures, and those who stayed on for years and years, making Renfro their home. Some of those who followed temptation but found the grass not greener elsewhere returned to Renfro, and Lair typically welcomed them back. Nor did Lair ever seem to hold a grudge against those who moved on to greater fame and money.

The performers' opinions of Lair varied enormously, as did their perception of what Renfro could offer. The contrasting views of Lair can be seen in the dramatically different memories of Jerry Byrd and Virginia Sutton, both of whom joined the cast in the early days. Still a high school student, steel guitar player Jerry Byrd joined the cast of *Renfro Valley Barn Dance* during the year they performed at the Memorial Hall in Dayton, Ohio. After graduating from high school, Byrd followed the barn dance down to Kentucky and played at Renfro for several years. Although most of the radio listeners found Lair to be warm and accessible, Byrd did not find him that way in real life:

> He was a reserved person . . . never felt a warm feeling, I never did, with him, although I never felt like I was ostracized or anything like that, either. He kind of kept a distance between . . . himself and the talent. I think that was for, more for business purposes than, than it was actually his personality, because he liked to be around entertainers and players of country music, the *real* country music. He was a kind of a purist, you know. So he was kind of hard to get to know, personally.

Byrd felt that even Lair's longtime favorites, such as the Coon Creeks and Slim Miller, would have said of Lair, "Well, I worked for him for years, but I never really knew him."[21]

Virginia Sutton also began her career while still in high school. Hearing her perform on radio in Indianapolis with her cousin, Lair extended an invitation to the girls to come to Renfro. The extremely nervous pair took a bus to the Renfro Valley Lodge to meet Lair:

> And so we were waiting to see him, and waiting for him to come in and talk with us. And in he walked, that's always one of my favorite stories, I thought it would be a man in a suit and a tie. In he came with an old pair of riding breeches on, they were torn in the knee and he was eating an ice

cream cone. So he put it at ease right now. So he hired us and we came down here, that was in the '40s, around '42 or 3.

Virginia Sutton Bray's career at Renfro would stretch over four decades. According to Bray, "we all loved Mr. Lair and we admired him."[22]

Byrd and Bray, however, also had noticeably different financial experiences with Lair. When he first moved to Renfro, Byrd only made room and board, and then finally moved up to $13.50 a week—not that his paychecks could always be cashed right away. Byrd noted: "John was tight with his money. . . . I had to run him down every week to get him to sign that check. I'd get the check, but nobody's signature would be on it."[23] Byrd did concede that Lair offered good opportunities to musicians at the beginning of their careers. Lair's emphasis on the ensemble benefited young performers, because it let each person have his or her moment in the spotlight. "John Lair was fair about that, you know. He never was unfair about his treatment, giving each person a chance to do his thing. He was smart that way, he got a lot out of his people for very little money because they felt like they were at least doing something on their own that could possibly bode well in the future. Whereas the Grand Ole Opry wasn't that way at all, it was, in fact, just the opposite." However, for a young and ambitious musician, this benefit did not ultimately outweigh the drawbacks of being at Renfro. As Byrd noted, "Well, people like Homer and Jethro and myself and Ernie Lee could see that if we stayed there, you'd dry rot."[24]

Virginia Sutton Bray, on the other hand, made $50 a week and felt that she "was really in the money." At one point, an offer to return to Indianapolis tempted her: "This person up there wanted us to come back, and offered us quite a bit more money—I don't remember what it was now—and we did go back for a little while, but we weren't happy. You're never happy after you've been to Renfro Valley."[25] Most of all Bray loved the informality and family feeling of the Valley. As she recalled:

> We would, we would do our programs, then we'd go up to the Lodge and eat breakfast. And lots of time someone would play instruments and some of us would get up and jitterbug and just, it was just a fun thing. But we would go and have breakfast together almost every morning over at the Lodge. And it was just a fun thing, we just enjoyed each other. And we would go, Lily May'd cook big meals and we'd go to their homes and eat, and you know, and it was just a lot of fun, it was a family affair, it really was.[26]

John Lair offered a family atmosphere as a perk, in lieu of fame and fortune. By providing an alternative to the peripatetic lifestyle typical of

Renfro performer Linda Lou Martin.
Photo courtesy of Southern Appalachian Archives, Berea College.

most radio barn dance performers, Lair could compensate for the other
shortcomings of Renfro Valley. Lair did send out various traveling shows,
but loyal performers could come in off the road. Linda Lou Martin began
performing professionally at the age of fifteen, after Lair saw her perform
at an amateur show. First Lair sent Linda Lou (whose name he changed
from Wanda) to work in a show he produced in Atlanta, and two years
later she joined Renfro Valley's traveling tent show. There she met the
one-armed banjo player Emory Martin and three months later they married. Although the Martins loved the life of the tent show, they knew
when it was time to stop. As Linda Martin recalled, "We came in when I
was about two months pregnant, we came in off the road and Mr. Lair got
Ballard and Ballard Biscuits . . . he got that sponsor. . . . You can't run
around all over the country when you have kids, unless you want to leave
them, you know. We never did want to do that, so we stayed, we just
stayed here. And Mr. Lair had programs, that program was on CBS [*Sunday Morning Gatherin'*], it started out, and it was pretty good."

Except for a brief stint in Louisiana and some road trips for Lair, the
Martins made Renfro their home. In 1956, Emory Martin leased a nearby
service station to provide additional means of support for their family. As
he explained, he "was fortunate to stay here long enough to get some
friends, and I really went to valuing them friends." Once their son reached
school age, the Martins wanted to stay in one place. As Emory Martin

explained: "I wanted him to finish here, and not do like I did. I went to several different schools, and just went through the eighth grade, you know. I didn't want that for him."[27]

For women performers, Lair offered what might now be characterized as a "mommy track" in country music. When members of different groups took time to have or care for a child, Lair had another young woman waiting in the wings to fill in. Both Linda Martin and Virginia Sutton, for instance, performed at various times as Coon Creek Girls, and Sutton also served as a temporary Farmer Sister. Both women, of course, also had their own acts, and backed up various other performers on stage.

While some of the young women who came to perform for Lair met their future spouses at Renfro Valley, others came as part of a family. Already seasoned performers, Jo and Russ Fisher joined the Renfro cast in 1955. When Lair created his own radio station a couple of years later, Russ Fisher became a popular DJ, and their thirteen-year-old son even became a radio announcer. Renfro Valley offered the Fishers full family employment. As Jo [Fisher] Simunick recalled, "Mr. Lair wanted the people that worked on the Barn Dance and *Gatherin'* to work in the little shops around the Valley to talk to the tourists and everything. So I worked in the gift shop. And when the tourists would come in, why they would recognize me and we'd talk and just, you know, enjoy it." Virginia Lair ran the gift shop at that time; to Jo Fisher, she "was just like my mother." Unlike Jerry Byrd, who felt that Lair held himself aloof from his performers, Simunick considered Lair "just like one of the gang." She went on to recall that "he and Mrs. Lair use to have all of us over for a little Christmas party and exchange gifts and things like that and it was just like a big family."[28]

While Renfro provided a clean country atmosphere to raise a family, during its heyday it also offered the performers some national exposure. Throughout the 1940s up until the mid-1950s, *Barn Dance* and *Sunday Morning Gatherin'* were broadcast on network radio. During a heady—albeit brief—time in the early 1950s, General Foods invested heavily in advertising through *Renfro Valley* broadcasts, one of the most lucrative radio sponsorships of that time. A few years later, Lair briefly had a television show sponsored by Pillsbury. But the days of the live radio show were waning, and Lair could not provide the one thing his most ambitious performers wanted: a recording contract.

Lily May Ledford came to believe that Lair deliberately kept her career from developing fully. However, Lair began his career during the

Renfro Valley, probably taken during the Pillsbury television show era. Although Lair manufactured a homelike setting at Renfro, his performers did create a family atmosphere. Photo courtesy of Southern Appalachian Archives, Berea College.

Depression, when live radio dominated the country music world. By the late 1940s, Lair perceived the growing power of the recording industry and, hoping to eliminate the middleman, attempted to create his own record company. Although Lair recorded a few records, the equipment he ordered turned out to be defective and the project stalled. The following year, the dream quite literally went up in smoke, when the recording studio, recycled as a walnut processing plant, burned to the ground. During the flush years of the General Foods deal, Lair's business associates attempted to lure representatives from Victor, Decca, and Columbia recording companies to Renfro Valley to audition the talent, but little came of these efforts.[29] Ultimately Lair had to settle for a deal with Golden Records, which produced a recording for a premium giveaway. Lair wrote to his advertising agency, "As you say I could not make any money on this but I think I see possibilities of building up a demand for records which might lead to national recognition of some of our talent."[30]

John Lair always claimed that the valley itself was the star of his show, but this statement, while perhaps reflecting his intentions, also served as a rationalization for the increasing difficulty he had in generating stars by the 1950s. His business correspondence from the decade indicates that Lair eagerly sought recording opportunities for his performers, but failed. Those performers who sought real success had to leave the comforts of the valley. Unlike Homer and Jethro, Jerry Byrd and others, Lily May Ledford never struck out on her own, and her choices, more than any actions of Lair's, hobbled her career. Late in her life, with two failed marriages behind her, Ledford may have regretted the choices she made, and Lair served as a convenient target to blame.[31]

Other performers, however, welcomed the fact that at Renfro they did not have to choose between performing and family life. Some did not even feel particularly deprived that they could not get a recording contract. As Linda Martin recalled, "You know, things was changing, too. All this record business started. And if you was lucky enough to get on a record, you have to get out and run around all over the road and plug that record. And you have to stay out on this road. And I tell you, when you're married and got a family, now that's not real good."[32] At Renfro, performers could maintain a family life and, according to Virginia Sutton Bray, Lair even proposed to build a nursing home at Renfro, in order to provide shelter for aging performers in their final years. The declining financial circumstances of Renfro made this dream an impossibility, but a number of performers did choose to retire in the area.

By the 1950s, John Lair's wife, Virginia, definitely had their own retirement on her mind and longed for a private life and the warm weather of Florida. Lair, however, found himself unable to accede to his wife's wishes until he had designated an heir to take over the business. Even though his wife apparently had better business sense than he did, it did not seem to occur to Lair during that time that one of his four daughters might be able to take over Renfro. Although he doted on his daughters, Lair simply did not have that expectation of them. His youngest daughter, Barbara, believed that it might have been for the best: "We've always felt like if he'd had a son, he would have been miserable. That, you know, Daddy might have really kind of pushed at him a little bit. I think because we were girls, it never entered his head that any of us would be interested or could be interested."[33] Lair instead searched for a surrogate son who could lift responsibility from his shoulders. Lair's hopes briefly settled on Tom Wood, the wunderkind who landed the General Foods contract, but, as Wood would later write, "Much as I would appreciate

Renfro Valley, it was not my dream & there is no way my limited talents could ever replace him."[34] Lair failed in his search for an heir apparent, and ironically, two of his daughters would ultimately help run the family business.

The 1960s were a bleak decade for Renfro Valley. Lair sold his radio show for a nominal fee and made do by relying largely on performers who would settle for the opportunity to perform as their main compensation. During the mid-1960s, Lair entered into a contract with Hal Smith to provide Nashville-style entertainment. After two years of a partnership fraught with tension, Lair sold out to Smith. Unfortunately, Lair waited too long to enjoy the travel and Florida retirement his wife always longed for. With his wife's health declining, Lair instead remained in his Renfro Valley home, watching the changes being wrought to his lifelong dream. In 1977 John Lair's life partner passed away. If it had not already been apparent, it became clear how little Lair knew about finances. As Barbara Lair Smith recalled, "I don't think we, we realized quite how . . . much until after she died. Daddy just couldn't do anything, as far as bills or that type of thing. . . . Like you hear of a lot of widows today, you know, then the husband died, they weren't aware of their insurance policies or how to do this or—that was Daddy. And I think we realized then how much of that Mother had handled for him all those years."[35] Although now in his eighties, Lair could not quit his life's work. A year before his wife's death, he purchased back Renfro Valley with two partners. His second daughter, Ginny Lee, entered the family business, handling public relations and bus tours for Renfro and seeking official recognition for Renfro Valley's contributions from the state of Kentucky. One of Lair's first priorities after purchasing back Renfro was to restore it to what it had once been, removing the traces of the previous Nashville-based regime. Lair removed the large sound system Hal Smith had installed in the barn and once again banned drums and most of the electric instruments. He also sought to bring a number of his former performers back to the Valley. Jo Fisher, who had left Renfro in 1966, recalled that in 1978 she returned home from work to find John Lair's Cadillac sitting in her driveway: "I said, 'Well what in the world are you doing in Bowling Green?' He said, 'I thought I'd . . . see if you would let me take you back to Renfro Valley.'" On returning to Renfro to play with her old band, Fisher felt "it was just like going home."[36]

Lair's daughter Nancy Griffin believed that Lair "came back to life again" in 1976 when he bought back Renfro Valley; he just had to have "people, and involvement, and adulation."[37] Although he energetically took on ambitious new plans for the valley, by the early 1980s Lair could no longer manage the workload. As Lair's health declined, daughter Ginny Lee's role at Renfro grew—and she began to realize just how active a man he had been. "Then when Daddy got sick, he had a stroke, I pretty much took over and I understood, sheesh. Seven days a week, writing a monthly newspaper, doing a half an hour show, being there for tapings and recordings, being there Sunday mornings, plus everything. I thought, how in the world this man did it, I don't know [laughs]. It was seven days, plus a week."[38] On November 12, 1985, at the age of ninety-one, John Lair died. After her father's death, Ginny Lee felt that she could no longer handle running Renfro Valley, and she turned responsibility over to her older sister Ann Henderson. The Lair daughters continued to own Renfro Valley until 1989, when the family sold everything but the Lair homestead.

Even though Lair has failed to win admission into the Country Music Hall of Fame, his legacy to country music has not been forgotten, particularly in his home state. In 2002, the elaborate horse stables he had had built for his daughters at Renfro Valley became the new Kentucky Music Hall of Fame, with Lair as one of its first inductees. There are two areas for which John Lair deserves recognition. First, Lair had a special knack for recognizing talent and shaping acts. During a time in which women performers in country music were few, Lair had a special interest in developing female acts. Certainly Linda Parker, Lulu Belle, and Lily May had the talent to succeed on their own, but would they have had the opportunity without Lair? Lair's other primary accomplishment lay in his ability to transcend the limitations of radio, through his creative imagining of what the audience wished to hear (and, at times, see) from his make-believe community. As artificial as Renfro Valley may have been, Lair's performers ultimately created real community, and this sense of family did not exist in Lair's promotional materials alone. Here, too, women reaped the rewards of Lair's vision. At Renfro Valley, female performers did not encounter the difficult choice between career and family that so many professional women of that time faced.

A complex man, Lair certainly had his share of failings. As with many visionaries, he often seemed selfish, for those things that did not serve his dream were of little interest to him. Lair, however, does not appear mean-spirited. He may have been tightfisted, but Lair seemed less interested in amassing wealth than in building dreams. If he had been truly obsessed with money, he probably would have paid more attention to accounting. Far from feeling manipulated and cheated, the women performers who worked for Lair largely seem to have liked and respected the man. Of course, there were exceptions, but even the ambivalent Lily May wrote warmly of the kindness the Lairs had shown her in her early years in Chicago, and she faithfully attended tributes to Lair in his final years. In general, Lair seemed to sustain far closer relationships with his female performers than with the male musicians.

If Renfro Valley might be seen as the product of a single man's vision, we cannot lose sight of the many women who helped build and sustain it. Lair's doting sister, mother, aunts, grandmothers, and great-grandmother shaped his dreams. A wealth of incredibly talented female performers made *Barn Dance* a success and transformed Renfro Valley into a real community. The levelheaded Virginia Lair deserves far more credit than she ever received for keeping Renfro Valley and the Lair family financially solvent. And finally, Lair's daughters ultimately helped ensure the continued survival of Renfro Valley into the present day, and saw to it that their father's memory remained alive.

Notes

The John Lair Collection at Berea College, as well as oral history interviews, served as the primary basis of this article. Thanks to Harry Rice for his assistance in negotiating the Lair Collection and for locating other valuable materials in Berea's collection. The oral history project was funded in part by the Kentucky Oral History Commission. My former graduate assistants David Baxter, Hillary Glatt Kwiatek, and Larry Morrisey conducted most of these interviews. Thanks also to my graduate assistant Rachel Baum for her meticulous editorial assistance in preparing this paper. I also owe thanks to Lisa Yarger for sharing her interview materials with Evelyn Lange Perry and her thoughts on Lily May Ledford.

1. Barbara Lair Smith, tape-recorded interview with David Baxter, Hopkinsville, Kentucky, 3 March 1995.

2. John Lair, tape-recorded talk to Loyal Jones's class, Renfro Valley, Kentucky, 23 June 1973. Tape available at Berea College, Special Collections.

3. Barbara Lair Smith, tape-recorded interview with David Baxter, Hopkinsville, Kentucky, 3 March 1995.

4. Nancy Griffin, tape-recorded interview with Hillary Glatt, Annandale, Virginia, 1 March 1995.

5. John Lair, tape-recorded interview with Loyal Jones, Renfro Valley, Kentucky, 15 April 1975. Tape available at Berea College.

6. *Stand By,* March 21, 1936, 16. For an analysis of the Lily May comic strip, see Lisa J. Yarger, "Banjo Pickin' Girl: Representing Lily May Ledford," Master's Thesis, University of North Carolina at Chapel Hill, 1997, 70–76.

7. John Lair, letter to Frankie Moore, 19 September 1935. John Lair Collection, Box 1, General Correspondence 1930–1936, Southern Appalachian Archives, Berea College.

8. John Lair, letter to Cousin Emmy, 12 August 1937. John Lair Collection, Box 1, Southern Appalachian Archives, Berea College.

9. Cousin Emmy, letter to John Lair, 11 February 1941; John Lair, letter to Cousin Emmy, 21 February 1941. John Lair Collection, Box 65, Southern Appalachian Archives, Berea College.

10. Evelyn Lange, letter to John Lair, 1 August 1937. John Lair Collection, Box 23, Southern Appalachian Archives, Berea College.

11. Evelyn "Daisy" Lange Perry, tape-recorded interview with Lisa Yarger, 13 August 1993, Frankfort, Indiana.

12. Esther M. Koehler, "Silent Singer." John Lair Collection, Box 19, WLS-Song Correspondence 1935–36, Southern Appalachian Archives, Berea College.

13. Evelyn "Daisy" Lange Perry, tape-recorded interview with Lisa Yarger, 13 August 1993, Frankfort, Indiana.

14. Margaret Lillie, letter to John Lair, 29 January 1937; John Lair, letter to Margaret Lillie, 11 February 1937; John Lair, letter to Margaret Lillie, 26 August 1937. John Lair Collection, Box 23, Southern Appalachian Archives, Berea College.

15. Mrs. T.A. Timmons, letter to John Lair, 23 September 1938. John Lair Collection, Box 1, Southern Appalachian Archives, Berea College.

16. Evelyn "Daisy" Lange Perry interview.

17. Freeman Keyes, letter to John Lair, 8 June 1938. John Lair Collection, Box 1, Southern Appalachian Archives, Berea College.

18. John Lair, letter to Freeman Keyes, 23 September 1940. John Lair Collection, Box 26, Russell Seed Co./Freeman Keyes 1939–1940, Southern Appalachian Archives, Berea College.

19. Ibid.

20. Ibid.

21. Jerry Byrd, tape-recorded telephone interview with Larry Morrisey, 14 February 1997.

22. Virginia Sutton Bray, tape-recorded interview with David Baxter, Renfro Valley, Kentucky, 14 April 1995.

23. Jerry Byrd, tape-recorded telephone interview with Larry Morrisey, 14 February 1997. During the early 1940s, Lair constantly asked Keyes to send the weekly payroll earlier. It is likely that Lair tried to appease his performers by handing out checks before he had the money from Keyes. By not signing the checks, he tried to delay the cashing of them, avoiding the explanation that he did not have enough money in the bank to cover the checks.

24. Jerry Byrd, tape-recorded telephone interview with Larry Morrisey, 14 February 1997.

25. Virginia Sutton Bray, tape-recorded interview with Larry Morrisey, Mt. Vernon, Kentucky, 22 May 1997.

26. Virginia Sutton Bray, tape-recorded interview with David Baxter.

27. Emory and Linda Martin, tape-recorded interview with David Baxter, 15 May 1995, Mount Vernon, Kentucky.

28. Jonelle [Fisher] Simunick, tape-recorded telephone interview with Larry Morrisey, 17 January 1997.

29. Tom Wood, "Summary Report on the Office and Radio Operation of Renfro Valley," 10 May 1951. John Lair Collection, Box 16, Tom Wood Correspondence

Folder, Southern Appalachian Archives, Berea College, 14. Tom Wood, memo to John Lair, 4 September 1951. John Lair Collection, Box 16, Tom Wood Correspondence 1951–52, Southern Appalachian Archives, Berea College.

30. John Lair, letter to Carl W. Stursberg Jr., 28 April 1952. John Lair Collection, Box 16, Foote, Cone & Belding, January-March 1952, Southern Appalachian Archives, Berea College.

31. See Lisa J. Yarger, "Banjo Pickin' Girl: Representing Lily May Ledford," M.A. Thesis, University of North Carolina at Chapel Hill, 1997, 159–72.

32. Emory and Linda Martin, tape-recorded interview with David Baxter, 15 May 1995, Mount Vernon, Kentucky.

33. Barbara Lair Smith, tape-recorded interview with Larry Morrisey, 25 October 1996, Hopkinsville, Kentucky.

34. Tom Wood Scrapbook, 9 May 1994. John Lair Collection, Southern Appalachian Archives, Berea College.

35. Barbara Lair Smith, tape-recorded interview with Larry Morrisey, 25 October 1996, Hopkinsville, Kentucky.

36. Jonelle [Fisher] Simunick, tape-recorded telephone interview with Larry Morrisey, 17 January 1997.

37. Nancy Lair Griffin, tape-recorded interview with Hillary Glatt, 1 March 1995, Annandale, Virginia.

38. Virginia Lee King, tape-recorded phone interview with Larry Morrisey, 27 February 1996.

THE VOICE BEHIND THE SONG

FAITH HILL, COUNTRY MUSIC, AND REFLEXIVE IDENTITY[1]

Jocelyn Neal

Introduction

In recent years, singer Faith Hill has taken both the country and pop music industries by storm, winning awards from most of the major music organizations, touring to sold-out arenas, airing television specials, and commanding astronomical fees for appearances.[2] All of her albums have been certified multi-platinum; her most recent album debuted at the top of the *Billboard* album charts, selling nearly twice as many units in its first week as her previous album had.[3] Meanwhile, fans and journalists alike have scrutinized and criticized the music on those albums regarding its place within the genre of contemporary country. The discussion is provoked, first, by the pop production elements, instrumentation, vocal techniques, and song structures to be found in her more recent work; second, by the business decisions Hill has made in marketing her own name and face through advertisements and commercial performances; third, by her self-professed roots in country music as her stylistic home; and fourth, by the ongoing polarity between crossover and traditionalist approaches that characterizes the whole arena of country music.[4]

Those debates and critiques typically fragment her work into individual songs, distinct musical styles, or differentiated biographical periods. A different perspective suggests that Faith Hill's music, taken in its totality, can be interpreted as a single artistic expression of her identity,

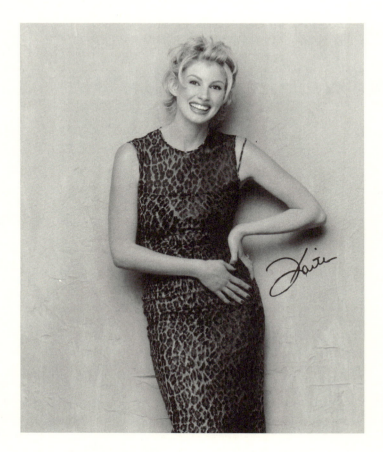

Faith Hill. Courtesy of Middle Tennessee State University.

projected by the reflexive, narrative voice through which those songs are presented.[5] In particular, her collective body of recordings can be viewed as a single text, from which four principal, consistent themes emerge: a search for personal identity, an articulation of desire, a contemplation of spirituality, and a reflection on the nature of love. Woven together, these four themes form the core representation of the artist behind the songs, as well as a tenable connection to country music's tropes and traditions.

The conventionally accepted interpretation of Hill's work describes a country-centered pair of albums, then a complete stylistic shift—accompanied by a change in personal identity—for three later pop-crossover albums. However, close examination of the lyrics, stylistic traits, and performances on all five albums indicates the existence of unifying threads that defy such superficial categorization. Furthermore, the popular bipartite interpretation of her musical output fails to recognize those elements of Hill's identity that have remained consistent across her entire career—there is something characteristic in all of her music that is uniquely and reflectively hers. Analytic theories of authorship, identity, and textual interpretation provide the tools to reveal that unifying voice, to identify the consistent themes of self-expression that persist throughout her work, and to represent Hill by the collective narrative of her recordings. Although her work is comprised of recordings, their accompanying videos, live performances, and her media presence, principally established through interviews, this essay focuses only on the recordings as a cohesive and self-contained representative collection.

Biography and Artistic Identity

Within the tradition of country music, artists are expected to connect with their fans through shared biographical experiences and the relevance of their personal backgrounds to a stereotyped country identity. These tokens of authenticity amplify the genre-identity of an artist's output—Loretta Lynn's coal mining roots, Merle Haggard's time on the wrong side of the law, or Dolly Parton's Smoky Mountain upbringing are all frequently invoked as synonymous with the content, meaning, and impact of their music. In keeping with those expectations, many aspects of Hill's biography are shared among her fans as common knowledge, and offer a significant contribution toward her recognized artistic identity.[6]

Born in 1967 in Jackson, Mississippi, Hill was adopted as an infant and raised in the nearby town Star. She started singing at an early age, took to performing in community settings, and set her heart on a musical career. Her biography resonates with the storybook fairytale of a young girl heading to Nashville to seek her fame and musical fortune: Hill's father dropped her off in "Music City, U.S.A." at the age of nineteen, where she found employment through a series of menial-labor jobs until her talent was "discovered." Her early career centered around a neo-traditionalist country sound, emulating Reba McEntire in particular. Two moderately successful albums later, she met Tim McGraw while on tour, fell madly in love, married him, and became the devoted mother of their daughters. After this brief hiatus from recording, Hill reappeared on the scene with a new look, a new sound, a new producer, and a new perspective on life and her music.[7] Three crossover pop albums were the product of this "new Faith" and her studio team.

Within this oft-repeated biography, elements of the requisite country identity are firmly in place: geographic association with the South, child-hood musical efforts, the devotion and ties to her family, and the influ-ence of her love life on her musical productivity. Considering only the biography (and temporarily disregarding the music she records), Hill's recent interviews include lengthy discussions of child-rearing, southern cooking (her cornbread dressing is her culinary specialty), and self-dep-recating statements that in spite of her $60-million tour two years ago, "success is far from assured."[8] These depictions invoke the girl-next-door status that is an expected part of a country artist's covenant with her fans, in spite of the irony that offsets such comments from her obvious celebrity status and commercial success. At the same time, celebrity en-dorsements, advertising contracts, and recordings in film music high-light the remote, pop-star aspects of her identity that threaten the country audience's acceptance of her.[9]

The Singer's "Voice"

In his 1971 biography of rockabilly star Buddy Holly, Dave Laing bor-rowed the principles of *auteur* theory from the field of film criticism and applied them to musical analysis; these ideas have since been embraced by musicologists working within popular music.[10] Within auteur theory, a single author, creator, or "auteur" is responsible for an artistic work, and that author's personal identity, thematic preoccupations, and dis-tinguishable control over the entire creative process govern the semiotics and interpretation of that work.[11] By extension, when an artist adopts the role of auteur, the specific lyrical content of each individual song is subsumed into the greater identity of the artist. In contrast, a performer who realizes a previously completed and independent work is perceived as a *metteur en scène,* in other words, a possibly talented singer who can interpret any song but does not project an autobiographical voice through that song. The lyrics "matter most, as words, when they are *not* part of an *auteur*ial unity, when they are still open to interpretation," explains mu-sicologist Simon Frith.[12] For such a performer, the interpretation and meaning of an individual song comes from within that song alone.

Within the canonical body of country music, there are many per-formers who emerge as author and voice through their entire repertoire. Merle Haggard, Hank Williams Jr., Loretta Lynn, and George Jones, for instance, infuse their songs with an autobiographical meaning that transcends the lyrics' interpretive potential. The country audience both expects and demands that these auteurs figuratively—and, to some extent, literally—"live out the songs they write," and each song is an expansion of the singer's self-expression through an ever-growing and cohesive output.[13] There are, likewise, artists whose ability to interpret a song as masterful performers provides them with their role within the genre— Kenny Rogers, Anne Murray, Tom T. Hall, or even Kitty Wells, all regarded as master storytellers, are craftspeople of the highest ability as singers. But they lack the same overt presence of a reflexive identity or autobiographical connection that consumes the work of other singers.

Within these two perspectives, Faith Hill is clearly capable of the vocal gymnastics and craft that are demanded from a *metteur en scène*. For the fifty-nine songs under consideration here, eighty-one different songwriters receive credit, and Hill herself cowrote only two, both of which appear on her first album.[14] Thus, the very words and melodies for which she is known are not products of her imagination. This interpretation positions Hill as a talented interpreter of standalone songs, a *metteur en scène* whose artistry lies in her vocal ability.

There is also a popular, if simplistic, interpretation of her work as fully autobiographical at the broadest level, which reads as follows: Hill's earliest two albums are primarily tales of heartache and heartbreak, recorded while she was embroiled in a seldom-mentioned divorce and an emotional search for her biological parents. Attention to this early period in her career is often neglected in Hill's officially distributed biography, but by the time Hill's first album (*Take Me As I Am*) debuted on the Billboard charts, she had already filed for divorce from songwriter Dan Hill (she married him on July 23, 1987; their divorce was finalized February 1994).[15] According to Jeremy K. Brown's biographical sketch, Hill chose to combat the pain of divorce by writing songs and recording her first album.[16] Her sophomore effort, *Who I Am,* followed in the same vein when Hill's personal life underwent a complete change: Hill reveled in the ecstasy of new love, true love, and the arrival of her first two daughters. The three most recent albums are filled with happy love songs, bubbly emotional satisfaction, and musical packaging in the glitz of pop stylings (*Faith, Breathe,* and *Cry*).[17]

Various supporting features for this interpretation include the physical transformation (a change in hair color and "look" from a redhead in jeans to a blonde in sequins) that is apparent in the album covers and liner art, and the ease with which the media adopted this reading—even a recent *New York Times* article on Hill featured a sidebar picture of Hill with second husband McGraw and the caption "She moved away from tradition [i.e., enacted a change in musical style] after they married."[18] The commercial development of her career also supports this reading: Hill's first album debuted on *Billboard*'s Top Country Album chart at little-noticed #73 (November 27, 1993), making few waves in a market dominated by Garth Brooks at his peak. Her second album fared some-what better, appearing at #6 (September 16, 1995), but was still far over-shadowed by Shania Twain, who was then claiming the attention of the entire country-music scene. After the shift in presentation mode (and personal situation), Hill's third album arrived with a #2 debut (May 16, 1998); this new success was followed by the two #1 debuts, *Breathe* and *Cry*. It seems quite justifiable to discuss her work "before" and "after" the shift, based on its commercial acceptance as well as the apparent change in audience reception. Among this interpretation's weaknesses, however, is its treatment of her songs in large, undifferentiated groups: not all the songs on her first two albums reflect heartbreak, for instance, nor do all the songs on her more recent albums echo with newfound happiness. Broad generalizations about the content of the songs weakens the rel-evance of the interpretation.

Neither focusing on her vocal ability as an interpreter of other people's songs nor over-simplifying her work into "sad-country" and then "happy-pop categories" accurately summarizes the arc of her career. Let me pro-pose a third interpretation of Hill's work, one that combines her recordings into a single reflexive text based on its own internal references, and one that gives rise to an auteurial construction of Hill as artist. The "voice" that emerges through the entirety of her songs offers consistent narrative threads that combine to form a portrait of the singer.

The Collection of Songs

Such an interpretation requires that Hill's musical output make up a single, collective, and inclusive text in spite of the diverse pool of songwriters credited with the lyrics. Justification for this interpretation is found, first, in the high level of control that Hill retains over song selec-tion, and second, in the connections, intertextual references, shared themes, and resurfacing phrase fragments that tie together the songs in substantial, easily perceived ways. Regarding song selection, Hill has co-produced all but her first album and in recent interviews has been very vocal about her role in the song-selection process: when choosing songs for *Cry,* for instance, she said, "I put the word out that there were no limits on songs. I said, 'If you think something is going too far, send it. If you think something's not far enough, send it.'"[19] On all of the albums, the result has been a collection of songs that share intertextual references and reflect Hill's own choices of expression; the three very brief samples of these numerous connections that follow will suffice to illustrate the interrelated nature of the texts.

Repetition of memorable phrases point to a personal rhetoric. For instance, beginning with her first single (and title track), Hill announces, "I don't need a bed of roses."[20] Two years later, not only is the sentiment the same, but the phrase itself reappears—albeit in a song by different writers—as a title: "Bed of Roses," the chorus of which includes the lines, "Don't want your bed of roses" and "I'm not gonna lay me down/In your bed of roses."[21] The assertive context of the lyrics has intensified since her initial statement, while the repetition connects the song to an evolving and growing body of text. I make no claim that these phrases are unique to Hill's songs—they most certainly are not—but their repeated presence does echo with her listeners from song to song and from one album to the next, weaving a cohesive rhetorical identity.

A more potent second example comes from her third album's extremely successful single, "This Kiss." The most salient lyrical characteristics of this song include the poetic patter of the chorus—a percussive use of consonants in a mesmerizing rhythm with a complex internal rhyme scheme and seemingly endless repetition of "this kiss."[22] The kiss becomes larger than life, and is indelibly associated with the hypnotic, up-tempo groove of the song. On her fourth album, Hill employs the same groove and up-tempo pop drive in her recording of "The Way You Love Me," where, again, the poetry overshadows the other elements of the song with its own internal rhythms. In this case, the song centers on the line "I'd wish you could see the way you kiss," whose hook is highlighted by the repeated use of assonance and matched voiceless fricatives.[23] The "kiss" from her third album is alive and well and openly referenced on her fourth; furthermore, both references invoke similar poetic devices in the surrounding lines of text.

A brief third example is contained on the album *Cry,* where three songs echo affirmations of self-worth through the following phrases: "You make me feel so beautiful," "There's someone out there for me/Who thinks I'm beautiful," "I wish you knew/How beautiful you are/In every way."[24] These three sets of lyrics appear on tracks 5, 6, and 8; their proximity on the album reinforces the listener's ability to recognize the connections, and the entire middle section of the album carries an uplifting affirmation of inner beauty and strength as its undercurrent.

Faith Hill and Reflexive Identity

It is not the individual textual cross-references but rather four themes running much deeper through the music that combine to form a network of connections and cohesion in Hill's work. The first is a continual reconsideration of a self-aware identity, expressed most simply by asking "who I am." The second theme is an increasingly specific articulation of desire, captured by asking "what I want." In recent albums, this theme has been de-emphasized, with an increased attention on an awareness of spirituality; in keeping with this, the third theme is an abstract acknowledgment of a divine presence and of spiritual strength. The fourth theme that emerges throughout her work is an exploration of the nature of love, primarily a metaphysical question about the definition of love.

This analysis does not discount Hill's own reported statements that she looks for very different content for different albums and is always interested in new and unique songs. Hill is quoted in *Country Music Magazine* as saying that she intentionally opted for a complete change in content for *Faith* and *Breathe*.[25] Rather, it is in light of these statements that the pervasive themes take on even more relevance to Hill's identity as an artist: in spite of her interest in diverse song material, these themes persist across the apparent diversity, thereby tangibly connecting her work into a reflexive portrait that she projects to her listeners.

Bear in mind that the majority of Hill's songs disregard the country-music tradition of third-person narratives ("story songs") and realistic descriptions in the lyrics ("real-world" or "realism" songs). Although the listening audience is used to hearing every detail of character and setting in story songs, which make up a sizeable part of the country-music repertoire, Hill rarely ventures into realistic story-telling mode—only eight times in all of her albums do third-person narratives appear—and almost always omits all contextualizing or real-world descriptive details in her songs.[26] Given this relative absence of story songs, the listener's attention is more intently focused on—rather than distracted from—the abstract philosophical musings that constitute the themes for the majority of her songs. Other trends in song selection also emerge in the progression through the albums—most obviously, an increase in the complexity of reference, image, and meaning on later albums is a manifestation of pop influences in construction of the texts. Country tradition dictates that songs be easily understood (at least on a surface level), while abstraction and obtuse interpretation have long been more valued in the world of rock and pop. Quite simply, this particular trend in song selection indicates her pop tendencies, but it also embeds some of the pervasive themes more deeply in the lyrics.

The first of those themes, summarized as "who I am," is continuously explored from her earliest work on, with increasingly complex revelations that culminate in an assertive statement on her fifth album. The singer's character and resilience is repeatedly questioned, then reaffirmed, as she poignantly defines herself through her responses to various situations. Hill's protagonist often finds herself caught in a bad relationship, where her reactions are occasionally contradictory. Sometimes the voice in the song succumbs in weakness, as in "Each time I tell myself that I can't stand the pain/You hold me in your arms and I start singin' once again."[27] But in a later song, she reconsiders when she sings, "I don't want to stop lovin' you, *but I will,*"[28] elsewhere asserting hopefully "I would be stronger than [a woman who stays in an abusive situation]."[29] This increased recognition of inner strength becomes a central element in the emergent voice: on *Cry,* a broken heart and a failed relationship still lead to the conclusion that "We both will be stronger" (when we finally emerge from the experience).[30]

Continuing on the topic of self-reflexive exploration, Hill presents a trio of songs that show specific thematic continuity, as well as evolution of "who I am." An early hit for Hill was "I Can't Do That Anymore," penned for her by Alan Jackson. In it, the narrator reaches a breaking point in selfless behavior and demands acknowledgment: she tells of sacrificing individuality and independence for her husband, cutting her hair, quitting her job, moving, and now concentrating on mundane domestic minutia. She concludes: "I keep on giving/But I can't stop living/A woman needs a little something of her own," concluding with the title line, "I can't do that anymore."[31]

Her third album amplifies these same sentiments from a new vantage point, and more resoundingly uses the same images and phrases in its lyrics. In the song titled "Me": "I've changed my hair, my clothes . . . /I can't believe I tried to be somebody I'm not . . . /It took finding you to finally understand what it's like to be loved for who I am."[32] The woman from "I Can't Do That Anymore" now tells of changing her priorities in the past tense, and in "Me," another chapter in the expanding text is delivered.

The third chapter in this series appears on *Cry,* through the song "This Is Me." Independent of any contextualizing love relationship, the woman announces her own identity through a catalog of attributes ("Yeah, I have my addictions/And keep my share of secrets . . . [the recitation continues with itemized descriptions]/But this is a part of me/Of what I do and *who I am*.").[33] What in earlier songs began as a quest for independence and a test of inner strength emerges here as an assertion of confidence, a recognition of self-reliance, and a recitation of the qualities that comprise her identity.

A second pervasive theme in Hill's recordings is the expression of desire, specifically apparent as statements of "what I want." This exploration becomes a thematic obsession from the outset of her work, even in the few third-person narratives that she has recorded. Her "Wild One" wants to chase her plans and dreams, and when she sings about "daddy's little girl and mama's little angel," the woman "means to make her life her own," and wants to wake up in her *own* dream for a change.[34] The voice speaking through Hill's songs wants to matter, wants to be accepted without pretense or compromise, wants to be free ("let go") from emotional restraints, and wants to know without a doubt, "what's in it for me?"[35] The simplest statement of this desire is tied very closely to the theme of searching for self-identity: Hill sings "All I really need is . . . someone with a strong heart/A gentle hand /Who'll take me as I am."[36] Hill's character does not want to compromise her own integrity and identity, yet she wants to find true love, a search that occupies many of her songs. In "You Will Be Mine," the singer lists quite explicitly that she wants to have held, kissed, claimed, and loved the object of her attention by the end of the night, a list of wants that is answered and apparently achieved in "I Got My Baby" ("Baby, I got you.") and reaffirmed in the line "Baby, you belong with me."[37]

A third theme characteristic of Hill's work is the reflection on the nature and presence of divinity and the recognition of spiritual strength. The songs navigate an expression of personal selflessness, spiritual reliability, and finally, transcendent salvation throughout their texts. Country music shares some historical roots with gospel songs, and sacred themes of spiritual and temporal salvation are ever present, either acknowledged or in the subtext, in country music's tropes.[38] The undercurrent of Protestant theology that runs throughout the genre is manifest in the tradition of placing a gospel song or "benediction" as the final track on an album. Even contemporary country artists like Garth Brooks and Shania Twain, who boast an overtly secular appeal, occasionally draw on this practice.[39] Hill's second, third, and fourth albums have followed suit. From its bluesy piano opening to its up-tempo preaching, "Keep Walkin'

On" wraps up *It Matters to Me* with a full-blown gospel celebration, with Hill and Shelby Lynne alternating the lines.[40] Sheryl Crow's "Somebody Stand by Me" closes *Faith* with piano and organ gospel accompaniment, leading into a soulful number, which includes the lines "Well, if God's here tonight/Are You here tonight/Maybe You could grab me up/Lord stand me on my feet. . . ."[41] Any momentary weakness in the woman's professed faith is answered by the prophecies that conclude *Breathe,* which ends with "There Will Come a Day." The song invokes a full southern gospel choir, including handclaps and rousing swells of sound, with the chorus: "There's another place where our Father waits/And every tear He'll wipe away . . ./Hold onto your faith."[42] Again, the audible organ plus the slow R&B groove support the shouts of "Hallelujah" and "Amazing Grace" in the gospel fervor.

Hill abandons this tradition on her most recent album, arguably one way in which *Cry* moves further from her established practice and country roots. Instead of a rousing gospel number, Hill uses another common device, closing the album with a heartbreak ballad hinting at an acoustic style ("You're Still Here"). The thread of tradition that Hill weaves into the second, third, and fourth albums is a particularly strong one—the appearance and placement of those three gospel tunes tie her to a long-established country music practice. Had she continued this on her fifth album, it would have been a link from her more adventurous stylistic work to past country connections, but the absence of a gospel tune stands out here.

While the specific gospel benedictions close only three of her albums, the themes of spiritual strength run throughout her work: her characters become sources of comfort and reassurance to those around them. On her second album, she sings, "You can't lose me/Bet your life/I am here and I will always be . . ."[43] The same sentiment emerges in the lines "Better days are comin' for you . . ./I know they will/'Cause I'll be right here makin' sure they do" on her third album.[44] In a song of outreach to a drug addict, Hill sings "When the world is falling down/Just kneel with me and pray," and "Count all your blessings/Instead of all your sorrows."[45] This song offers another glimpse of the spiritually resourceful character offering to be a pillar of strength for someone in need.

In *Dreaming Out Loud,* Bruce Feiler describes the transformation that occurred in Garth Brooks's sense of purpose when he attained sufficient commercial success, his music changing from addressing the microcosm of one individual's world to addressing the global philosophical stage: "With success, Garth had embraced the sixties ideal of what a pop star should be: He began believing his music could change the world. Witness 'We Shall Be Free,' an application for saintdom of the highest order."[46] Along similar lines, Hill's tropes of spirituality have evolved through the albums from viewing herself as a pillar of reliability and comfort, through a prophecy of salvation, to the abstraction of "What would you do if I did somethin' outta the blue/That made the world a better place?"[47] Even in the absence of a definitive gospel number, *Cry*'s entire textual content supports a moral code defined quasi-spiritually: "I try to love Jesus and myself"—and make the world a better place.[48]

In his seminal book on topical themes in country music, Jimmie N. Rogers writes that "approximately three out of every four popular country songs relate to some facet of love."[49] That love is a central theme in Hill's music is hardly surprising or even worth comment. However, more specifically it is not tales of romance, nor even reflections on having loved and/or lost that occupy Hill's music. Rather, the fourth recurring theme is a philosophical contemplation on the nature of love, questioning what love is. There are certainly plenty of conventional love and heartbreak songs throughout the five albums, keeping with popular music's fixation on those topics, but the more philosophical reflections that appear are rather distinctive within the genre of country and form a continuous thematic thread in her music.

On her first album, in one of her few self-penned lines, Hill sings, "It's time to find out what love is really all about," a statement that, to some extent, is addressed in her entire subsequent work.[50] The majority of the songs on the first two albums explore situations characterized by love, but on her third album, she attempts a definition of love by cataloging all that it isn't: "You can't buy it at the store, try it on for size . . ./You can't trade it in like an automobile . . ./It don't fall from the sky like a tiny drop of rain . . ."—while the process of elimination points to an answer of what love might be, in the end, our singer concludes love "ain't easy to define."[51]

The *Breathe* album continues to explore the question of "what is love." The song "Love Is a Sweet Thing," leads to the description of the emotion's effect: "Caught up in the touch/Slow and steady rush/Baby, isn't that the way that love's supposed to be?" Notice that her evolving definition moves in the direction of the physiological.[52] *Cry* features a metaphorical treatment of the topic that offers ". . . love's the moon/. . . love's the flame/. . . love's the jewel/. . . love's the rising sun," a kind of response to the earlier list of all that love isn't (although here the descriptions are ironically embedded in a heart-wrenching ballad of lost love).[53] "That's How Love Moves" continues to contemplate the mystery in all its manifestations.[54]

Potentially the most profound treatment of the question "what is love" emerges in the song "If I'm Not In Love."[55] This ballad is ostensibly a beautiful contemplation of happy love—the voice within the song is reflecting on the realization that she's in love, based on her heart aching to hold her lover, to feel his arms embrace her. However, the recognition of love is continually cast as a question in the lyrics, and both the musical setting and the text suggest that perhaps the question is not entirely rhetorical. "If I'm not in love with you/What is this I'm going through?" can be read as a literal question as the singer tries to explain the emotions and experiences she encounters. She asks, "How do I explain this feeling?" Perhaps a simple answer of "love" does not suffice.

The performance juxtaposes images of pain and loss, beginning with the initial statement's appearance cast in the negative: "If I'm *not* in love . . . " The singer describes her heart aching, how much she misses the object of her infatuation, the risk that this is someone she could lose, and repeats the question throughout the song. It is only in her fantasy that the lover embraces her, and only in her dreams that she surrenders to his touch. The recording opens with a solo piano, soon reinforced by melancholy strings. Hill's vocal performance draws on the throaty, close-microphone work that characterized her earlier neo-traditional ballads, which were more closely aligned with the mainstream country sound.

All of the musical signifiers point to a ballad of heartbreak, and the performance suggests that the opening question be read literally, not rhetorically. Hill's personal explanation of the song, which she posted on her website as part of a song-by-song description of *Breathe,* positions it as a tender, beautiful account of falling in love.[56] I contend, instead, that the references to love interlace a much darker emotional state, and the song's interpretive ambiguity keeps the investigation of "what love is" open and ties this utterance to the larger body of Hill's work as a thematically continuous text contemplating the nature of love.[57]

Echoes of the Country

While these four themes together weave a compelling reflexive identity that is projected throughout Hill's work, it is the anomalous inclusion of a single song on her third album that highlights both the continuity of her work and her embrace of country signifiers. The third album, *Faith,* is most noted as the newly-blond, upbeat, "reinvented" Faith Hill's re-entry into the country music scene, and the first of her recordings to openly embrace pop production and songwriting modes. In the midst of

Hill's abstract, reflective, pop-tinged love songs appears an unexpected insertion of realistic description and country pastiche, which echoes with the sounds of an old-fashioned country story song.

In "My Wild Frontier," Hill recounts a journey through Kansas, north to the farmlands of Calgary in Alberta, Canada.[58] She leaves civilization, finds a simple means of support in farm labor, and emotionally thrives in love. The cornfields and the peach trees are vividly painted for the listener, who can feel the icy snow, and hear the wind howling across the prairie, as Hill describes the change in seasons, both literal and metaphoric, in a throaty twang, her audible southern accent coloring the vocal performance. The event-driven narrative then concludes with the death of her loved one, and toward the end of the song a cowboy refrain is heard across the "lonesome prairie": "Get along, get along, get along . . . ," accompanied by a solo acoustic guitar and haunting fiddling with the classic western refrain "get along little dogies" just out of earshot. Her narrative, imagery, and performance invoke the most grounded signifiers and icons of traditional country music. The story is told in the empathetic first-person voice, but the level of detail in describing the physical surroundings, the events, the locale, and the narrator's activities are entirely uncharacteristic of most of Hill's recordings.

Using this song as a reference point, both her earliest and her most recent recordings include songs of lost love that are easily interpreted as mourning brought on by death. Eerily similar themes of a widow imagining the return of a now-departed love are found in "Just About Now" ("Just about now/I'd be watching you wake up . . .") and "You're Still Here" ("Thought I saw you today/You were standing in the sun . . ./ I knew it couldn't be . . .").[59] More than any other genre of popular music, country narratives often describe parent-child relationships and anchor themselves in a circle of life that spans multiple generations—wisdom, experience, and love passed from grandparent to parent to child. Such a reference is invoked in "You're Still Here" when the woman says she can see her absent loved one in her baby's eyes. The parent-child bond referenced here is also reminiscent of "My Wild Frontier." The text in that particular song ("While my baby lay sleeping/An angel slipped past . . .") leaves open to interpretation whether the departed one is a lover or a child.[60] The ambiguity between lover and child is also in place in "Baby You Belong," but within the context of the other country signifiers, even the possibility of interpreting these songs as about mother-child relationships enriches the emotional landscape of the work.[61] Through three songs that span the entire career—"Just About Now," "My Wild Frontier," and

"You're Still Here"—the singer tells a story of mourning and remembrance, colored with country signifiers and icons, and touching on the generational breadth of country music.

While description of detailed settings and events are extremely rare in Hill's work, stories about other individuals are even less common.[62] Of the only eight songs that recount third-person narratives of any kind, the most vivid characterizations are of working-class people inhabiting a world of dive bars and late-night diners. Hill introduces her listeners to a couple of guys sitting around a bar drinking; their bartender Sam pouring martinis; another bartender sweeping up and closing his run-down bar for the night; Linda, who works as a waitress at a diner; her abusive, alcoholic husband, Jimmy; a homeless man sitting on a street corner drinking a beer; and a young Texan girl who sings in the pool halls and dive bars.[63] The bulk of Hill's work—abstractions of love, reflections where "you" broke "my" heart or "I" love "you," and songs where the narrative is reflective rather than plot-driven—is equally non-specific in terms of cultural setting. To place Hill's songs in a cultural context requires the sort of environmental detail and description of characters, settings, events, and actions that only her few story songs provide. The inhabitants that we meet through those songs unquestionably live in the working-class, alcohol-drenched environment of dive bars and honky tonks, which are not the exclusive purview of country music, but which certainly resonate with country music's strongest images.

Only one character in Hill's songs seems out of place in this world: a former Hollywood star whose popularity has dissipated and left her friendless, driving around aimlessly in her Mercedes-Benz.[64] Unsurprisingly, this character appears on *Cry,* and the song provides Hill's audience with a concrete disjuncture in characterization between the earlier work and this moment. Although the song argues that emptiness and loneliness pay no heed to social class, Hill's story songs clearly do, and this character is an anomaly.

"Who I Am"

The first impression one gets of Faith Hill's recordings is the musical setting: the beat, the soundscape of guitars and synthesizers, the texture of her voice, and the melodic, harmonic, and the timbral content of her songs. Obviously the impact of these elements is primary, and the music itself draws on both traditions and creative innovations in the general arena of popular music. The musical complexity and construction of her last three albums in particular threatens to overshadow and overwhelm the narrative elements of the songs. Furthermore, a radio station or video television broadcast offers the audience a single song by Faith Hill, surrounded by work by other artists, commercial advertisements—perhaps even a weather report. These factors leave a song as an isolated instance of musical creation in the minds of many listeners: Hill vocal performance brings to life a single text within an elaborate vehicle of musical presentation arriving independently for the audience's consumption. In such a context, one might question the need to investigate any consistent artistic identity of the singer. Yet Hill has repeatedly defended the integrity of her music as a whole, and her affiliation with the world of country music, both of which motivate examination of her artistic output for continuous threads of personal identity and the thematic roots of her work.

Considerations of superficial gestures of "country" identity (her cornbread recipe, her Mississippi upbringing) are not particularly relevant. Yet the popular journalistic approach—to claim that Hill has simply left behind a relevant population of "country traditionalists" with her pop-crossover albums—is both unhelpful and historically naïve when it comes to understanding the music she has made. First of all, the claim that Hill's "most recent album" is the one where she broke with country tradition has been applied to each successive album since 1998's *Faith,* devaluing the argument even if only through repetition (as well as confusing the position of the previous album with each iteration). Second, the frequent association of Reba McEntire's name as an early idol and prototype for Hill's sound on her first two albums is often used as a reference to country traditionalism, but the strong R&B presence in McEntire's sound from the mid-1980s onward is equally often overlooked—McEntire's recording of "Little Rock," for instance, is an obvious example of more soul-drenched R&B than traditional country.[65] Exploration of crossover influences in the country-music genre over the past two decades far outstrips the scope of this analysis, but even in Hill's earliest sounds (and in the country music of the early 1990s in general), there was no stream of traditionalist-pure country in the musical mainstream.

The interesting question that arises from Hill's music is not whether any given album is pop or country—that decision is best left to the employees of record stores who must stock the relevant bins, and to the fans who submit requests to radio stations. Nor is it whether or not her musical output is subjectively "good": no analysis should masquerade as a review, and I make no such claims here (furthermore, reviews of Hill's albums abound, and some are admittedly scathing).[66] Instead, the question worth contemplating is whether or not there is some essential characterization or reflexive identity that emerges from her collective recordings—specifically whether Faith Hill as an artist claims any sort of auteurial design over her work.

There are clear topical themes running throughout Hill's work, each of which has developed and matured from one album into the next. The voice that emerges from these themes is increasingly confident in the recognition of her own identity and desires, repeatedly acting as a comforter and source of strength through the invocation of spiritual reassurance, and philosophically intrigued by the nature and definition of love. The vast majority of song texts remain unencumbered by details about context, characters, or plot, yet in the few instances where settings, events, locales, and individuals are depicted in realistic detail, those settings resonate with country signifiers—this trait holds throughout her work, both before and after the putative country-pop change in style. Such an understanding need not discount the other parameters of her work—musical production techniques and music style both change dramatically from album to album, as does the autobiographical relevance of individual songs, and her admirable vocal technique is displayed throughout her recordings. Instead, such an analysis seeks only to add another dimension to our portrait of Faith Hill as an artist, and to understand the connective, thematic elements that define a narrative "voice" across her entire musical work.

Notes

1. A version of this essay was presented at the International Country Music Conference, Nashville, Tennessee, 1 June 2001.

2. Among the most prominent of her awards are a Grammy for Best Female Country Vocal Performance, 2000; the Country Music Association's Female Vocalist of the Year, 2000; and the Academy of Country Music's Top Female Vocalist, 1998, 1999, and 2000.

3. Sales figures for *Cry* report 472,000 units for the first week, and the album went platinum shortly thereafter, multi-platinum within six weeks. These figures appear on Hill's official web site as well as in common reviews and press about the album; see, for instance, James Hunter, "Faith Hill: Redrawing Country's Borders," *New York Times* (Arts section), 24 November 2002, and Robert Hilburn, "No Tears for Faith Hill," *Los Angeles Times* (Calendar Weekend), 24 October 2002.

4. Although tangential to the study at hand, the dichotomy between pop country and traditionalist country has been significantly amplified in recent years by a resurgence of interest in old-time, acoustic, and folk-roots infusions in country

music. The primary catalyst for this development was the soundtrack to the Coen Brothers film *O Brother Where Art Thou?*, produced by T-Bone Burnett and released in December 2000.

5. The reader is invited to consult the liner notes for Faith Hill's five albums in conjunction with this article. All albums are readily commercially available, and the liner notes include complete lyric transcriptions. Only brief references to specific lyrics are included in this article.

6. Biographical details are readily available to fans—Hill has been profiled in *Current Biography* (March 2001, 25–28), *Country Music* (December 2000/January 2001, 50–54), VH1's "Behind the Music," (most recent version broadcast 25–26 November 2002) and even on her official website (http://www.faithhill.com). In addition, literally dozens of magazine articles propagate fans' knowledge of Hill's biography; see, for instance, Sara Switzer, "Ya Gotta Have Faith," *Glamour*, January 2000, 160–61, 177 or Jeanne Wolfe, "Keeping the Faith," *Redbook*, June 2000, 118–21, 148–49.

7. Producers Dan Huff and Byron Gallimore worked on *Faith, Breathe,* and *Cry.* Huff's resume contributes to the trend in mid-1990s country music toward rock and pop producers working on country albums—Huff's other production work includes work with the artists Megadeth, Celine Dion, and Barry Manilow, for instance.

8. Jim Jerome, "Every Reason to Smile," *People,* 17 October 2002, referencing Hill's 2000 "Soul 2 Soul" tour with Tim McGraw.

9. Hill recorded the theme song for the Hollywood blockbuster *Pearl Harbor* and has done ad campaigns for products ranging from cell phones to makeup. While other country stars, notably Shania Twain and Toby Keith, have done a significant number of product endorsements, it is not a generally accepted practice within country-music culture, as seen by the wave of controversy that accompanied Garth Brooks's 2001 acceptance of a contract with Dr. Pepper after more than a decade of publicly denouncing product endorsements.

10. Dave Laing, *Buddy Holly* (New York: MacMillan Company, 1971), 74–76. Musicologist Simon Frith, for instance, discusses this theory in "Why Do Songs Have Words" in Frith's collection *Music for Pleasure: Essays in the Sociology of Pop* (New York: Routledge, 1988), 105–28.

11. Discussions of the auteur theory are readily available in texts on film criticism; see, for instance, Tim Bywater and Thomas Sobchack, *An Introduction to Film Criticism* (New York: Longman, 1989), 53–60, 222.

12. Frith, "Why Do Songs Have Words," 123 (emphasis Frith's).

13. Hank Williams Jr. famously offers this opinion verbatim in "Family Tradition" (his recording of this self-penned composition dates from 1979). Honky tonk and the outlaw movement are both known within country music for the importance they place on singers who write and live their own material.

14. Most of the songs feature two or more cowriters. Hill's name appears on "I've Got This Friend" and "Go the Distance," both on *Take Me As I Am* (Warner Bros 9 45389-2, 1993).

15. Faith Hill filed a complaint for divorce with the Fourth Circuit Court for Davidson County, Tennessee, on 28 July 1993, citing irreconcilable differences.

16. Jeremy K. Brown, "Faith Hill," *Current Biography,* March 2001, 25–28. The sketch was updated and re-published in the *Current Biography Yearbook* 2001, 253–55.

17. This interpretation of a two-part split in her oeuvre is bolstered by the observation that between her 1993 debut and the later recordings, country music itself was hit with a pop music evolution sparked by Shania Twain's abs. In this reading, Hill's so-called new sound and look are seen as merely keeping up with the times.

18. James Hunter, "Faith Hill: Redrawing Country's Borders," *The New York Times,* 24 November 2002, http://www.nytimes.com/2002/11/24/arts/music/24HUNT.html?ex=1039141869&ei=1&en=5d9e0014ab1ea00f (registration required).

19. This quotation reported in Wendy Newcomer, "No Tears," *Country Weekly Online* http://www.countryonline.com, 11 October 2002.

20. "Take Me As I Am," by Bob DiPiero and Karen Staley, track 1 on *Take Me As I Am.*

21. "Bed of Roses," by Will Rambeaux and Jaime Kyle, track 4 on *It Matters To Me* (Warner Bros 9-45872-2, 1995). Although the musical settings of these texts is not addressed in this analysis, it is worth noting that the shared phrase here is set to almost an identical pitch motive as in "Take Me As I Am." "Take Me As I Am," recorded in the key of F major, sets the text "bed of roses" over melodic pitches B-flat4, A4, and descending to G4. In "Bed of Roses," recorded in the key of E major, the text is set over melodic pitches A4, descending through G-sharp4 toward E4. The similarity in melodic motive reinforces the relationship of the shared text in the two songs.

22. "This Kiss," by Robin Lerner, Annie Roboff, and Beth Nielsen Chapman, track 1 on *Faith* (Warner Bros 9-46790-2, 1998). This single is generally credited with launching the "second phase" of her career and moving her into the pop-crossover arena.

23. "The Way You Love Me," by Keith Follese and Michael Delaney, track 7 on *Breathe* (Warner Bros 9-47373-2, 1999).

24. "Beautiful," by Aimee Mayo, Chris Lindsey, and Shaye Smith; "Unsaveable," by Bobby Terry and Bekka Bramlett, and "If You're Gonna Fly Away," by Alicia B. Moore and Linda Perry, tracks 5, 6, and 8 respectively on *Cry* (Warner Bros 9-48001-2, 2002).

25. Tamara Saviano, Nick Krewen, and Michael McCall, "The Four Faces of Faith," *Country Music Magazine,* December 2000/January 2001, 50–55.

26. Third-person depictions occur only in the following songs: "Wild One"and "I Would Be Stronger Than That" (*Take Me As I Am*); "Someone Else's Dream," "A Man's Home Is His Castle," and "You Can't Lose Me" (*It Matters to Me*); "The Secret of Life" (*Faith*); "Love Is a Sweet Thing" (*Breathe*); and "When the Lights Go Down" (*Cry*).

27. "Piece of My Heart," by Bert Berns and Jerry Ragavoy, track 4 on *Take Me As I Am.*

28. "But I Will," by Troy Seals, Eddie Setser, and Larry Stewart, track 7 on *Take Me As I Am* (emphasis added).

29. "I Would Be Stronger Than That," by Gary Burr, track 10 on *Take Me As I Am*.

30. "Stronger," by Hillary Lindsey and Troy Verges, track 9 on *Cry*. The recognition of inner strength follows on that album in the form of the song "I Think I Will" (by Anthony Smith and Steve Robson, track 13), which includes the line "The longer I live, the stronger I get."

31. "I Can't Do That Anymore," by Alan Jackson, track 7 on *It Matters To Me*.

32. "Me," by Aimee Mayo and Marv Greene, track 9 on *Faith*.

33. "This Is Me," by Hillary Lindsey and Troy Verges, track 11 on *Cry* (emphasis added). It is worth noting that this song shares distinct melodic, harmonic, rhythmic, and topical similarities with an extremely successful single, "Who I Am," also written by Troy Verges (co-written by Brett James) and performed by country star Jessica Andrews. Andrews's song appears on her album *Who I Am* (Dreamworks 450248, 2001). The commonalities are musically significant and easily perceived, even without a musical transcription to highlight them; musical analysis can isolate the similarities.

34. "Wild One," by Kaime Kyle, Pat Bunch, and Will Rambeaux, track 2 on *Take Me As I Am*, and "Someone Else's Dream," by Craig Wiseman and Trey Bruce, track 1 on *It Matters To Me*.

35. "What's In It for Me," by Billy Burnette, Bekka Bramlett, and Annie Roboff, track 1 on *Breathe*.

36. "Take Me As I Am," by Bob DiPiero and Karen Staley, track 1 on *Take Me As I Am*.

37. "You Will Be Mine," by Rob Honey, track 9 on *It Matters To Me,* "I Got My Baby," by Bob DiPiero and Annie Roboff, track 2 on *Breathe,* and "Baby You Belong," by Keith Follese, Wade Kirby, and Bill Luther, track 7 on *Cry*.

38. This spiritual side manifests itself in the use of gospel songs to close albums, concerts, and historic events—"I Saw the Light" remains Hank Williams's final association, engraved on his tombstone, and according to legend and reinforced by the movie *Your Cheatin' Heart*, it was the song sung by his waiting fans upon hearing of his death. See Curt Ellison, *Country Music Culture: From Hard Times to Heaven* (Jackson: University Press of Mississippi, 1995), 120–21.

39. Two recent illustrations of this practice are Brad Paisley's "In the Garden" and "The Old Rugged Cross," the traditional gospel hymns that conclude his first and second albums, respectively. Shania Twain's *The Woman In Me* closes with "God Bless the Child"; Garth Brooks's *Sevens* concludes with "Belleau Wood," as close to a gospel song as anything the artist has recorded. Brooks's *The Chase* opens with "We Shall Be Free," another often-referenced gospel number in his work.

40. "Keep Walkin' On," by Karen Staley and Tricia Walker (*It Matters To Me*) is the only definitively gospel number on her albums.

41. "Somebody Stand by Me," by Sheryl Crow and Todd Wolfe, track 12 on *Faith*.

42. "There Will Come a Day," by Bill Luther, Aimee Mayo, and Chris Lindsey, track 13 on *Breathe*.

43. "You Can't Lose Me," by Trey Bruce and Thom McHugh, track 6 on *It Matters To Me*.

44. "Better Days," by Bekka Bramlett, Billy Burnette, and Annie Roboff, track 5 on *Faith*.

45. "If You're Gonna Fly Away," by Alicia B. Moore and Linda Perry, track 8 on *Cry*.

46. Bruce Feiler, *Dreaming Out Loud* (New York: Avon Books, 1998), 189–90.

47. "I Think I Will," by Anthony Smith and Steve Robson, track 13 on *Cry*.

48. "This Is Me," by Hillary Lindsey and Troy Verges, track 11 on *Cry*.

49. Jimmie N. Rogers, *The Country Music Message: Revisited* (Fayetteville: University of Arkansas Press, 1989), 47–48. He further specifies that "most of the love songs depict a relationship that is unhappy, or to use the vernacular, hurtin'."

50. "Go the Distance," by Trey Bruce, Thom McHugh, and Faith Hill, track 9 on *Take Me As I Am*.

51. "Love Ain't Like That," by Tim Gaitano and A.J. Masters, track 4 on *Faith*.

52. "Love Is a Sweet Thing," by Brett James and Troy Verges, track 3 on *Breathe* (1999), and "Breathe," by Holly Lamar and Stephanie Bentley, track 4 on *Breathe*.

53. "If This Is the End," by Steve McEwan, track 10 on *Cry*.

54. "That's How Love Moves," by Jennifer Kimball, Fitzgerald Scott, and Ty Lacy, track 12 on *Breathe*: "That's how love moves/Like a river running through you/Sometimes it lifts you high as Heaven/It consumes you."

55. "If I'm Not In Love," by Constant Change, track 8 on *Breathe*.

56. http://www.faithhill.com, posted during the marketing of her fourth album, 1999–2000.

57. Hill's hit song "The Secret of Life," by Gretchen Peters (track 7 on *Faith*), is closely linked to philosophical contemplation about the nature of love, focusing more broadly on that which is significant in life in general. Adopting a similar catalog-list approach to the narrative structure, this song offers a number of paradoxical definitions of the secret of life. Notably, love is not specifically part of the formula (except to "find the right woman"), and the song concludes with the self-parodic comment that "thinking won't get you too far."

58. "My Wild Frontier," by Franne Golde, Robin Lerner, and Marsha Malamet, track 6 on *Faith*. The absurdity of comparing herself to a "sad armadillo" in the opening of the song can be read as a reference to Texas as the starting point of the journey.

59. "Just About Now," by Gar Burr and Jon Vezner, track 3 on *Take Me As I Am*, and "You're Still Here," Aimee Mayo and Matraca Berg, track 14 on *Cry*. Neither of these songs specify that *death* has parted the lovers, but the text, tone, and presentation of these songs is consistent with mourning, as opposed to the tainted heartbreak of a relationship that ended.

60. Faith Hill has explained that "My Wild Frontier" is a story of widowhood in which the lover dies, leaving behind a single mother. See Jim Brown, *Country Women in Music*, (Kingston, Ontario: Quary Press, 1999), 243.

61. "Baby You Belong," by Keith Follese, Wade Kirby, and Bill Luther, track 7 on *Cry*. Nothing in the text of this song explicitly points to a mother-child relationship, but both individual lines and the underlying sentiment of the song support such a possible reading, without ruling out the interpretation of a more conventional romantic relationship.

62. Not only are story songs extremely common in country music, but many of the most memorable and significant songs employ third-person, plot-driven narratives. Garth Brooks's controversial "The Thunder Rolls" and the Dixie Chicks' "Goodbye Earl" are two prime examples. First-person story songs, centered on a sequence of plot events and colored with detailed descriptions of the setting and characters, are even more common and foundational in the genre.

63. These characters appear in "The Secret of Life" (*Faith*), "When the Lights Go Down" (*Cry*), "A Man's Home Is His Castle" (*It Matters to Me*), and "Love Is a Sweet Thing" (*Breathe*). The only other named character in her songs aside from Sam, Linda, and Jimmy is Bill, rebel boyfriend to the teen-aged "Wild One" in the song of the same name.

64. "When the Lights Go Down," by Craig Wiseman, Jeffrey Steele, and Rivers Rutherford, track 4 on *Cry*.

65. "Little Rock" appeared on *Whoever's in New England* (MCA 31304, 1986).

66. Among the more critical reviewers of the recent *Cry*, for instance, are Alanna Nash, writing for the website Amazon.com ("the album itself is a self-conscious mess . . . a miserable failure"). See also Robert Hilburn, "Nice try, Faith, but go back to the studio," *The Los Angeles Times* (Sunday Calendar), 13 October 2002, which includes the line, "*Cry* is so filled with vocal histrionics that it borders on the unlistenable."

THE COW THAT'S UGLY HAS THE SWEETEST MILK

Rebecca Thomas

"It's a great life for dogs and men but it's hard on women and steers."

DuBose Heyward on mountain life

"It's the dumb gals that count on their fingers. The smart ones count on their legs."

Cousin Minnie Pearl

In his sermon to a Nashville congregation, the nineteenth-century evangelist Samuel Porter Jones taunted the town mothers that it would be better for their tender daughters to join with the town's Negro men than with their beer-guzzling, card-playing, back-sliding beaus (Eiland 8). The good reverend hit his mark. They were galled. As the birthing bed of the Ku Klux Klan, Nashville projected the sentiment of most southern cities and towns by assuming the separation of races above all other matters. In the first decades of the twentieth century, as the Klan renewed its commitment to white supremacy, white communities expanded the idea that the differences between black and white were more far-reaching than skin color. Emphasizing behavior as well as appearance, the division was steeped in moralism (Williamson 108). Plainly put, a person of color was savage by nature, a white person inherently decent, and a white woman, above all, a vessel of virtue. This gilded propriety would change the history of country music by ignoring black influences on the music. It would also continue to limit the role of women in country music.

The therapeutic code of moralism that developed in southern culture justified the growing nativist sentiment during this period and soothed the insecurities of the larger nation. Nostalgia grew in popularity as industrialized people looked back over their shoulders and wondered if they were really progressing. They fancied notions of a simpler era that included segregation and revised the history of interplay between the races. Whiteness became an allegiance to wholesome nationalism. African Americans who had grown up in the same religious culture and followed many of the same moral guidelines as whites were discounted, as blackness summarily became a sign of depravity (Williamson 3). Lynching increased between 1889 and 1909 with the revival of the bestial view of black men (Grantham 32). The white woman, the "shield-bearing Athena" of domestic Christian virtue described by W.J. Cash, was sanctified anew (Cash 89). Floating above corruption in angelic gleaming clouds, she eclipsed the real woman. Reduced to symbolism, she remained the celestial source of sermonizing and regional tribute.

A new class of savvy businessmen utilized technology and mass production to anticipate and feed the appetites of the era. With one eye squarely on profit, the first generation of commercial music managers mastered the sophisticated balance between art and science by mass-producing emotional authenticity. In country music, traditionalism took center stage and lined the pockets of men like Ralph Peer, Judge Hays, and Art Satherley. Female talent continued to defer to codes of femininity, and public performances by the few remaining African American string musicians were brought up short (Wolfe 17). By drawing moral distinctions based on race and reinforcing gender stereotypes, commercial country music was politicized, and decency itself became the product.

The fragmentation of southern music in the early twentieth century was emblematic of the nation's prevailing racism. Most of white America agreed with Woodrow Wilson that the unfortunate legacy of the Civil War was racial coexistence. In a period when the president sang the praises of D.W. Griffith's *Birth of a Nation,* Americans embraced whiteness as a sign of righteousness. Tantalizing his audiences with the silent moving picture, Griffith combined the best that innovative film artistry had to offer with the undisputed message of a powerless gender and a depraved race. It was an old story, beaten down but not destroyed by the Civil War. As the theater pianist pounded the ivory keys, vigilante law made heroes of men in sheets riding in a trail of dust and vindication. White actors with blackened faces aped across the screen, demonstrating their unworthiness by their degenerate actions. Audiences could plainly see that this was no blackface minstrel or plantation rube, but evidence of a new generation of enfranchised blacks who threatened decency itself by intruding on the white order.

Fear of race-mixing produced whiteness campaigns in traditional southern music. Troupes, festivals, and tent shows traveled the landscape as showcases for white propriety and erased as much evidence of black influence on the music as possible. Even though black fiddlers, guitarists, and banjo pickers had been a constant presence in traditional southern music dating to the colonial period, those remaining found fewer audiences willing to tolerate them. Instead, annual gatherings such as the Whitetop, Virginia, musical festival stressed the preservation of "the folk," veneration for Anglo-Saxon culture, and the exclusion of vulgarity and outsiders (Cantwell 32). Old-time music and parlor songs paid tribute to home, hearth, and motherhood because commercial decency demanded it. Before the start of the Doc Hauer Medicine Show, Hauer himself reassured his guests of his intentions. "And I'll guarantee you one more thing," he announced, "you're gonna see a *family* show. You'll never see or hear a thing in one of Doc Hauer's shows that you wouldn't go home and tell your dear ol' grandma" (Acuff 103). A playbill for the Carter Family promised ticket buyers that their program was "morally good" (Hagan 119). Radio sponsors and advertisers demanded decent spokespeople for their insurance, medicinal concoctions, and self-rising flour. Comedy was acceptable only if it was clean. Country personality Grandpa Jones called his favorite brand of humor "real and honest." "I don't like smutty things," he said, "they're not funny to me at all" (Jones 178).

Women in the early commercial period, having been relegated for generations to singing parlor ballads or playing the dulcimer on the front porch, were particularly vulnerable to public scrutiny. The Carter sisters were pivotal in gaining acceptance for their gender in traditional music, but they did so within the confines of convention. Traveling under the protection of husband and brother-in-law A.P. Carter, the family's decorum in dress and presentation was uncompromising. Physical expression didn't happen. When they performed happy tunes like "Keep on the Sunny Side," their stoic faces were a direct contradiction to the words of the song. Guitarist and friend Chet Atkins laughed at the contrast, comparing their stiff driving lyrics of joy to a "funeral dirge." Standing for publicity photos in wool coats and a man's suit that revealed only their heads and hands, the trio's message was all business (*America's Music*).

White lies protected the sensibilities of the country audience. The stars were expected to behave themselves, and those who weren't up to it learned to cover their tracks. Managers approached the duplicity as good business practice. When Sara Carter divorced her husband of seventeen years, the Victor Records executive Ralph Peer asked her not to damage the reputation of the Carter Family. She and A.P. agreed to maintain the façade, and the public never knew of their split while they toured (Bufwack, 58). Roy Acuff also worked fast in damage control when speculation about a single woman in his company threatened his sales. Assigning B.B. Oswald as Cousin Rachel's "Bashful Brother," Acuff diffused the tension and freed the comedienne banjo player to perform under the watchful eye of her pseudo-relative (Green 43). Proving a star's religious devotion could challenge even the most gifted public-relations practitioner. When the often lewd and suggestive Uncle Dave Macon became a star on the early Opry, the manager George Hay made excuses for him by explaining away his vices. "Uncle Dave knows the Bible from 'kivver to kivver,'" Hay wrote, adding that Macon was known to "put down his banjos" to preach a sermon. While Hay admitted that Uncle Dave was "familiar with the other side of the King's English," he called Macon's profanity "cute and never off-color. He is a child of nature and enjoys each day for what it is" (Hay 6).

Decent Christian southerners considered the banjo, fiddle, and guitar nothing less than divining rods for evil. The fiddle's bad reputation preceded its arrival in America, conjuring up satanic images in Europe before continuing in the colonial period in ads linking the instrument to runaway slaves. Eighteenth-century newspapers warned that the runaway devil fiddler could conceal himself as a beggar or drunk, linking deception and fiddle music to black skin (Malone 36). The threat of depravity by association continued into the next century. William Frost linked stringed instruments to places of ill repute in 1899, noting that the banjo was "commonly accounted wicked" (Frost 314).

Such fear took its toll on white mountain communities. In 1904, Emma Bell Miles sensed the repression and hunger for sensation in mountain communities when she referred to religious music as their "one emotional out." "A high-strung race," she added, they must "find vent" somewhere (Miles 119). Writing for *Harper's Monthly Magazine* in 1915, William Bradley blamed the disappearance of the ballad from the mountains on the "aggressive puritanism" of the Old Regular Baptist Church (Bradley 913). Fundamentalist sects only approved of hymns and psalms, and children learned that they would be punished for singing, playing a fiddle, or dancing. When Maud Karpeles traveled with Cecil Sharp into the mountains collecting songs at the turn of the century, she noted that the "Holiness" sect thought it was wicked to sing love songs, and dancers at a square dance had to call their behavior "playing" instead of dancing (Karpeles 164). Janette Carter adds that in Poor Valley, "it seemed everyone was supposed to sing hymns" (Carter 47).

The most conservative wouldn't admit that they knew the songs, publicly disassociating themselves from these "devil's ditties." William Bradley told of the difficulties in gathering information about secular songs from a remote southern white woman: "[S]he may turn on you with singular vehemence and assure you that, no, indeed, she knows only 'good songs!'" he wrote. Only after the glare faded from her eyes and her "toothless mouth" stopped working would she agree to resume conversation on more acceptable topics (Bradley 914). Carter remembers "a few scattered square dances in the valley, but we couldn't go . . . as there might be drunks!" (Carter 47). Mountain preachers denounced dances and "play-parties" as sinful diversion, and the church became the only site for recreation. As Horace Kephart concluded in the 1920s, "they certainly have put a damper on frolics" (Kephart 340).

For the southern musician, the choice between public approval and the temptations of catgut could be daunting. Devil ways and the promise of danger were appealing references for men, but they meant virtual excommunication from the church. "His Puritanism might at a pinch move him to outlaw the beloved fiddle from the church as an instrument of Satan," noted W.J. Cash, but it would also "lead him habitually to regard pleasure as in its very nature *verboten*" (Cash 59). Musical talent could enhance a man's sexual prowess if he was willing to risk respectability for delicious infamy, but a fiddler knew that if he attended church, he had a decision to make. A minister in particular would earn the reputation of a "no good" preacher if he listened to or played stringed instruments, so men such as Richard Bridgett of Hannibal, Missouri, made the sacrifice for the sake of their congregations (Marshall 45). The conviction that the music was removed from God was a powerful force. When a fiddler named Clarinda "sallied forth" to play and dance in the mid-eighteenth century, she was suddenly "seized with fits." After her religious conversion, she put aside her fiddle for God (Epstein 114).

Those who had to scratch the itch became closet players, hiding their instruments and risking exposure at any moment. "He must lay aside his bow," warned William Bradley, "or else take it out only when he is secure against all surprises" (Bradley 913). Some men who were "saved" into the church couldn't bring themselves to destroy their fiddles, so they hid them in cabin walls and exterior buildings. When Maybelle Carter's future mother-in-law found her son's fiddle under some straw in an outhouse, she demolished it (Orgill 45). The Appalachian musician Jean Ritchie tells a story about a neighbor named "Cedarhead" who destroyed every fiddle his sons were able to construct. When he found more hidden in a log, he forced the boys to roll the log down the hill with the instruments inside. "Purty soon the fiddles begun to fly ever which way," writes Ritchie. "Strings a-popping, gourds a-bustin. . . . 'Courding to Cedarhead, he personally tore up Hell in the new ground that day!" (Ritchie *Singing Family,* 145). A few of the faithful tried to reconcile their talents with their church by playing religious tunes. Howe Teague, a Missouri fiddler born in 1913, describes his discomfort in taking a fiddle to church: "[O]ne time, when I was about seventeen . . . they had a church over here about three mile and they wanted me and another boy to come over there to church one night and play a tune or two. . . . And I never felt so much out of place in all my life. . . . So we played 'Ole Rugged Cross' and it went over big, you know" (Marshall 45).

Southern blacks, too, shared ambivalence about religion and stringed instruments. In African American folklore, the lutelike instrument was the devil's own riding horse, and judgments on musicians could be severe. They also knew the pressure of having to choose between masters. W.C. Handy recalls taking his violin into church choirs only to hear the women whisper "Yonder goes the devil," and his Grandpa Brewer played the fiddle to earn money before he "got religion" (Handy 5). Another musician claims "They used to be no bigger devil in the world than I was," but after his conversion he "let a 'ligion get me, I quit all sick o' that" (Ramsey 170). When Muddy Waters started playing the harmonica, his grandmother warned him "Son, you're sinning. You're playing for the devil. Devil's gonna get you" (Rooney 105). Eugene Jones started singing spirituals after his conversion, but when he is alone he still plays the blues because, he says, "The old Devil gets in you" (*Bootheel*). Like the fiddling sons of Cedarhead, black musicians also hid their instruments (and their talent) in order to continue playing music. Big Bill Brody and his friend Louis made a guitar and fiddle out of boxes and used his mother's thread to make a bow. They hid the instruments under the house "because," he writes, "our mothers wanted us to be preachers" (Lomax 428). When the mother of twelve-year-old Eddie "One-String" Jones discovered his banjo, she burned it and warned him that the instrument would make him a "trifling boy" (Evans 229).

Some musicians of both races simply refused to be shamed by the religious community. B.B. King learned to play the guitar at age seven from the minister at his church, but the congregation wouldn't let him join in the gospel groups (King 67). The reverend disagreed with his followers, calling the guitar a "precious instrument" and "another way to express God's love" (19). King carried this belief into his adult life, describing the music of T-Bone Walker as "Jesus Himself" playing the guitar (83). White country musician Willie Nelson responded to conventional pressures by turning his back on organized religion. Nelson considered becoming a minister until church leaders forced him to choose between teaching Sunday school at the Baptist church or playing music in Fort Worth bars. The hypocrisy wasn't lost on Nelson, who noted that he was singing to the same crowd at both places (Nelson 251).

Women black or white were only a token presence in the male-dominated circuit. African American women who liked to play stringed instruments or sing traditional blues were often morally chastised. Thirteen-year-old Lillie May Glover defied her minister father and sang the blues in a carnival show in Nashville, Tennessee. "I was brought up in a sanctified church but I wanted to be a blues singer," recalls the African American blues woman. When her family found out, "They like to killed me" (McKee 146). The African American singer Martha Turner of Louisiana had to reconcile her desire to play the guitar with the taboo against women playing it. Her father encouraged her to play the piano instead because it was "pretty." "Dad said, 'Guitar is not a feminine instrument,'" Turner recalls, "but I never wanted to learn to play piano. I wanted to play guitar" (Fraher 51). Carol Hascall, an old-time white fiddler from Polk County, Missouri, remembers trying to learn the fiddle against her father's wishes. "I wanted to play the fiddle. We only had one fiddle; it was Dad's. His mom could play the fiddle, [although] nobody had told me. She never did it around the family noooo, that was a no-no. Women didn't play the fiddle, that wasn't lady-like." To get around the father, Carol's grandmother taught her the fiddle, and her mother accompanied on the guitar while he was away at work. When her father discovered their secret, he "put a stop to it right then and there. He said 'there is only going to be one fiddler in this family, and I'm it'" (Marshall 26).

Public performances by white women wouldn't penetrate the commercial market until the 1920s. In this decade the secretary of a Georgia fiddlers' association responded to their first female applicant, a self-taught country fiddler, with backhanded approval. He wrote that he had no objection to her attempt, even though "women are running the men out of every kind of job." He warned, however, that the mountain men attending the conventions might not be so obliging since they still believed that a woman's place is "in the cabin, doing the cooking and looking after the children, with some plowing and hoeing in season. And they certainly are not used to women fiddlers" (Daniel 39). The first rule for such women was never to find themselves in a position of competition with men. Minnie Pearl knew that her job as a female comic in the 1930s and 1940s was secure because she posed no threat to the male musicians. "I didn't sing and I was a woman. Men, at that time, *never* figured a woman to be a threat" (Cannon 141). White women were also restricted in their choice of songs. Jean Ritchie recalls her mother's disapproval of a "low" song that Jean's sister sang. In "God Bless the Moonshiners," a man wants to "go to the alehouse" and drink with his friends, with "No woman to follow/To see what I spend." Ritchie explained that "[b]oys could sing them if they wanted to, and pick the banjer too, but a girl who thought anything of herself should not do either one" (Ritchie *Folk Songs*, 44).

The only women who successfully challenged the conventions of female propriety in southern music were classical African American blues singers. Bessie Smith, Memphis Minnie, and Mamie Smith toured in black vaudeville circuits and performed at nightclubs, flaunting their sexuality to a world that had historically exploited it. While the mere existence of a black man in the South was a sexual affront to white women, black women could turn the jezebel stereotype on its head and render bittersweet justice from their unbounded sexuality. Black men might be lynched for singing a suggestive song in front of white women, but the classical blues woman could sing to anyone she liked. Unbound by the paternalistic system that girdled her white sisters, she could travel alone, direct the genre, and sing about herself with abandon. In Bessie Smith's 1926 release of "Baby Doll," she sang, "I wanna be somebody's baby doll so I can get my lovin' all the time/He can be ugly, he can be black, so long as he can eagle rock and ball the jack" (Angela Davis 24). In Sara Martin's "Mean Tight Mama," she sings of her hidden talents. "Now my hair is nappy, and I don't wear no clothes of silk," she sings, "But the cow that's black and ugly, has often got the sweetest milk." Martin claimed that when a man "starts jivin', I'm tighter than a pair of shoes" (Barlow 151). Managers and producers banked on the heightened sexual image. Okeh Race Records published a "Book of Blues" describing the featured female singers as "smilin', teasin' brownskin gal[s]" who "jes got it natchely." Regarding Martin, they write: "there's none finer or grander when it comes to warblin' mean and hot the low-down ravagin' Blues." Another brochure says of a blues woman named Alberta, "Naughty! Naughty! Alberta's at it again? There's just nothing will make that girl behave" (*Okeh*).

Blues women learned to look after themselves in a culture where white paternalism translated into danger, rather than protection. In the music, at least, they made the rules in defining their relationship with men. While a white woman's identity was based on marriage and mother-hood, the blues woman could sing, "I don't need no man, Lawd, Lawd, I don't need no man" (Cohn 102). Ray Charles remembers such independence among the women of his youth: "In those days no man just took his pussy—not unless he had his gun. No, sir. You got what you were given. And there was no way you could throw your weight around. Gals were used to real labor. And if they didn't want to give you a piece, Jack, you just weren't gonna get any. Fact is, I'd say the average gal of 125 pounds back then could whip the average cat of 160 pounds today" (Charles 29). Bluesmen answered the female call with thrill and torment, moaning about the ability of such women to break them down and then take them to a level of pleasure that transcended sex. Even though white bluesmen pushed the boundaries with lyrics on white female sexuality, the lust was generally one-sided. Not so in black blues culture. While white women were teetering on their biblical pedestals, black women were bringing down their own miracles. Sonny Boy Williamson sang about black women who were so good in bed that they could make a blind man see, a lame man walk, and a dumb man talk (Spencer 116).

Southern white culture viewed such displays alone as evidence of racial depravity. There was no mistaking the godlessness of the blues; the lusty, raw sentiment was the devil's handiwork; the sexy lyrics and wanton wails of the slide guitar were an affront to Christian society. The translation of African customs onto American soil held no interest. Dismissive of the centrality of sex and fertility in the religions of Africa, whites labeled blacks as uncivilized savages who—more shocking still—seemed proud of their depravity. They didn't consider that within the context of African American culture the language of eroticism could transcend sex, or that sensuality was not obscene to those who did not accept shame (Bayles 71).

White southerners also failed to consider the desire among blacks to distinguish themselves from the hypocrisies of a sexual culture that they knew all too well. Plantation stereotypes of the "black male buck" and the "female jezebel" had fueled behavioral blindness and justified the denial of black humanity in exchange for the forbidden act. White participation in a sexual history of eroticism and domination was at the root of a racial tension in which white women were rendered asexual, black women were used and discarded, and black men were lynched to cover the guilt. African American men, wrenching their identity from those who would take it from them, took whatever liberation they could find in dismissive white contempt. Where whites expected to find shame they were confounded by pride. Sexual prowess was one of the few traits that had historically awarded any kind of status to African Americans, and the price was dear. The sexuality expressed in blues music was more than reactionary, but if whites were offended by it, all the better.

As the country industry removed racial immorality from its product, the sexual content of country blues songs went unaccounted for. This blind-eyed revisionism would shape the history of the music over the next century. The first decades of the twentieth century were a hot time for men who became known as white bluesmen, but advancing moral amnesia circumvented honest reckoning. The radio personality Paul Harvey recalls from his childhood that country music radio "did not sing dirty." Country music, he argues, historically reflects "apple pie patriotism, virtue, boy-girl romance." Harvey concludes that modern tunes are "down right porno," and the format is at risk of becoming "a *Hustler* magazine of the air" (Harvey). But the overwhelming evidence demonstrates that a healthy vein of lust ran uninhibited in country music well into the 1930s, as white men produced some of the genre's most explicit material.

As in the blues, foodstuff was a metaphor for sex in early country numbers. Merle Travis grew up listening to black men in Kentucky sing "Sweet jelly roll, /Once you taste that jelly/Yo' mama can't keep you home" (Green x). In a Jimmie Davis copyrighted verse of 1935, he sang: "Like my ice cream in a bowl/Can't get enough to save my soul/But it ain't like jellyroll." Rodgers also sang about peaches and bread: "I smell your bread a-burning, turn your damper down,/If you ain't got no damper, good gal, turn yo' bread around" (Paris 168). Reave's White Country Ramblers sang in 1928 about jumping into bed to get their hands on "shortenin' bread," and Skyland Scotty Wiseman sang in 1937 about loving his "biscuit sopped in gravy" (Averill 387). For Uncle Dave Macon it was keeping his "skillet . . . good and greasy" by giving his sweetheart a jug of brandy to keep her "drunk and boozy" (Malone 59). One of Fiddlin' John Carson's tunes tells how he "met her on the road," "laid her on a board," "tuned up" his fiddle and gave her "sugar in the gourd." "I can't get it out," sings Carson, " [the only] way to get the sugar out's [to] roll the gourd about" (Wiggins 84).

Animal metaphors in white dance numbers also told of the undercurrent of sexual tension. A well-known figure dance in Missouri was the "cheat or swing," which started with a fiddle tune called "Hell Up Skunk River." The caller tells the men, "now you dance, and now you swing, and how can you cheat that purty little thing" (Broadfoot 112). In another fiddle tune the caller tells the male dancers to "dip that hunk in a whole lot of gravy. Rope the bell, bell the calf, Swing your corner one and a half. Treat 'em all alike." Titles such as "Forky Deer" and "Clabber Cod" were full of innuendo, including phrases such as "Sally upstairs with a hog-eyed man." "Old-timers today won't tell a stranger what 'hog-eyed' means," writes the editor of *The Illustrated History of Country Music,* "but they grin when somebody asks them" (Carr 18). When Irene Spain transcribed Fiddlin' John Carson's early recordings, she was so embarrassed at the content of his songs that she closed her windows and doors. "Daddy [Jenkins] and my husband were both ministers," she recalls, "and we were quite ashamed to be playing such records in our house" (Wiggins 82).

Emulation may be the simplest explanation for the similarities between black bluesmen and this generation of white men in country. White men listened at train stations, street corners, and in cotton fields with callused fingers and a hunger to express themselves using the black man's technique. The songs may also reveal a broad cultural envy of the bluesman's ability to embody unrestrained sexuality. When the inclusion of race stopped being a possibility in traditional country music, the shame of the sexual metaphors was minimal because there was no threat of black men participating on that level. In Roy Acuff's "Gonna Raise a Ruckus Tonight," the word "hell" was edited out while the word "nigger" remained (Schlappi 28). It was a rare period for white men in country music as they safely visited the ways of the "immoral" race, tasted the wickedness that was their own construction, and remained free of the bondage of being black. Some, like Jimmie Davis, went a step further by suggesting a liaison with a black woman in "Sewing Machine Blues." Wanting an angel from Heaven, he sings that if he can't get one, then he'd like a "high steppin' brown" (Averill 761). This seductive notion expressed itself in the culture at large, too. In 1941, a white woman entertained the notion that her inner inhibitions might be due to a secret black heritage: "I have always thought how nice it would be to really be [a mulatto woman]," she says, "you could just do anything you wanted and it wouldn't make any difference" (Allison Davis 20).

As the twentieth century progressed, even the musicians seemed to forget about the sexual content of their early material. Roy Acuff began his music career singing tunes like "Bang Bang Lulu," the sexual fantasy of a man who wishes he was a ring on his girlfriend's hand so that every time she took a bath he would be "a lucky man" (Escott). Later in life, Acuff professed that it was difficult for him to "write a song and not bring

Christianity into it" and criticized obscenity by adding, "I can't write on that type of stuff" (Nash 14). A young Jimmie Davis sang about a "triflin' mama," who was "tomcattin'" with a man who took honey from his "beehive" (Russel 82). When Davis ran for office in 1944, his opponent used Davis's suggestive Victor releases against him. Years later Davis told an editor of a Baton Rouge tabloid that he only liked gospel and country music if it wasn't "vulgar" (Tosches 130).

With each passing decade, the construction of a "pure" country history became easier to believe. Most songs marketed as white blues were cleaned up as the commercial market grew. The bawdy numbers that were popular in the early years among singers such as Acuff, Rodgers, and Davis never fully penetrated the commercial mainstream. A few years later Hank Williams would challenge the boundaries of sexuality again, his angular pelvis and raw crooning voice reaching out for feminine comfort to ease the pain of a woman he couldn't stop loving. Williams would revive the wanton abandonment of the early bluesmen and revitalize the outlaw image in country and western music. But even his suggestive lyrics in "Lovesick Blues" were mild in comparison: "She'll do you, she'll do me, she's got that kind of lovin.'" The tormented Williams was kicked off the Grand Ole Opry, but when he died at age thirty-three from prescription drug and alcohol abuse, all was forgiven. The prodigal white son, wrapped in the bosom of eternal marital discord, is enshrined underneath a monument to postmortem royalties.

For women in country music, there is no such thing as a prodigal daughter. Instead, the age-old double standard reinforces the rule that while boys will be boys, a young lady should know better. Honky-tonk angels aside, a white woman who wanted to establish herself in the business kept her morals high, her skirts low, and her Christian virtue front and center. The flags for femininity—subordination, humility, and self-effacement—were non-negotiable. One writer describes Kitty Wells, country music's first female star, as a woman of "all deference," too placid to compete with anyone. A Tennessee governor agreed, calling the Bible-carrying wife and mother the best representation of southern womanhood (Dawidoff 66). Women in the business were among the strongest supporters of the code. The country comedienne Minnie Pearl, who makes it clear in her autobiography that her husband is the undisputed head of the house, says Wells was successful because she was "a lady . . . some tramp could never have done it." Kitty, who always traveled with her husband, says, "I always had somebody to look after me" (Dawidoff 66). June Carter Cash explains that her former marriages failed because she didn't follow God's word and become a dependent wife. Female ambition is a dangerous trait, she warns, "especially for a wife and mother. . . . A woman is truly liberated when she gets these things into perspective" (Cash 100).

Country television and radio personality Charlie Chase writes that the culture protects women, but it also holds them accountable for their conduct: "If the word spread that a female artist was sleeping around, chances are good she would be rejected by her audience," Chase explains. "Yet fans don't seem to reject a male doing the same thing. It's just the way society views the sexes." Chase's cohost Lorianne Crook found this out when she joked on the air about going home and relaxing with a drink. "Charlie can joke about having a Jack Daniel's after the show," Crook explains, but after her comment "the phone lines lit up." Irate mothers claimed that Lorianne was a role model for their daughters and criticized her for setting a bad example (Crook 110). George Jones, lamenting the alcoholism that destroyed his friend Lefty Frizzel, explained that a good wife might have saved him. "He needed a woman like I found in Nancy," remarked Jones. "If Nancy hadn't done for me what some wives have failed to do for their husbands, I might have wound up like Lefty" (Jones 52).

Loretta Lynn recognizes the double standard in her industry, and she doesn't like it. The writer of such songs as "The Pill" and "You Ain't Woman Enough" says, "I've heard people say men are bound to run around a little bit. It's their nature. Well, shoot, I don't believe in double standards" (Lynn 55). Lynn notes the irony between the culture's expectations of women and the reality of performing on the road. "It's a funny deal," she says. "In country music, we're always singing about home and family. But because I was in country music, I had to neglect my home and family" (Lynn 105). The disparity between image and reality persists in the culture. Mrs. Fred Frailey, a member of a Missouri Bootheel fundamentalist congregation, demonstrates in the late twentieth century how some traditions die hard. Although she co-pastors their church alongside her husband, she insists that he is the head of her, saying "I'm old fashioned that way." Having married her when she was only sixteen, she explains, he "picked me green off the tree and raised me to suit hisself" (*Bootheel*).

Female country artists must also remain mindful of their public image. Although the number of exceptions is expanding due to crossover concerts and music videos, those who rebel beyond the level of comfort are usually chastised publicly. A young girl who attempted to wear a hula skirt at a music festival was escorted off the stage and told to "go home" and "put on some decent clothes like a lady is supposed to wear. . . . You are a disgrace to the five-string banjo" (Loyal Jones 65). The singer k.d. lang drew comparisons to the legendary Patsy Cline until enough people got a good look at her; Lang's deliberate androgyny contributed to her short-lived career on the country charts. When Reba McEntire and Tanya Tucker appeared at the 1993 Country Music Association show in outfits that critics considered risqué, a ministerial coalition of Nashville pastors called for repentance, prayer, and spiritual renewal (Ferraiuolo). The standard is by no means consistent, and may vary according to the history of public affection an artist receives. Dolly Parton's autobiography reveals a less than conventional attitude about sex, monogamy, and love between women, but her attributes of voice and breast have made her a top-heavy icon of women in country music.

With the help of commercial management, recording technology, and mass production, southern white culture overhauled its image through a publicity campaign at the turn of the century that would forever change the history and meaning of country music. It was a reconstruction not unlike that of the post–Civil War period. Distinctions of race and gender were the cornerstones of the new foundation. With moralism and racism rejoined, the gender stereotypes of the Jim Crow era were reinforced. When blackness became the very definition of immorality, country music became pure of the sin of race. Dividing music into camps of character, country became the righteous stronghold in the face of an encroaching moral pall. The sad legacy would continue as the century progressed when a group of southern white men declared in the 1950s that the rising "negro" music, rock 'n' roll, was an NAACP plot to mongrelize the races (Carney 264). But the sexuality of these early country stars was undeniable, the scandals were often true, and the intangibles between black and white southern men and women were legitimate. The public relations campaign for moralism came too late. The "dye" was cast, and no amount of moral whitewashing could erase country music's all-too-human lineage.

Works Cited

Acuff, Roy, and William Neely. *Roy Acuff's Nashville: The Life and Good Times of Country Music.* New York: Putnam, 1983.
America's Music: The Roots of Country. Turner Broadcasting Company, 1996.
Averill, Patricia. "Can the Circle Be Unbroken: A Study of the Modernization of

Rural Born Southern Whites Since World War I Using Country Music." Ph.D. diss., University of Pennsylvania, 1983.

Barlow, William. *"Looking Up at Down": The Emergence of Blues Culture.* Philadelphia: Temple University Press, 1989.

Bayles, Martha. *Hole in Our Soul: The Loss of Beauty and Meaning in American Popular Music.* New York: The Free Press, 1994.

Bootheel Collection. Missouri Historical Society. AC28, 1994.

Bradley, William Aspenwall. "Song-Ballets and Devil's Ditties." In *Harper's Monthly Magazine* 130 (1915).

Broadfoot, Lennis L. *Pioneer of the Ozarks.* Lithographed and bound in the U.S., 1972.

Bufwack, Mary A., and Robert K. Oermann. *Finding Her Voice: The Saga of Women in Country Music.* New York: Crown Publishers, Inc., 1993.

Cannon, Sarah Ophelia Colley, with Joan Dew. *Minnie Pearl: An Autobiography.* New York: Simon and Schuster, 1980.

Cantwell, Robert E. *When We Were Good: The Folk Revival.* Cambridge: Harvard University Press, 1996.

Carney, George O., ed. *The Sounds of People and Places: Reading in the Geography of American Folk and Popular Music.* New York: University Press of America, 1987.

Carr, Patrick, ed. *The Illustrated History of Country Music: The Editors of Country Music Magazine.* Garden City: Doubleday & Co., Inc., 1979.

Carter, Janette. *Living with Memories.* Hiltons, Virginia: Carter Family Memorial Music Center, 1983.

Cash, June Carter. *Among My Klediments.* Grand Rapids: Zondervan Publishing House, 1979.

Cash, Wilbur Joseph. *Mind of the South.* New York: Vintage Books; Random House, 1941.

Charles, Ray, and David Ritz. *Brother Ray: Ray Charles' Own Story.* New York: Da Capo Press, 1992.

Cohn, David Lewis. *Where I Was Born and Raised.* Notre Dame: University of Notre Dame Press, 1935.

Crook, Lorianne, and Charles Chase, with Mickey Herskowitz. *Crook and Chase: Our Lives, the Music, and the Stars.* New York: William Morrow and Company, Inc., 1995.

Daniel, Wayne W. *Pickin' on Peachtree: A History of Country Music in Atlanta, Georgia.* Urbana: University of Illinois Press, 1990.

Davis, Allison, et al. *Deep South: A Social Anthropological Study of Caste and Class.* Chicago: University of Chicago Press, 1941.

Davis, Angela Y. *Blues Legacies and Black Feminism: Bertrude "Ma" Rainey, Bessie Smith, and Billie Holiday.* New York: Pantheon, 1998.

Dawidoff, Nicholas. *In the Country of Country: People and Places in American Music.* New York: Pantheon, 1997.

Eiland, William U. *Nashville's Mother Church: The History of the Ryman Auditorium.* Old Hickory, Tennessee: Thomas-Parris Printing, 1992.

Epstein, Dena. *Sinful Tunes and Spirituals: Black Folk Music to the Civil War.* Urbana: University of Illinois Press, 1977.

Escott, Colin. *The Essential Roy Acuff, 1936-1949*. Liner notes. Columbia Country Classics. Sony Music Entertainment, Inc., 1992.

Evans, David. "Afro-American One-Stringed," *Western Folklore* 29 (1970).

Ferraiuolo, Perucci. "The Devil in Country Music?" *Christianity Today,* 8 November 1993.

Fraher, James. *The Blues Is a Feeling: Voices and Visions of African-American Blues Musicians*. Wisconsin: Face to Face Books, 1998.

Frost, William Goodell. "Our Contemporary Ancestors in the Southern Mountains." *Atlantic Monthly 83* (1899).

Grantham, Dewey W. *The South in Modern America: A Region at Odds*. New York: Harper Collins, 1994.

Green, Douglas B. *Country Roots: The Origins of Country Music*. New York: Hawthorne Books, Inc., 1976.

Hagan, Chet. *Country Music Legends in the Hall of Fame*. Nashville: Thomas Nelson Publishers, 1982.

Handy, W.C. *Father of the Blues: An Autobiography*. London: Sidgwick and Jackson, 1957.

Harvey, Paul. "'New' Country Music Is in Poor Taste: Singers Polluting Country Sunshine," *Nashville Banner,* 1 April 1980.

Hay, George D. *The Story of the Grand Ole Opry*. George D. Hay, 1953.

Jones, George, with Tom Carter. *George Jones: I Lived to Tell It All*. New York: Villard, 1996.

Jones, Louis M. "Grandpa," with Charles K. Wolfe. *Everybody's Grandpa: Fifty Years Behind the Mike*. Knoxville: University of Tennessee Press, 1984.

Jones, Loyal. *Minstrel of the Appalachians: The Story of Bascom Lamar Lunsford*. Boone, North Carolina: Appalachian Consortium Press, 1984.

Karpeles, Maud. *Cecil Sharp: His Life and Work*. Chicago: University of Chicago Press, 1967.

Kephart, Horace. *Our Southern Highlanders: A Narrative of Adventure in the Southern Appalachians and a Study of Life Among the Mountaineers*. New York: The MacMillan Company, 1926.

King, B.B., with David Ritz. *Blues All Around Me: The Autobiography of B.B. King*. New York: Avon Books, 1996.

Lomax, Alan. *The Land Where the Blues Began*. New York: Pantheon Books, 1993.

Lynn, Loretta, with George Vecsey. *Loretta Lynn: Coal Miner's Daughter*. Chicago: Henry Regnery Company, 1976.

Malone, Bill C. *Singing Cowboys and Musical Mountaineers: Southern Culture and the Roots of Country Music*. Athens: University of Georgia Press, 1993.

——, and Judith McCulloh, eds. *Stars of Country Music: Uncle Dave Macon to Johnny Rodriguez*. Urbana: University of Illinois Press, 1975.

Marshall, Howard W., et al. *Now That's a Good Tune: Masters of Traditional Missouri Fiddling*. Columbia, Missouri: University of Missouri Cultural Heritage Center, 1989.

McKee, Margaret, and Fred Chisenhall. *Beale Black and Blue: Life and Music on Black America's Main Street*. Baton Rouge: Louisiana State University Press, 1981.

Miles, Emma Bell. "Some Real American Music." *Harper's Monthly Magazine* 108 (1904).

Nash, Alanna. *Behind Closed Doors: Talking with the Legends of Country Music.* New York: Knopf, 1988.

Nelson, Willie, with Bud Shrake. *Willie: An Autobiography.* New York: Simon and Schuster, 1988.

Okeh File, Race Record and Catalogue. Jonathan Edwards Memorial Foundation, Chapel Hill.

Orgill, Michael. *Anchored in Love: The Carter Family Story.* Old Tappan, New Jersey: Fleming H. Revell Company, 1975.

Paris, Mike, and Chris Comber. *Jimmie the Kid: The Life of Jimmie Rodgers.* London: Eddison Press, 1977.

Ramsey, Frederic Jr., *Been Here and Gone.* New Brunswick: Rutgers University Press, 1960.

Ritchie, Jean. *Folk Songs of the Southern Appalachians as Sung by Jean Ritchie.* New York: Oak Publications, 1965.

———. *Singing Family of the Cumberlands.* 1955. New York: Geordie Music Publishing, 1980.

Rooney, James. *Bossmen: Bill Monroe & Muddy Waters.* New York: The Dial Press, 1971.

Russel, Tony. *Blacks, Whites and Blues.* New York: Stein and Day, 1970.

Schlappi, Elizabeth. *Roy Acuff: The Smoky Mountain Boy.* Gretna, Louisiana: Pelican Publishing Company, 1978.

Spencer, Jon Michael. *Protest & Praise: Sacred Music of Black Religion.* Minneapolis: Fortress Press, 1990.

Tosches, Nick. *Country: Living Legends and Dying Metaphors in America's Biggest Music.* New York: Charles Scribner's Sons, 1985.

Wiggins, Gene. *Fiddlin' Georgia Crazy: Fiddlin' John Carson, His Real World, and the World of His Songs.* Urbana: University of Illinois Press, 1987.

Williamson, Joel. *New People: Miscegenation and Mulattoes in the United States.* New York: The Free Press, 1980.

Wolfe, Charles. "Black String Bands: A Few Notes on a Lost Cause." *Old-Time Herald* 1 (1989).

WOMEN IN TEXAS MUSIC

A CONVERSATION WITH THE TEXANA DAMES

Kathleen Hudson

Texas music contains the voices of many women. Once relegated to the role of backup singers, women have stepped into the new spaces that have opened up. Some women led the way in this revolution, and some still feel they are relegated to a backup role. The Texana Dames, originally from Lubbock, Texas, are forerunners. They began playing music as a family, the Supernatural Family Band. As the family evolved and changed, so did the music.

Speaking to women in music today, one finds that old attitudes still prevail, even as new steps are being taken. Ms. Lavelle White feels that discrimination against age is as threatening as racial and gender discrimination. Ms. White has been playing blues, soul, and jazz for a long time.

Pauline Reese, a new face in the Austin country music scene, says that the club owners still discriminate against women. Her husband and manager says it pointedly, "When we finish a gig, we want to go home. It's still a boy's club out there; they hang out after the gig and socialize with the owners. Just look at who's still getting the attention—Robert Earl Keen, Pat Green, Cory Morrow, Jack Ingram. Where are the women in this lineup?"

Pauline plays honky tonk music at the Broken Spoke in Austin, Texas, and the Europeans on tour get up and dance. The Texana Dames also play a regular gig at this classic honky tonk dance hall. Dancing is part of their story. Dancing is a part of the definition of good Texas music, that and the writing. The Dames first entertain and play for dances, typically a man's field. Their songwriting supports the idea that music provides a release, a healing, a way to have fun.

After hearing the Dames for the first time, I had the chance to promote their music worldwide while attending Midem, a music conference in Cannes, France. Rod Buckle loved their music. As the man who first produced Doug Sahm's music, he knew good Texas eclectic music when he heard it. The subsequent album took them to the Frutigen Songwriters Festival in Switzerland. I traveled with them, watching the reaction of over seven thousand Europeans gathered under a big tent in this small Swiss German town at the base of the Alps. I stayed with them on this thirteen-day tour, quickly feeling that I was part of a family.

Since then, I have been to many Sunday afternoon sessions at Guero's on South Congress in Austin. My favorite Dames recording captures these Sunday afternoons. "Texana Dames Live" features the soulful voice of Traci singing soulful songs in Spanish and playing accordion, the guitar and steel guitar rhythms of Conni, and the bass and keyboard of Charlene, the "grand dame." Often accompanied by Tomas Ramirez on saxophone, John Reed on guitar, and Paul Mills on drums, the Dames kept up this regular Sunday afternoon gig for many years. Charlene finally requested a break in 2002, five years after the 1997 CD came out.

Conni writes the liner notes, expressing her soulful connection to music. The title is "There's Something about Music on Sunday Afternoons," and this note contains a powerful story about the role of music in building community and creating family. She talks of attending the Mexican-style dances (*tardiadas*) on Sunday afternoons, led by Keith Ferguson, former bass player with the Fabulous Thunderbirds and an aficionado of the music of Mexico, and of hearing the music of Los Tigres del Norte, Flaco Jimenez, Cuatitos, and more. The Texana Dames found their own home, first at La Zona Rosa for three years, then Guero's. There I discovered my favorite Dames' interpretation, Traci playing accordion and singing "Quiero Ser Solo Tuya," a song written by Felipe Martinez.

Conni says, "It's a cleansing of sorts. We forget the past week and prepare for the next." I took my daughter and granddaughter to meet the Dames; I had had the realization that the family of women had a distinct place in my life. Knowing the Dames helped me see the women in my own family with new eyes.

After Tommy Hancock, Charlene's husband, took off to follow his own dream of teaching, the women formed their own group and began another journey through Texas music. All three women have many stories to tell. The following conversation captures the essence of two women, honoring their mother as a source. It also reveals Charlene Hancock, who has a heart as big as Texas.

Women in Texas Music: A Conversation with the Texana Dames

The Ladies Lynching League at Luckenbach, Texas, headed up by Maggie Montgomery, decided to showcase women in Texas music. I always enjoy an evening in Luckenbach, where "everybody is somebody," so I went. The showcased writers on May 30, 2002, were Los Dos Dames, Conni, and Traci Hancock. Maggie Montgomery, hostess of this show, is herself a songwriter. Her interview with these women is part of a film documentary on women in Texas music. I sat in on the conversation and joined in. Maggie welcomed us to a balmy Texas afternoon—about 106 in the shade. "When I first met them, they were the Texana Dames, originally from Lubbock, Texas, and the Supernatural Family Band with Charlene and Tommy Hancock. I remember those days." And she began by asking them about their folks: "Your mom has been in the music business for fifty years, and you've handed me this CD documenting her musical life."

TRACI: This CD, *Charlene Condray Hancock: 50 Years,* is twenty-five songs and fifty years of singing and recording. She should get an award for all the miles she's traveled and all the gigs she's played. It begins with her first recording when she was twelve, and she recorded in the same studio as Buddy Holly. She joined my dad's band when she was sixteen years old. They played for many years around Lubbock at the Cotton Club, and we became the family band in the early seventies, and we traveled all over the country. No way to say exactly how many were in the band because lots of friends joined in from time to time.

MAGGIE: I remember visiting your house, coming into the living room and meeting your family. It was all very formal. Then your father said, "Okay, everybody, we've moving to the music room. If you can't hear what the singer is saying, you're playing too loud." [Lots of laughter.] It was organized, but it was supernatural. Such fun. I'll never forget it.

FELIPE MARTINEZ: Well, Kathleen Hudson, as I live and breathe. What are you doing here? Have a seat and join us. Tell us who you are, Kathleen.

TRACI: Well, first of all, she's a Texana Dame. She has played her egg and her bones with us.

KATHLEEN: I got really interested in oral history in about 1986. My first book is a collection of interviews with Texas songwriters. Now I am focusing on the voice of women in Texas music. I've traveled thirteen days in Europe with this family, documenting their effect on audiences in Frutigen, Switzerland, and Bad Ischl, Austria. I introduced them to Rod Buckle, and he produced an album on them in England—he also produced the Sir Douglas Quintet. Yes, I have a long history with the Texana Dames. I've watched them perform weekly at Guero's on South Congress in Austin. Here I am today, and I'm pleased to join this conversation. I live in Kerrville, and I'm fascinated by the distinction that women have in Texas. I would love to hear a comment from all three of you, describing what is distinct about being a woman in this scene.

CONNI: Well, I don't know anything else.

TRACI: You're around a lot of men. Which is fine. [Laughs.] We do everything in our business ourselves. We are totally self-sufficient. I think it takes a lot of strength. This may go for everybody in the business, but for a woman to be in a traveling band, you have to be really strong. There's a lot of late nights on the road by yourself. You have to stand up for what you want. You can't let anyone run over you. You have to be real clear about that. We like to have a balance between the women and the men in the band when possible. For me, as a woman in the audience, I always like to see a woman in the band. It's kind of a sisterhood there, with other women performers. We know each other and support each other. There's a real kinship there.

CONNI: For me, it's probably pretty different from lots of others. With my dad and brothers, the men in our lives have been so supportive. John Reed and Paul Mills have been so supportive in our band. And then there's our mom. She's been singing professionally since she was about eight years old. They have all made life beautiful and easy for us. Might be tougher for a woman folksinger trying to break into the business.

KATHLEEN: Support seems to be so important, and we know men and women communicate differently. Women seem to provide support for each other. You have provided a lot of support for me over the years!

TRACI: Conni wrote a song that I think is really poignant and something that women need to hear. It's called "Same Taste in Men," and it's how we're not in competition with each other. Let's love each other. I think more women are starting to see the value in each other. We are not on opposite sides.

CONNI: One reason I wanted to settle in Austin is that I felt welcome right away. Marcia Ball and Angela Strehli and Lou Ann Barton made us feel so welcome when we came. We have lived in New Mexico and Colorado, traveled to Europe, Mexico, and South America. Austin felt like home.

KATHLEEN: I was so glad to hear that you were playing Luckenbach. Combining your family history with the heritage at Luckenbach creates a special moment in Texas music history. Historical or hysterical!

CONNI: On the way out I saw a sign that said "Thanks, Waylon." Right away I felt a connection. Waylon used to be a deejay in Lubbock and play my dad's records on the radio. He and my dad stayed in touch over the years. When he died, I felt a strange loss. I never saw him anymore, and I didn't have a personal friendship with him. But I had this connection that he supported my dad by playing his records.

KATHLEEN: You can't escape the the line, "Let's go to Luckenbach, Texas, with Willie and Waylon and the boys."

MAGGIE: Or "with Traci and Conni and the girls." [Laughter.]

KATHLEEN: Ah, the Luckenbach Ladies Lynching League. . .

MAGGIE: Literally!

TRACI: It's wonderful to be here.

KATHLEEN: What do you think of when you hear "Luckenbach"?

TRACI: First, a vision of the Willie Nelson Picnic. What these people who attend look like. These buildings are amazing.

MAGGIE: We just celebrated our 150th anniversary for the fourth year in a row. We had so much fun the first time that we decided to keep it.

CONNI: When you're from Lubbock, there's a deep appreciation for the hills and the trees and the wildflowers. When I think of Luckenbach, I think of this little piece of heaven.

KATHLEEN: What is most important to you in your career right now?

CONNI: Just for people to know that these CDs are available. My mom's and this one by my dad and John X. Reed. It has a compilation of music from each decade. It will take you back.

TRACI: We feel it's very important to get people to hear this music. I'm working on a solo project—an all-Spanish CD.

KATHLEEN: Will it have my favorite song on it? "Quiero Ser Solo Tuya"?

TRACI: That's a gorgeous song.

MAGGIE: You can interview me anytime, Kathleen.

KATHLEEN: Yep, but you need to speak up now.

MAGGIE: I've been singing all my life. I moved from Birmingham, Alabama, when I was thirty. My brother went off to Vietnam and left me his dog and his Gibson guitar, saying take care of my dog and learn to play the guitar. Well, the dog was killed by a neighbor's dog, so I figured I better learn to play the guitar. I moved to Texas with that guitar on my back, and all of a sudden there was this little child on my lap strumming. I was chording and he was singing. One day he said, "I think I can play a little lead on this song, 'Someday Soon.'" I said to go ahead. He started doing my breaks, then sets by himself. Pretty soon he started doing all of my gigs. I moved into promotion and administration. And I still play and sing.

CONNI: I remember your bringing him to our gigs when he was just a toddler.

MAGGIE: Oh, he loved you girls!

CONNI: He was the sweetest thing. [The women are referring to Monte Montgomery.]

MAGGIE: That's sort of my story. Luckenbach is my favorite place to play, under this tree. I've gone off in many directions, but I've always returned. Now I'm president of the Ladies Lynchin' League. What I'm trying to do is make sure the women know they are welcome here. There are so few of us. One woman and fifteen guys. It's fun for a while, but we need more women. Hondo also named me "the Luckenbach Songbird." That's my most treasured title. We're big on titles around here. I'm also the editor of the world famous *Luckenbach Moon,* our newsletter, so I get to write about everything. I want us to be noticed. I don't want us to have to stand in line and say, "Is it my turn? Is it my turn?" That's my story.

KATHLEEN: When you are traveling around the world, do you run into anything distinct about being a woman on the road.

CONNI: We're three women.

TRACI: Not many people are going to mess with us!

CONNI: I can remember getting the flu, being very ill a couple of different times. I was so thankful I was in a band with my mother and my sister, women who would take care of me. I can remember hearing rockabilly musicians talking about hating each other by the end of the tour. For me, it was a bonding experience.

MAGGIE: The noise in the background is not really noise. That's the sound of the Luckenbach pickers. It goes 24/7, and we love it. It's time to move over to the dance hall now.

Several months later, I caught up with the matriarch of this group in Austin, Texas. The following conversation evolved at Vinnie's on August 1, 2002:

KATHLEEN: Charlene Hancock, you are a woman who has been a real source of inspiration for me. When I think of someone who has really woven all the threads together I think about you. We've traveled together in Europe, and I've sat in Guero's on South Congress on Sunday afternoon and danced to your music with Tommy "Zen and the Art of Two-Step," your husband. I've seen the big shows and the little shows.

Let's have another conversation to pull all these times together into one story. Each woman I've talked with has a distinct story. Let's talk about the music business, relationships—you and Tommy have a unique one—choices you've made and things you've learned about yourself.

CHARLENE: Tommy inspires me to get up and move. I'm a pretty passive person, but when you raise four kids, you lose that. I was really young, seventeen, when we married. He was ten years older than me, and everyone said, "Oh, you're marrying that older man." Some worried. We could both tell that there was something that we shared that was just meant to be. We decided to make a try of it. Over the years it has all come about and worked itself out. We've been together for forty-five years now. After we played music together for thirty years, he got tired of the music business. He always wanted to teach; he kept his teacher's license up so he could do that. He asked me to go out to Presidio with him. Conni, Traci, and I had just begun the Texana Dames band, and Conni was writing music for the three of us to sing. That was something I did with my mother when I was growing up, sing harmony. I just couldn't pass up that opportunity. I really wanted to sing with them. He and I both had enough trust and faith in each other that he could go to Presidio and pursue what he wanted to, and I could go to Europe with the Texana Dames and pursue what I wanted to do. Here we are. We were together constantly for forty years. It got to the point where we didn't have any stories to tell each other. It seemed like we were stepping on each other's toes out of habit. Nothing intense. It just seemed like we needed some space.

When he moved out to Presidio, we missed him badly. And the same was true for him. But he had his work teaching out there, and I had my music.

KATHLEEN: Isn't it great that you didn't have to call it quits. A lot of people get to that point and just quit.

CHARLENE: We couldn't. We have too much history. It's not like we didn't love each other, we were just too close. We're both back in Austin now. He has a place in town. He's in town a lot more than I am. I like staying out by the lake where it's quiet. It's a retreat for me. I need that balance in my life. I need the intensity of the music business, but at the same time, I need the balance of a retreat.

KATHLEEN: I remember some of our conversations in Switzerland, and we talked about that balance then. I do think our needs change, mine have. It's a different perception for each of us, balance. You seem really be in touch with your own needs. What are some experiences that have served as a teacher for you?

CHARLENE: Moving to New Mexico from Lubbock in 1970. We lived there for three years in an isolated canyon in a log cabin with no electricity or plumbing. This was quite different from where we lived in West Lubbock with central air. Over in New Mexico we had to work with everything we got. I came from a family that did that. My mother's family moved to West Texas for free land. It was dry-land farming, and it was hard on them. I heard those stories when I was younger, and I thought, "Man, that was tough." I've seen some old pictures recently that I never saw before, and I realized how tough they were to do that. It was kind of that way with us moving to New Mexico. It looked irresponsible to everyone; they thought we were crazy. But, that experience bonded all of us as a family. We had to make it through those winters. Tommy told the kids that he really wanted to do it, but he could wait until they were out of school. They were all ready to go with us. We had a simple life. You draw the water out of the creek, you make your own fire, you chop that tree down.

KATHLEEN: What did you do for money in a traditional sense?

CHARLENE: We still owned the Cotton Club with Tommy's parents, and we rented that out for parties. They didn't have a regular booking going on at that time. We had some income from that and some money saved. We would go back once a month and play the Cotton Club with our old band. Then the kids got interested in playing because there's nothing to do out there in the canyon. Tommy and I did the proverbial thing, saying, "These kids are good. We can do something with this." And that's how the Supernatural Family Band got its start. Also, Tommy and I are both big readers. We began to read the red-letter edition of the Bible just to see what Jesus had to say about living. And we tried to go by that. That led us to more spiritual books about all kinds of religions. We both always had this questions, "Is this all there is? Is there something better?" Someone was hitchhiking through and spent the night with us in New Mexico and told us about Maharaji. We went up to Denver to check that out. We got the techniques to meditate and have continued with that since then. It's not a religion, rather a technique to meditate to connect with yourself.

KATHLEEN: Is this the same person that Jimmie Dale Gilmore connected with?

CHARLENE: Yes. Maharaji is very low-key. He goes around the world, and we see him when we can. That was the first time I went inside myself just to see what I want. I always knew I wanted music; that was a given. I always loved my family and knew I wanted that. It was important to me that Tommy and I enjoy each other and enjoy our kids. This is a completely personal thing for me. He's in his forties now.

KATHLEEN: He must have been very young when you first saw him?

CHARLENE: He was. And the things that came out of his mouth really struck me. That's the truth as I see it. He said things like, "You know the truth when you hear it because it's already there, you know the answers to your questions because they are already there."

KATHLEEN: I can see where that would open up a lot of space for peace.

CHARLENE: And self-reflection. I've been doing music for many years, and now I'm asking, "What else is there?" The question is answered by my love for my family. I have more time for my family this summer, but I still have the need to play.

KATHLEEN: I noticed the last couple of times that I've seen the Dames, that it has been "Dos Dames." I wondered if you had made a decision to stop playing.

CHARLENE: For a couple of months I haven't played much. Before that I never took a break. Conni and Traci needed and wanted to go on. I understood that, and I was real pleased that they went on with their music and have done more things.

   I don't want any of us to feel like we're joined at the hip. I want them to have their own dreams. Maybe they are like I was. My music came from my mother. She sang and played and loved it. She would just beam when things were just right. I remember that. Everything I do, I think of her now. I always think of my mother.

KATHLEEN: Those of us who have these great relationships with our mothers do carry our mothers with us. I know I do.

CHARLENE: My mother was the greatest influence on me in all ways. She was beautiful and had a beautiful heart.

KATHLEEN: Your new CD has all those wonderful shots of you and some of your mother. Let's talk about that. It says "family."

CHARLENE: I'm glad it does. My mother and her brother played music together. Their father played banjo, and I have a picture of him playing banjo in Kentucky. I'm so thrilled to see that thread going back a little bit further. My mother was sixty-five when she died of a heart attack. It was a sudden thing. She lost a baby when I was about four years old. He was nine months old, and, at the time we were living in Dayton, Ohio. My mother would have her songbook and guitar. I could tell she would get sad and lonely, and she would sit down at the kitchen table and sing every song in her songbook and just let it out. Let those feelings be soothed by those songs she was singing. She taught me some harmony. Then we got back out to West Texas, she kept getting so much joy out of her music.

KATHLEEN: So, this is just one big supernatural family!

CHARLENE: I know. You can't draw a line around it.

KATHLEEN: What do you think your kids will say about their mother?

CHARLENE: I know they're going to say, "She's tough." And I am! I'm well honed by my experience. The music was the thing that kept our family together. When we moved to New Mexico, we felt we needed a little more time before everyone moved off. When we found they could play music, we started booking gigs. Tommy was big on showing them about the music business, how to run a gig on the stage. He showed them things music alone can't show you. They know how it goes.

KATHLEEN: I know these girls. Do you have sons?

CHARLENE: Tommy and I have four kids. Conni and Traci and our son Joaquin and our daughter Holly, who lives in Lubbock. Then Tommy has four other children. They are my friends, too. Tommy became such a good dad just thinking about what he wanted for his family. Holly sang with our band when we started. She was only nine then. She liked to dance. She's out in Lubbock now, married to a musician. They sing in church. Her dad played in Tommy's band. Joaquin got married and didn't want to be on the road. That's when Tommy quit playing too. I still see that bond we all have from being on the road together and meeting our goals together.

KATHLEEN: My bonding came through barrel racing, a family affair for us.

CHARLENE: Now we all remember our time on the road fondly. Conni and Traci and I have been doing the Texana Dames Band about fifteen years now. It seems like we just started. It's still exciting to play with them.

KATHLEEN: I saw the beautiful poster advertising the Broken Spoke gig next Wednesday. Tell me about that gig.

CHARLENE: John Reed, of course, is playing with us. And Paul Skelton from the Cornell Hurd Band is playing with us. He's like John, they can do anything. The whole saga continues on. I wouldn't trade my life for anything. I'm so glad I've been able to do what I've done. Tommy always had the understanding that I needed this in my life and supported me in this. We missed each other terribly, but we had plenty of stories to tell when we got back together.

KATHLEEN: What's ahead?

CHARLENE: What's most important to us now is to get our Supernatural Family recordings on CD. Conni is working on the record label on a full-time basis. I want to go into the studio. I'm ready to create some new music. I feel rested enough to focus my energy on new music. Right now, I'm not into traveling. I'm spending a lot of time with Ruth, Tommy's mother. That's my priority. She's ninety-five and still lives at home. She has been going to the senior center for thirty years. She's a beauty.

[Charlene joyfully greets Conni, as if she hasn't seen her in a while. The strong mother-daughter bond is evident as Conni joins us.]

KATHLEEN: Conni, tell us something about women in Texas music.

CONNI: I find the Hispanic women so inspiring. In some cultures, they take what little money they have and make something so beautiful.

KATHLEEN: In a male world, being strong is "winning." A lot of women who work in a male environment take that on. You all are part of my own learning about the value of sitting and talking to women, of certain kinds of energy.

CHARLENE: The music really makes you focus on the strength that comes from inside, from the music. And you find that you are stronger when you can learn to wait. In music, you can't jump ahead or you will miss the moment. Being a bass player, I really know that.

CONNI: Also the power and strength of female energy has to do with nurturing. I really believe that the best music does nurture us. As

Texana Dames, when we play music we are nuturing ourselves and our audience. Very rarely is a honky tonk dance band perceived as a nurturing experience.

KATHLEEN: I was watching Pauline Reese play at the Broken Spoke last night. There were about nine people there from Holland. They got up and formed lines to dance. They really were happy to dance to her honky tonk tunes. There is something different about a woman up there singing than a man. It's not the same.

CHARLENE: It makes you allow yourself to be more vulnerable, some way. Women can accept their vulnerability better than a man. Men seem to have to put up a front of strength at all times.

KATHLEEN: I love the conversation in education about nature versus nurture. Some of who we are is our biology, and some is our culture.

CHARLENE: My mother was a traditional wife. Daddy insisted that she not work outside of the home. She set out to make our home the best home it could be. I realized something when I was pregnant and playing music. I played until I was about seven months at least. I realized that the main things I got from my mother came from the womb. When she would be lonely and sit down and play music, I was there! I knew that music as comfort before I got here. I felt that in myself.

CONNI: I can remember being a toddler at their gig for the first time. I remember focusing in on mother and feeling it like a memory, kind of connecting in my mind, somehow, that this was the outside of it.

CHARLENE: Looking back I can really see what happened. When the kids started playing with us, they followed us much better than any other players. It was easier to do with them.

KATHLEEN: Who are some women who come to mind as strong influences?

CHARLENE: Peggy Lee comes to mind. I always loved her voice and material. I learned much later that she was writing much of that music. Ella Fitzgerald. Any woman playing music caught my eye. There are so many. When I started singing in Tommy's band, there were no singer/songwriters around. There was the "girl singer" in the band.

KATHLEEN: So you were a forerunner.

CHARLENE: I remember thinking, "Why can't I do something here? My own thing?"

CONNI: I noticed the same thing. I paid attention to the women who were playing an instrument. I specifically loved blues and steel guitar, so I loved Bonnie Raitt from the beginning. What my mom experienced was transferred further with me.

KATHLEEN: I was talking to Pauline Reese's husband last night, and he said that in Texas music today, it's still the boy's club. He said, "Look at the songwriters. Look at the guys who stay later and socialize at the club. Pauline and I finish up the evening and want to go home."

CHARLENE: We really never wanted to draw a line around our music. You have the purists in any field, and I just shy away from that.

KATHLEEN: What other band is as eclectic as you?

CONNI: Doug Sahm was.

CHARLENE: But he compartmentalized it. He didn't do all the styles he knew in one gig like we do!

We ended our conversation at Vinnie's in Austin. I was left with my memories, not only of the Dames but of the women in my own family: Annabel, my mother; Carolyn, my sister; Lisa, my daughter; Jessica and Angel, my granddaughters, and my memories of my grandmothers, Hilda "Daddo" Pillow and Alice Maud McClary.

Note

This interview is part of a manuscript for a book on Texas women being prepared by Kathleen Hudson for the University of Texas Press in Austin, Texas.

IF YOU'RE NOT IN IT FOR LOVE

CANADIAN WOMEN IN COUNTRY MUSIC

Linda Jean Daniel

Introduction

The following article is based on data gathered for a doctoral thesis entitled *Singing Out! Canadian Women in Country Music*. It explores the experiences of thirty Canadian women country music singers in order to learn more about women's lives as performers. Since the number of artists is actually much greater than most sources would suggest, the data collected here will merely begin to provide more knowledge about the present situation of Canadian women and country music.

Methodology

Field research in the form of interviews and questionnaires generated the major data. While this essay presents mainly qualitative work, some of the information is presented in tabular form for ease of understanding. Although the statistics do not come from a sufficiently large or randomized population to be generalized, they do reveal some interesting trends from which further, valuable research questions could be generated for future study.

The target population consisted of women who were Canadian citizens and currently performed or had once performed country music. A list of names was compiled; it included women country music artists from a number of different locales across Canada. The main body of information was collected through face-to-face interviews (twenty), with nine additional participants completing and mailing back questionnaires. One interview was conducted over the telephone. A total of thirty women participated in the study. In spite of the unique and individual experiences of each participant, common patterns emerged. An analysis of the information provided by these women is the subject of this article. Pseudonyms are used in order to protect the identities of the respondents. Quotes are attributed to individuals using last names only.

In order to discuss the data collected in a historically relevant manner, the responses of the thirty women were divided into three categories according to year of birth. The first group consisted of women born before the year 1950, referred to as the Pioneers. The next group, called the Middle Group, was composed of those born during the 1950s. The youngest participants formed the Newcomers, with birth dates 1960 and after. Respondents who chose not to specify a year of birth were placed within one of the three groups based on other information obtained during the course of the interview that would locate them within an approximate time frame. At the time of the interviews, the age of the respondents ranged from twenty to sixty-nine years. The mean age was thirty-nine.

Defining Country Music

Defining country music is a difficult—if not impossible—task. There are probably as many definitions as there are people who write, perform, play, or listen to it. Country music is a genre that has developed over time and continues to grow and change. What became known as "country music" was brought to North America by early settlers and developed in pockets throughout the continent. While originating mainly from the "folksongs, ballads, dances, and instrumental pieces brought to North America by Anglo-Celtic immigrants," over time it has absorbed many other musical forms, most notably "from the culture of the Afro-Americans" and has eventually become "a force strong enough to survive, and even thrive, in an urban-industrial society" (Malone 1).

While some may argue that country music originated in the southern United States, independent development also took place in other parts of the continent. The same kind of music that gave rise to "country" in the U.S. was also present in certain regions of Canada during the nineteenth and early twentieth centuries. Neil Rosenberg states: "Maritimes country music, earlier labeled 'cowboy' or 'western' music, has been typically thought to be a popular American form rather than part of a viable, local

Canadian, folk music tradition. In fact, country music in the Maritimes is both of these things" (418). In the Canadian West, what was then termed "country and western" music was beginning to take hold. Immigrants of varying backgrounds settled in the prairies and this music provided a means of sharing common experiences in a new land. In *Canadian Women Making Music,* K. Linda Kivi explains: "The many kinds of folk music from the old countries did not flourish in the same way because immigrants who couldn't understand each others' languages weren't able to share their culture in that particular way. Country music, on the other hand, was homegrown, North American prairie music that spoke of their experiences in an adoptive land: English was the common language" (36–37).

There are many differing opinions about what defines distinctly Canadian country music if, in fact, it exists as a separate entity. On this point, many would agree with Mitch Potter of *The Toronto Star* when he writes: "When it comes to country music, Canada is not Nashville. From Vancouver Island to St. John's harbor, the argument goes, nearly a dozen distinct variations on the Canadian country equation add up to something very different from its American counterpart" (C10). Defining Canadian country music by what it is not, Potter separates it from its country cousin to the south by acknowledging the differences between the kind of music emanating from the Mecca of American country music and that found in various regions across the vast expanse of Canada.

Brant (Pioneer) is an artist who has been involved with music since the early 1960s. As Canadians, she believes that we are still learning "what works for us." For her, being Canadian is to possess a unique identity. She states: "We're not Americans and we don't think like Americans" as much as some people would like to have us believe. Canadians are different. "I think we have a different concept of music up here. I think that Canada has always had great singer/songwriters and that that's a very strong tradition. I think we've always had very strong regional singer/songwriters who sing about the places where they are and where they come from."

Brant admires the tradition of music originating from one's location and experience. As an example, she cites Rita MacNeil, who is "a star in Canada because she addresses with a marvelous voice very Canadian concerns." While MacNeil may not fit Nashville's conception of a country star, she has been very successful in Canada. Brant sees the regional nature of Canadian music to be very powerful: "That tradition here is still very strong and still is a major driving force in the industry here. And I hope that that continues to be, that we don't lose that." Riley (Middle Group) concurs: "We are unique, we are different than the Americans, we have our own style, we have our own things to sing about that...have a bit of different flavor." Cullen (Middle Group) adds, "I think Canadian country music has a tendency to be more with a rootsy country, down-home feel. And in the States, it's still got that homogenizing, a bit of "love 'em or leave 'em material. . . . They've had an uphill swing to a more pop feel." McPherson (Middle Group) sees country music as "a very natural folk music of Canada. . . . It's almost an indigenous kind of music for our country." She believes it to be a part of the Canadian identity and who Canadians are as a people.

Clark (Newcomer) views country as "the music of the '90s." Her definition reveals the all-encompassing attitude of some of today's artists when she claims: "It can be anything you want it to be. There are no limitations with country music." Clark describes the warm acceptance she feels Canadian performers receive around the world, asserting, "The world is always ready for good music regardless of where it comes from. And everyone I've met around the world loves Canada."

The Subculture of Country Music

The women interviewed for this study can be described as belonging to the subculture of country music. While most upheld many of the beliefs and values of the society at large, they were drawn together as a group due to their special interest in this particular type of music. As James E. Curtis and Ronald D. Lambert state, "Any group that has a great deal of interaction within itself and whose experiences set it apart from the rest of society will tend to develop local cultures, or what sociologists call subcultures" (43). Those belonging to a particular subculture may feel that their beliefs and values are what they consider to be "right." It is this belief that provides the cohesion that keeps the group together. They view the rest of the world and their place within it from this perspective.

As members of the country music subculture, many of the participants used a common language to describe their beliefs and values. They employed a discourse that spoke to their inclusion in a group of people for whom country music plays an important part in their lives. The frequent use of terms such as "real," "honest," and "down-to-earth" expressed their perception of the genre and their connection with it.

In attempting to define country music, the following quotes show the significance given to the word "real":

The real life experience—emotions and everything—are all in country music, all in the songs, daily dramas, yes. [Stone, Pioneer]

Just real music. . . . it's about real things and about real people. [Laurence, Middle Group]

It's very real. . . . The songs are written about real life situations that most people can relate to . . . and I think that's why it's becoming so popular today. [Baker, Newcomer]

Respondents from all three groups spoke about the importance of the music being "real." John Shepherd states: "People situated differently in the social structures of industrial capitalism experience and articulate reality in different ways" (134). In other words, in the subculture of country music, what may be considered to be "real" for many of these women is not necessarily what those from other levels of society or, indeed, from other subcultures would view as "real." Depending on one's racial, ethnic, sexual, or socio-economic background, what constitutes that which one perceives to be "real" varies greatly.

Many of the respondents' responses revealed a strong relationship with country music. For several, being a professional country music singer was more than just a "job," it was a way of life. Clark (Newcomer) says, "I never actually 'became' a country singer, I just always was as far back as I can remember. By the time I was eight I was singing professionally." For her, country music is an integral part of who she is as a person.

This display of emotional attachment reinforces the concept described by Curtis and Lambert in which they acknowledge both the external and internal aspects of belonging to a culture. "Culture is external to individuals, in the sense that they learn about it, but it is also internal—it becomes part of them and bestows meaning on their lives. So people's loyalty to their culture is an intensely personal matter" (34).

While human beings are not merely "puppets on a string" manipulated by the society in which they live, they are influenced by that society. One's cultural surroundings tend to influence the way one feels about particular musical styles. Peter J. Martin postulates: "The ways of thinking, acting and feeling which we assume are normal and natural are in fact the results of a lengthy and complex process through which we learn to operate in accordance with prevailing conventions—the process of 'socialization'" (4). The music that some of the respondents described as "real" or "natural" may be in fact the effect of their socialization within the particular subculture of country music, one that results in a feeling of comfort. Martin explains: "As a routine part of the process of socialization, we absorb the music of our cultural environment, just as we learn its language. The music which we thus 'internalize' comes to sound right and natural, even though we many subsequently realize that the conventions which organize it are arbitrary, in the sense that they are not shared by other cultures, and represent only a fraction of the possible ways in which melody, harmony and rhythm may be combined" (8). References to "feeling at home," "a natural progression," or having been "chosen" by country music are perhaps more indicative of the process of socialization of which Martin writes. Children raised in an environment in which country music plays an important role will develop an appreciation for that style of music and regard it in a positive light. While not all participants were exposed to country music while growing up, the majority had some direct contact with the genre during their formative years.

The similarity of the participants with respect to their perception of country music may have to do with the working-class background shared by most of the women—it may have played a part in their attraction to the music and what they felt it represented to them. However, it is important to note that while most participants' parents were working class, the number of variables impacting on each individual artist makes the issue of defining her class problematic with respect to an analysis of choosing a career of performing in this genre, especially since the level of income was unknown.

Curtis W. Ellison, in his book *Country Music Culture,* characterizes those in country music as behaving "like a vast extended family at an endless church supper" (xvii). In agreement with this feeling of "family," some of the respondents described the country music industry in Canada similarly. Barry (Middle Group) states: "There's a big feeling of family across . . . the board between artists, radio people, . . . management companies, record companies. It just seems like there's a real family feeling in Canada. It's a unifying kind of thing. And the industry's growing and there's a lot of talent that keeps emerging every year and it's great." Wilson (Newcomer) agrees: "Everybody is recognized for what they do and how they do it." She feels Canada is special in that the industry has kept its simplicity, family orientation, and closeness.

However, others disagreed. McPherson (Middle Group) considers the industry in Canada to be very "regionalized." Her experience has been that the music she produces is limited to the area in which she lives. She has found it difficult to be heard across the country. She relates, "My career as an artist really is only tak[ing] place out where I live [in the west] because I don't have airplay out here [in the east]." For McPherson the "unifying kind of thing" described by Barry does not exist. She finds the term "regionalism" to be more descriptive of the present music scene in Canada. This situation probably has little to do with the fact that she is a woman but is rather more reflective of the regional nature of Canada and the difficulty that country artists experience in promoting their music due to the great distances from coast to coast—to coast.

Being a Woman Country Music Singer

Gender has become an important area of academic discussion. What was formerly accepted as "just the way things were" has been replaced by new ways of looking at our social environments and our roles as women and men within society. Gender is a relevant area of study since issues like power and economic independence are so tightly bound with one's gender and role expectations within a community. Sylvia Hale states: "Gender relations are moving into the center of cultural, social, and political struggles in the 1990s. Much of the taken-for-granted character of relations between women and men, and also between men and men, and women and women, have been challenged by feminist theory, the active politics of the women's movement, and the emerging struggles around gay and lesbian sexual orientation, and men's liberation movements" (85). With regard to country music, studying the treatment of women in the early years of the business provides us with an account of the difficulty female singers faced when attempting to secure a place within the industry. In recognition of this adversity, Craig (Pioneer) pays tribute to those who "paved the way" and believes had it not been for these early women breaking down the barriers, women in country would be much further behind than they are today. Through the accomplishments of these early female artists, it was established that women could sell records and could be more than just "fillers" on a show. As Craig says, "The first lady I so admired was Kitty Wells and there was Jeannie Shepard, also. They were very different, they were unique, and you know, they were the beginners in this business because it was always men who had all the hits and seemed to get all the breaks. And the women on the shows were what we call 'filler' or whatever. And these ladies came along and had tremendous hits and opened the door for a lot of other women artists to be recognized as people who could sell records."

Stone, another Pioneer, also notes some of the difficulty women had: "They didn't even want to play women on the radio. . . . For one thing, they said women were the ones who bought the records and they want to listen to the men. So, it was a hard grind—a hard grind. Until Loretta Lynn and Kitty Wells started to come out with stuff. And then Patsy Cline, of course. But we're there now. But it's still a struggle though. But they are taking us more seriously as writers now. So that's good." In Canada, the beginnings of country music saw few female artists. Laval (Pioneer) recalls: "When I started out, it was. . . . I can almost count on my hands the female singers in Canada. . . . It was myself and Anne Murray and Carroll Baker. Lynn Jones had a show out of Hamilton. Julie Lynn was playing the club circuit here. . . . But it was just a handful of us and look how it's grown. And I'm glad to have been part of the beginning." Proud to have been one of the few female performers in the early years, Laval emphasizes the importance of educating younger singers so that they realize that what they now enjoy was always there. She feels that they need to be made aware of what has gone before: "They might think that it's just started now and it really started like twenty years ago or more with Lucille Starr and those people. So I'm glad to have been a part of the early era."

The type of song material available for women to record during this period was rather limited, according to Laurence (Middle Group), who began performing at a young age. "They were singing cutesy songs— songs that men wrote for them that didn't really kind of touch on how they felt. And so I think a lot of women found it frustrating." In *Finding Her Voice: The Saga of Women in Country Music* by Mary A. Bufwack and Robert K. Oermann, Kitty Wells comments on the scarcity of songs from which women had to choose and how her hit, "It Wasn't God Who Made Honky Tonk Angels," was a turning point in the writing of songs to which more women could relate: "They didn't seem to write songs for women before then [referring to Wells's hit song 'It Wasn't God Who Made Honky Tonk Angels']. . . . Mostly, [songs] were for men. . . . There weren't a lot of songs to choose from. You had to sing them or not sing at all. . . . ['Honky Tonk Angels'] was kind of the womenfolk getting back at the men" (179).

In addition, the way in which women were introduced on a show could be demeaning. Laurence (Middle Group) recalls: "I just remember even in the introductions, 'Here's the pretty little lady,' and that's all you were— was kind of a little novelty thing or something—for a long time." Clifford (Middle Group) concurs: "Years ago, the women—'girls,' the 'girl singers' in the band . . . they were sort of just there. 'Well, we gotta have a "girl." You have to have a "girl singer," you know. We better have a "girl" on stage to make it look good,' kind of thing—not really taken that seriously."

As singers of country music, women were sometimes expected to do more than they bargained for in order to gain access to the industry.

Termed "the old couch theory" by Laurence (Middle Group), she explains: "You go to meet the record people and you were sometimes expected to do more or, you know, to go along with it just to get anywhere. And I think that happened a lot, too, and that a lot of women just kind of said, 'I don't need that.'"

According to Monica Boyd, "Sexual harassment is essentially a display of power in which one person attempts to control, and often succeeds in controlling, another through sexual overtures" (3.4). Its history is rooted in an ideology of gender inequality, which discriminates against women. "Sexual harassment is the result of the general belief that men are superior to women and may impose their will on women. It is also the outcome of patterned ways of behaving that are based on this belief and that serve to reinforce it" (3.5).

One of the Pioneers recounts a disturbing story of when she was seventeen and was asked to sing on a country music television show. She describes herself as quite naive and "unknown to the ways of the world." She tells what happened in preparation for the show:

> I went to quite a few rehearsals . . . thinking I was going to go on the show, really excited—thrilled, of course. And then at the eleventh hour . . . I was told that—this was *really at* the eleventh hour—I was told that I would have to come across sexually to go on the show. . . . And, of course, I was absolutely shattered, you can imagine! So I said, "No, I'm going to— there's no way." I said, "I'll make it on my singing." And he said, "Oh, well, you'll be lucky"—that sort of thing, a real downput [*sic*]. So that was very, very shattering because I often feel that if that had not happened to me and I had been on the show, my whole future could have been different. It could have been a lot easier. I'd have had the exposure and the financial assistance that I needed. So that was horrendous when that happened.

She also mentions incidents of club owners "coming on to you." Early in her career, she felt that, as a woman, one had to accept it as part of what one was trying to do. Acknowledging that sexual harassment is still being perpetrated, she now believes steps can be taken to counteract this type of behavior. "Those things happened and unfortunately, I guess, they're still happening. But today, you do something about it. But in those days, you just thought, 'Well, that's life,' you know, like having a backache. But you're brought up kind of stupid and naive. And I don't think anyone could have been more naive than I was *then*. But I've changed. *Boy*, have I changed [laughs]." It was not until the 1960s that the term "sexual harassment" even came into existence. Since there was no name for the experience, it clearly was considered to be unimportant or simply nonexistent.

Another respondent reveals her experiences as a woman in a leadership role. While singing in clubs, Riley (Middle Group) explains the difficulty some people had perceiving her as the leader of the band. She states:

> I think women still are—and women in music are still—thought of, "Oh, she's *just* the singer," or "She's flighty," or "She's a ditz," or "She's the chick in the band." . . . I used to get people coming up to me all the time and saying—like people who didn't know who I was—they would say, "Who— what's your band's name?" or "Who's the leader?" And it's like, "Well, it's me, it's my band." "Well, what's the name of your band?" "Well, it's just [Riley]." It's like, "These people work for me, I'm the leader." You almost had to spell it out. They don't expect the woman to be the leader. It's just sort of—they still see you as a "girl" singer, the "chick" up there. I found that.

Riley chooses not to perform in clubs anymore in part due to the negative attitude toward women with which she was confronted. At times, it was an uncomfortable environment.

Although Riley enjoys traveling with her own band—she describes the members as "friends"—working with an unfamiliar back-up band can have its challenges. In these situations "It might take a while for the guys to get used to—this 'girl' is your boss. And some of them would have a problem with that." The following excerpt reveals Riley's sense of frustration in her repetition of the word "hard," meaning "difficult":

> It was hard sometimes to throw around your authority or to take a stand on things. It was hard. It's hard because you're a woman and you've got these four men—boys. . . . Sometimes it took extra courage to get up the nerve to stand up and say . . . "I don't like the way you're doing that," or "I don't want you to drink on stage." It's hard. And then, of course, if you're too aggressive, then you get called a bitch, you know. Well, any woman in any business, that's the way it is, you know.

If a male were the bandleader, perhaps saying what Riley said would be interpreted as being "strong." Yet, the same assertive behavior exhibited by a woman can result in being called a "bitch." Emmons (Middle Group) agrees that being a woman in country music is like being a woman in any other kind of business: "You have to work harder than a man would to get the same amount of respect."

"The stuff women can't see, feel, or touch are interactions that leave them feeling ignored, excluded, patronized, insulted, or undermined" (Reardon 166). By openly discussing the problems faced by women aspiring to or already in leadership positions, Reardon insists that women "must take control" of these situations and learn effective ways of dealing with them instead of just "letting them go." Recognizing "the subtle stuff" and responding effectively are important to both women and men in opening up the lines of communication and improving working conditions.

The participants in this study found being a woman country music singer to have both its advantages and disadvantages. As women, most of the participants did not perceive any difference in the way they experienced the country music business and, in fact, viewed being a woman as an advantage in the present market, with so many female artists doing so well.

Women in country music have made unprecedented gains since the 1950s. Over time, women have come to represent more of the top-selling records. There were several respondents who thought the present (i.e., when they participated in the study) was the best time to be a female performer of country music. They believed it was a distinct advantage even if the phenomenon could not be explained or its duration known. Many observed that people seem to be paying more attention to women performers of country music, and they are perceived to be doing well on the charts, especially in Canada:

> I think women are doing very well in country right now. There's a lot of interest in women performers in country—just at this time. Whether that will continue or not, I don't know. [Brant, Pioneer]

> It seems to be an OK thing to be right now. . . . There seems to be a lot of women in the top ten in Canada right now. And, like I say, I don't know why that is. But I certainly don't see any disadvantages at the moment. [Edwards, Middle Group]

> I feel that the women are very strong and very much accepted. And it's evident in the artists. It's evident in our track record of artists, female artists in Canada. [Wilson, Newcomer]

Baker (Newcomer) describes now as "probably the greatest time" to pursue a career in country music, "for women especially."

Edwards (Middle Group) recalls a conversation among performing artists at Country Music Week in 1993: "We were talking about this last night—about how in Canada there are way more women singers, women Canadian singers in country music than in the States, for some reason. I don't know why, but most of whom I really like—I like their statements." Laurence agrees with the notion that women seem to be more popular in the Canadian country music scene: "I think it's an exciting time for women to be in music. . . . I think it's more of an advantage now just because the whole industry's hot on female artists. I think in Canada, . . . it's the strongest category. I think we have more stronger females than we have in any other category." As a Canadian, Clifford (Middle Group) credits performers such as Anne Murray and, years later, k.d. lang with changing attitudes towards female performers. She thinks women have become "quite a force in music," not only as performers but behind the scenes as well: "Women are taking more of an active role in power positions of companies and making decisions in the music business rather than just being the secretary in the office or whatever." Women are far more recognized than they have ever been.

Working Lives

Exploring how the respondents deal with their everyday lives while at the same time pursuing a singing career is a relevant area to examine due to the impact that their lives as women outside the realm of singing has on their careers. The home situation seems to play a fundamental role in many of the basic and, therefore, very important contradictions these women experience. Gender is significant when discussing issues of childcare and homecare since, for many, the female performer's experience differs greatly from that of the male artist when dealing with these realities.

Trying to be successful in one's occupation while at the same time raising children and maintaining a home is a daunting task for many women. The number of women having to deal with this situation is increasing all the time. "There has been [a] particularly sharp growth in the employment rate of women with children in the last decade" (Almey 64). Yet although there are more women with young children working outside the home, childcare and homecare are still mainly relegated to them. "Even when employed, women are still largely responsible for looking after their homes and families" (70).

Childcare is a significant issue for those women country music entertainers who have them. Since singing usually requires several hours of work at night, in addition to preparation time for performances and, in many instances, extensive traveling time, childrearing is a concern. Being responsible for caregiving in an occupation such as performing is difficult.

There were 14 respondents (47 percent) who had children and 14 (47 percent) who did not. (Two remained unknown.) Craig (Pioneer) expresses the guilt she still feels about being "on the road" and leaving her child behind. Although her son is now an adult, she thinks of the time when he was young and she was not there to watch him grow up. Brant (Pioneer) was also involved in childcare several years ago. She describes how she dealt with traveling, having a young child, and then experiencing the end of her marriage. A live-in housekeeper made touring possible, but after the breakup of her marriage, decisions were made that directly affected her singing career.

Other artists also were forced to make so-called "choices" due to relationships involving childcare responsibilities, which, in turn, affected their careers. Bailey (Pioneer) recalls her experience with the fatigue of "trying to do it all" and her ultimate decision:

> There were nights when I don't know how I made it either. 'Cause then you work till one in the morning and by the time you get home, it's two. And then you've got to get up for two kids in the morning. You don't get any rest, so you're really exhausted. . . . I used to come home and cry—I was so tired—just sit downstairs and cry. . . . It got to the point that I just had so much of it that I couldn't take it anymore and that's when I said, "I'm finished, I'm quitting. I can't handle it anymore."

Although Bailey had some support from her family, she still found it difficult to cope and eventually left the music business. Having to choose between career and family is troublesome. To feel one cannot do both is a disconcerting issue with which to deal especially when you love both your family and your chosen occupation.

Stevens (Middle Group) explains a decision she made as a result of childcare demands on her time: "I had to pull back totally from my career for at least three or four years, which was fine, but I don't know if as many men [put their careers on hold]—unless they were involved in being the major caregiver, which is still, you know [rare]." To Stevens, having children is a commitment and proper childcare is a necessity: "When you have children, someone has to be there to take care of these kids and give them what they need." The average performer usually cannot afford daycare or full-time babysitters, so making outside arrangements for the care of children is a significant factor with which a woman in country music must deal. Since there are apparently few male performers who are the major child caregivers in their families, Stevens believes that female entertainers' careers are definitely more likely to be adversely affected by childcare concerns than their male counterparts are.

McPherson (Middle Group) observes that there are fewer women in the business who have children than men. She provides the following explanation:

> I feel that the women in country music, fewer of us that I know of, have families—than men. Mainly because [the male performers] leave the woman in charge at home and they're able to go and tour and pursue their careers and there's still someone "holding the fort" at home. There's not too many women with families like myself who can just sally forth and leave somebody nurturing the children—not just meeting their physical needs but actually involved in their lives.

McPherson's situation is unusual, in that her husband is currently not working outside the home and is therefore able to provide the essentials for their children. This affords her the opportunity to tour without worrying about proper childcare.

Homecare is another issue. Although women's participation in the labor force is greater than it has ever been, in most cases their work at home has remained unchanged. As Bonnie J. Fox notes, "Despite having assumed part of the responsibility for breadwinning, women remain largely responsible for the full range of tasks known as 'housework'" (9.17). Margrit Eichler states: "Under the patriarchal model of the family, wives were responsible for all housework and other unpaid family work, for all service work for the household members . . . and for everything else that was needed to keep the family and the household on an even keel. To a large degree, unfortunately, this still describes today's reality" (59). Participating in the country music scene and maintaining the major responsibility for the household is a combination of pressures that many women in the business face. As a performer of country music for many years, Stone (Pioneer) talks about her experience with what she terms the "double shift": "It's working the nightlife plus trying to do the day scene. You know, 'double shift.' It takes its toll. Still having to get up in the morning when you haven't gone to bed till four, maybe, at least fallen asleep till that time because you're so geared up." Laurence (Middle Group) explains how she deals with both childcare and homecare:

> When we go away and travel [performing, recording, and so on], we have a lady that comes in and stays with the kids. She doesn't live with us all the time. . . . When I'm at home, I cook probably 99 percent of the time . . . . I find now we've gotten so busy . . . that I've decided to kind of delegate some stuff to—like getting a housekeeper so I have more time with the kids when I'm at home and just so I can have more time to write. . . . I fall into bed every night at like 10 o'clock and I'm exhausted. But I still carry most of

the weight around the house. And I think, you know, probably that's still the case for most working women, unfortunately. So it is very tiring.

The word "unfortunately" summarizes Laurence's feelings well. Although she would like the situation to be different and believes that it should be, she recognizes the reality and copes with it as best she can.

Janet Saltzman Chafetz states: "Domestic and familial obligations *are* work, and hard work at that. The tasks required of those who run a household and raise children are time, attention and energy-consuming. Full-time jobs also consume substantial time, attention, and energy some more so than others. Conflicts arise in the family largely because domestic work is not shared equitably by women and men" (122–23). A career singing country music comes with a cost to one's private life. McPherson (Middle Group) explains the amount of commitment required by women who choose to perform:

> They sacrifice. You make choices that involve—"I will do this, I will spend my money on this and not that. I won't have a home. I will have a good press kit and stage clothes that are expensive, and good equipment. I won't have a family in the form of children. I will have quite a bit of profile in radio because I'm out working my singles and touring and talking to all the radio stations as I go. I won't have time with my boyfriend or husband on a regular and predictable basis because I'm out of town three months coming now and I love him very much but this is what I have to do for my career." So everybody makes sacrifices and it just very much is a matter of how much you feel comfortable giving to this industry and what's appropriate for you.

Being a country music performer can affect every aspect of a singer's existence.

The Role of Radio

It is important to discuss the role of radio, since it plays such an important part in the career of a country artist. Having a song played on the radio can become a major component of a singer's success because airplay significantly augments the number of people who hear an artist's music. Radio airplay is required in disseminating a singer's music to a broader audience. The following discussion outlines the relationship between radio and country music and also addresses the continued importance of this association in the lives of Canadian women country music singers.

In 1971, the Canadian Radio-Television and Telecommunications Commission (CRTC) established Canadian content regulations (known as "Cancon") in order to give Canadian musicians more opportunities to be heard in Canada. Cancon was introduced to support the promotion of Canadian talent by forcing Canadian radio stations to play music "made in Canada." The CRTC created a system whereby every musical selection received a rating according to the input Canadians had in its creation. Known as the MAPL (Music, Artist, Production, and Lyrics) system, it states: "A musical selection must generally meet at least two of the five criteria set out . . . in order to qualify as a Canadian selection" (CRTC Public Notice 38–39).

Cancon regulations were met with mixed reviews, especially by those in private broadcasting. Yet, according to Rowland Lorimer and Jean McNulty, the effect of Cancon's original implementation on the Canadian music industry has been very positive: "The most important government action taken in Canada to support the domestic recording industry and Canadian musicians was the CRTC's 1971 establishment of Canadian content quotas for all radio stations" (198).

At the time of the data collection for this study, Canadian content regulations stated that 30 percent of the music played on Canadian radio must be classified as Cancon. The opinions of the women interviewed concerning Cancon ranged from considering it a necessity to viewing it as a detriment. While some described Cancon as a benefit (57 percent), others wished it did not exist (17 percent). A few remained neutral on the subject or stated that they did not want to reveal their opinions (13 percent). Four were unknown.

By far the most positive response towards Cancon came from the members of the Pioneer group—those who had been in the music business the longest. Out of a possible seven within this group, six, or 86 percent, believed its implementation to be necessary in order to aid the Canadian country music industry in its survival. Although several wished that Canadian artists could succeed without it, their experiences had led them to the conclusion that it was difficult to establish oneself in the Canadian music business without some kind of protection against the overwhelming deluge of foreign material. They believed it was only due to Cancon that Canadians received significant airplay:

> It was through Juneau who insisted on it—that it had to be Canadian. That's the only reason that Canadians got played is through that coming in. Otherwise they still would be playing all American. [Bailey]

> Most assuredly, a lot of Canadians would not be getting their records played [if it were not for Cancon]. Because, you know, the big labels dictate. It's always been like that, and it'll always be like that. That's just the way it is. That's why artists try to be on big labels. Money talks, doesn't it. [Craig]

> We would never have gotten airplay in the first place to create the industry we have without [Cancon regulations]. [Murray]

Brant can see both sides of the issue but she believes that Cancon regulations are essential: "It is a necessity because, unfortunately, unless they were made to do so, Canadian broadcasters would not play as much as 30 percent." When asked why, she responds: "Because they fall back on the old thing which was true twenty years ago—that there wasn't enough good Canadian material. Further to that, we're on the border with the United States. We are constantly bombarded with American programming. That's where our charts come from. But whether we like it or not, it's a fact of life. And we do need to protect our own industry. There's no two ways about it." In fact, Brant thinks the CRTC should be even stricter when it comes to protecting the rights of Canadian artists. Like Brant, Stone considers the situation to be unfortunate and wishes that Canadian radio would play Canadian music of its own volition. She views it as a disparagement of talented Canadian singers that radio has to be forced to play Cancon material but also acknowledges that if it were not mandatory, Canadian artists might not receive any airplay. "So in one way, it's a put-down that [Canadian radio stations] *have* to [play Cancon material]—not that they're willing to do it." Her exasperation comes through loud and clear in the following quote:

> I just don't know. It's pathetic really because it would help Canada—it would help Canadians. You shouldn't have to feel that you have to leave Canada and make it somewhere else to prove that you're a success or that you're good at your trade. But that's the way it is. . . . The fact [radio stations] don't play Canadian, I guess that is the biggest disadvantage [in being a Canadian woman in country music]. I'm not making back what I'm putting into it.

When Stone asked some Canadian radio stations why they were not playing her song, they replied that they only play "hits." She questions how songs ever become "hits" if they are not played on the radio and the listeners never hear them. "The public out there would probably love to hear [Canadian country music]. . . . This other thing [songs from the American hit list] is being forced on [the general public]. They don't have their own free will. Because if you phone in for a request for a Canadian song, you don't get it." The excuse that radio DJs mention for not playing a requested Canadian song is that it is not on the play list and the musical director has not chosen it. Stone thinks that Canadian radio stations are "gutless" and that they should forget the top American songs and start playing Canadian music, because people would accept it.

There were eight respondents—more than half of the Middle Group (57 percent)—who, like the majority of Pioneers, believed that Cancon was important in helping to provide Canadian artists with the opportunity of receiving airplay. Many had serious concerns that if it were not in place, Canadian artists would simply not be played on Canadian radio. These women felt Cancon played a very important role in establishing and maintaining a career in country music in Canada:

> Very positive. Without [Cancon] we would never get played. The egos of radio music directors would choose U.S. music every time. They are so cowardly. Radio caters to U.S. artists to our exclusion and detriment. Foreigners set our sound standard. We are a 30 percent minority in our own land. [Burgess]

> I think it's great. . . . I don't trust those radio people. I don't trust that they would play Canadian music if they didn't have to. . . . I think it's a great thing. . . . I think it's just really important. It's too bad but it is important. [Edwards]

> It's necessary here. It just is. . . . We've got to protect ourselves. . . . The States has been into protectionism for years and years. We hardly protect anything that's ours. This small gesture is hardly, you know, worth mentioning. That's my attitude. [Richmond]

Phillips affirms that the geographical reality of "a sleeping giant like the States beside you" exerts an extremely strong cultural influence on Canadians that necessitates a system like Cancon. Without it, "I'm not sure how much exposure Canadian artists would get. And I think it's really important." Legislation is essential because "people would be more tempted to play the glossy American stuff first." She regrets the fact that well-known Canadian musician Stompin' Tom Connors, who writes and sings about his own country, has rarely received airplay on major Canadian radio stations. Connors, a nationalistic singer/songwriter, writes, "We have been blessed with one great big young and beautiful country of which we can all be proud. And I'm talking about the kind of pride that we should all be writing and singing about. And not the kind of shame and embarrassment that big radio stations feel when they refuse to play the music that should always be encouraged to flow freely from the hearts of all true Canadians" (634–35).

Emmons is a Canadian country music artist who not only performs but also has a business that promotes independent artists to Canadian country radio stations. She states adamantly that Cancon is absolutely necessary but points out its drawback—that many times the 30 percent *minimum* requirement is implemented by radio in the form of a 30 percent *maximum*. Radio stations usually play only 30 percent Cancon and nothing more, instead of well over the 30 percent regulations. Her sense of frustration is clear in the following quote:

> [Cancon regulations] are the only reason we have a few stars now, at least at radio level. Canadians as a society have this *huge* problem with recognizing their own. I operate a business . . . which promotes Canadian independent artists to Canada's country radio stations. Without Can-Con regs of 30 percent we wouldn't stand a chance of getting on radio because 90 percent of the music directors are afraid to stick their neck out and play somebody new that they really like unless everybody else is—"i.e." chart action. The problem with Can-Con is that most music directors treat it as a maximum instead of minimum.

Emmons describes the situation in Quebec as an example of the effect higher mandated percentages of Cancon could have on promoting more Canadian country music singers. She explains the difference between Quebec and the rest of English-speaking Canada: "In Quebec, French-language stations are forced to play 65 percent French vocal music and a Quebec 'star' sells more records in Quebec than an English 'star' does in all the rest of Canada; all the proof I need to say it's time Canadian radio played more Canadian music and (unfortunately) the only way it will happen soon is if they are forced to by regulation." If English radio stations were mandated to play 65 percent Cancon, Emmons believes this would help to improve the exposure of Canadian country music artists and, in return, increase their popularity.

In direct contrast, Thompson (Newcomer) feels that although Cancon has most likely aided Canadian artists, she does not believe it is necessary: "I fully believe in free market. So I'm not a big—I know Cancon has probably helped a lot of people. Philosophically, I don't believe in government regulation of anything. So you know, we are—if we're good enough to compete, then that's how we get on the radio. If we're not good enough to compete, then we've got no business being on the radio." The Newcomers had the lowest percentage of positive responses to Cancon, with only three of the group, or 33 percent, agreeing with its implementation. As a whole, this group was more evenly spread among the categories (Positive, Negative, Neutral, Unknown) than the Pioneers or the Middle Group. This result may be in part due to the fact that these women have been in the singing profession for considerably less time than most of the women in the other two groups and their experiences have therefore been quite different from a historical point of view.

As an example of the percentage of Canadian artists played on a Canadian radio station and the time of day in which their songs were played, Table 1 examines a play list for CISS-FM, in Toronto, Ontario.

On Sunday, March 24, 1996, the percentage of Cancon songs (40.12 percent) was higher than the mandatory 30 percent. However, throughout the entire day, only eight Canadian "hits" were played, representing only 3.31 percent of the total number of songs. This contrasts significantly with the 106 American "hits" played, which accounted for 44.66 percent of airplay. From 6:00 a.m. to 7:00 p.m., there were only five Canadian "hits" played compared to 103 American "hits." Sunday evening, a less popular listening time, was left for Canadian artists.

To compare a weekend with a weekday, Table 2 shows the hours of radio airplay on Wednesday, March 27, 1996.

The percentage of Cancon songs played was 40.11 percent. Most of the Cancon material on that particular day was aired after the dinner hour, during the "evening" time slot (between the hours of 7:00 p.m. and midnight). Of the total number of Cancon songs receiving airplay during the entire day (eighty-six), over half, forty-five (52.3 percent), were heard during this less popular time slot.

To gain perspective, CHFX-FM from Halifax, Nova Scotia, was studied with reference to number of Cancon songs, gender, and country of origin. Table 3 illustrates Cancon and non-Cancon material on a weekday (Monday, February 26, 1996) and a weekend (Saturday, March 2, 1996).

On Monday, February 26, 1996, the percentage of Cancon material played was slightly above the required 30 percent at 31.5 percent. However, on Saturday, March 2, 1996, the percentage of Cancon fell from 31.5 percent to 27.2 percent, below the mandated Cancon quota. Non-Cancon songs received an overwhelming 68.5 percent and 72.7 percent, respectively, of the total songs played each day.

Table 4 categorizes the female/male and Canadian/American artists receiving airplay.

On Monday, February 26, 1996, the percentages of airplay received

Table 1
Radio Airplay by the Hour for Radio Station CISS-FM, Toronto, Ontario, Sunday, March 24, 1996

Time	Cancon Songs		Canadian Female Lead		Canadian Male Lead		Canadian "Hits"		American "Hits"		Total Songs
	N*	%	N	%	N	%	N	%	N	%	N**
6 am	2	20	2	20	0	0	0	0	8	80	10
7 am	3	33.3	0	0	3	33.3	0	0	2	22.2	9
8 am	3	25	0	0	3	25	1	8.3	9	75	12
9 am	3	23.1	2	15.4	1	7.7	1	7.7	7	53.9	13
10 am	2	15.4	1	7.7	1	7.7	1	7.7	8	61.5	13
11 am	3	20	1	6.7	2	13.3	0	0	10	66.7	15
12 am	3	21.4	2	14.3	1	7.1	0	0	11	78.6	14
1 pm	2	15.4	1	7.7	1	7.7	1	7.7	10	77	13
2 pm	2	13.3	1	6.7	1	6.7	0	0	10	66.7	15
3 pm	6	42.9	6	42.9	0	0	0	0	7	50	14
4 pm	5	35.7	2	14.3	3	21.4	0	0	8	57.1	14
5 pm	6	50	2	16.7	1	8.3	0	0	6	50	12
6 pm	5	31.3	1	6.3	4	25	1	6.3	7	43.8	16
7 pm	10	71.4	4	28.6	5	35.7	0	0	2	14.3	14
8 pm	11	78.6	4	28.6	6	42.9	1	7.1	0	0	14
9 pm	10	77	6	46.2	3	23.1	1	7.7	0	0	13
10 pm	10	77	2	15.4	7	53.9	0	0	0	0	13
11 pm	10	71.4	6	42.9	4	28.6	1	7.1	1	7.1	14
Total	96	-	43	-	46	-	8	-	106	-	238
Ave.	-	40.12	-	17.8	-	19.3	-	3.31	-	44.66	-

*The total number of Cancon songs played does not equal the total number of Canadian Female Lead and Canadian Male Lead since some songs classified as Cancon are written and/or produced by Canadians but are not performed by Canadian artists. In one case, the gender of a group's lead singer was not known.

**The total number of songs played per hour

Table 2
Radio Airplay by the Hour for Radio Station CISS-FM, Toronto, Ontario, Wednesday, March 27, 1996

Time	Cancon Songs N*	%	Canadian Female Lead N	%	Canadian Male Lead N	%	Canadian "Hits" N	%	American "Hits" N	%	Total Songs N**
6 am	1	14.3	0	0	1	14.3	0	0	6	85.7	7
7 am	1	14.3	1	14.3	0	0	0	0	6	85.7	7
8 am	2	33.3	1	16.7	1	16.7	0	0	4	66.7	6
9 am	3	23.1	2	15.4	0	0	0	0	10	77	13
10 am	4	28.6	1	7.1	2	14.3	0	0	8	57.1	14
11 am	4	28.6	3	21.4	1	7.1	0	0	9	64.3	14
12 am	3	23.1	3	23.1	0	0	0	0	10	77	13
1 pm	5	35.7	0	0	4	28.6	1	7.1	9	64.3	14
2 pm	4	30.8	2	15.4	2	15.4	1	7.7	6	46.2	13
3 pm	3	21.4	1	7.1	2	14.3	0	0	8	57.1	14
4 pm	3	25	2	16.7	1	8.3	0	0	7	58.3	12
5 pm	3	27.3	2	18.2	1	9.1	0	0	8	72.7	11
6 pm	5	41.7	2	16.7	2	16.7	2	16.7	5	41.7	12
7 pm	7	58.3	3	25	4	33.3	0	0	1	8.3	12
8 pm	9	75	3	25	5	41.7	0	0	0	0	12
9 pm	8	72.7	4	36.4	3	27.3	0	0	0	0	11
10 pm	11	91.7	5	41.7	3	25	2	16.7	0	0	12
11 pm	10	77	3	23.1	5	38.5	0	0	0	0	13
Total	86	-	38	-	37	-	6	-	97	-	210
Ave.	-	40.11	-	17.96	-	17.26	-	2.68	-	47.89	-

*The total number of Cancon songs played does not equal the total number of Canadian Female Lead and Canadian Male Lead since some songs classified as Cancon are written and/or produced by Canadians but are not performed by Canadian artists. In one case, the gender of a group's lead singer was not known.

**The total number of songs played per hour

Table 3
Playlists for CHFX-FM - Halifax, Nova Scotia
Cancon and Non-Cancon Songs

| | Monday, February 26, 1996 | | Saturday, March 2, 1996 | |
	Number of Songs	% of Total Number of Songs	Number of Songs	% of Total Number of Songs
Cancon Songs	81	31.5	73	27.2
Non-Cancon Songs	176	68.5	194	72.7
Total	257	100.0	267	99.9

Table 4
Playlists for CHFX-FM - Halifax, Nova Scotia
Canadian and American Female and Male Performers

| | Monday, February 26, 1996 | | Saturday, March 2, 1996 | |
	Number of Songs	% of Total Number of Songs	Number of Songs	% of Total Number of Songs
Canadian Country Females	42	16.3	35	13.1
Canadian Country Males	39	15.2	38	14.2
American Country Females	42	16.3	51	19.1
American Country Males	134	52.1	143	53.6
Total Number of Songs	257	99.9	267	100

for Canadian country females, Canadian country males, and American country females were all around the 15 percent to 16 percent percent mark, making the three groups surprisingly equitable in this particular example. In fact, both the Canadian country females and the American country females were tied exactly at 42 songs for each group, or 16.3 percent of the total number of songs played. The most interesting fact was the overwhelming majority of music sung by American males—134 songs, or 52.1 percent. Over half of the airplay was given to one group of singers (American males) leaving less than half of the remaining airplay to be divided among the other three groups (Canadian females, Canadian males, and American females). This pattern continued on Saturday.

The examples above document the lack of support given to Canadian country music artists by two Canadian radio stations during prime listening times. The data analyzed revealed that in several instances, Canadian country music artists were treated as "second best" after American country music artists, who received the vast majority of airplay during the most popular listening times.

Conclusion

Gender has an effect on the life of a Canadian woman country music performer. Although most of the participants did not feel they were treated differently because they were women, some structural barriers became obvious. Many spoke of the amount of energy required to realize a performing career, while at the same time usually being held responsible for the majority of homecare and/or childcare.

An analysis of some radio stations' play lists revealed that Canadian content regulations as to content—30 percent Canadian programming—were fulfilled, but as to timing—when Canadian artists received airplay—were usually not followed. Various singers expressed their disappointment with the reality of trying to establish a country music career in Canada when it was so difficult to receive consistent radio airplay, and several spoke of the importance Cancon regulations had had in their musical lives. Many believed that due to the overwhelming influence of Canada's neighbor to the south, whose close proximity necessitates the protection of Canadian culture, Cancon is the impetus behind Canadian country music artists receiving more recognition on Canadian airwaves.

The data gathered for this study are evidence that women who sing country music come from diverse personal and musical backgrounds and that there is no set formula or prerequisite for becoming a country music singer. The commonality among the participants was their passion for the music they sing and each performer's sense of self. While each woman reflected her own individual circumstances, the general pattern of responses appears to suggest that achieving and maintaining a career in the country music business over a substantial length of time remains a challenging vocation, but one with which Canadian women persevere due to the music they love.

Works Cited

Almey, Marcia. "Labour Force Characteristics." In *Women in Canada: A Statistical Report. Third Edition, Target Groups Project.* Ottawa: Statistics Canada, August 1995.

Boyd, Monica. "Gender Inequality: Economic and Political Aspects." In *New Society: Sociology for the 21st Century,* edited by Robert J. Brym. Toronto: Harcourt Brace & Company, 1995.

Bufwack, Mary A., and Robert K. Oermann. *Finding Her Voice: The Saga of Women in Country Music.* New York: Crown Publishers, Inc., 1993.

Chafetz, Janet Saltzman. "'I need a (traditional) wife!' Employment–Family Conflicts." In *Workplace / Women's Place: An Anthology,* edited by Dana Dunn. Los Angeles, California: Roxbury Publishing Company, 1997.

Connors, Tom C. *Stompin' Tom and the Connors Tone.* Toronto: Penguin Books, 2000.

"CRTC (Canadian Radio-Television and Telecommunications Commission) Public Notice 1998–41." *Commercial Radio Policy 1998.* April 30, 1998.

Curtis, James E., and Ronald D. Lambert. "Culture." In *Sociology,* 4th ed., edited by Robert Hagedorn. Toronto: Holt, Rinehart and Winston of Canada, 1990.

Eichler, Margrit. *Family Shifts: Families, Policies, and Gender Equality.* Toronto: Oxford University Press, 1997.

Ellison, Curtis W. *Country Music Culture: From Hard Times to Heaven.* Jackson: University Press of Mississippi, 1995.

Fox, Bonnie J. "The Family." In *New Society: Sociology for the 21st Century,* edited by Robert J. Brym. Toronto: Harcourt Brace & Company, 1995.

Hale, Sylvia M. *Controversies in Sociology: A Canadian Introduction,* 2nd ed. Toronto: Copp Clark Ltd., 1995.

Kivi, K. Linda. *Canadian Women Making Music.* Toronto: Green Dragon Press, 1992.

Lorimer, Rowland, and Jean McNulty. *Mass Communication in Canada,* 3rd ed. Toronto: Oxford University Press, 1996.

Malone, Bill C. *Country Music U.S.A.,* rev. ed. Texas: University of Texas Press, 1991.

Martin, Peter J. *Sounds and Society: Themes in the Sociology of Music.* New York: Manchester University Press, 1995.

Potter, Mitch. "Roots Music: Get Ready for Country TV Without the Twang, Maybe." *The Toronto Star,* 9 January 1994, C10.

Reardon, Kathleen Kelley. "Dysfunctional Communication Patterns in the Workplace: Closing the Gap between Women and Men." In *Workplace/Women's Place: An Anthology,* edited by Dana Dunn. Los Angeles: Roxbury Publishing Company, 1997.

Rosenberg, Neil V. "Ethnicity and Class: Black Country Musicians in the Maritimes." In *Canadian Music: Issues of Hegemony and Identity,* edited by Beverley Diamond and Robert Witmer. Toronto: Canadian Scholars' Press Inc., 1994.

Shepherd, John. *Music as Social Text.* Cambridge: Polity Press, 1991.

THE YODELING COWGIRLS

AUSTRALIAN WOMEN AND COUNTRY MUSIC

Andrew Smith

They dressed in fancy western clothing, wore wide-brimmed cowboy hats, played guitars and yodeled, just like their American counterparts. More often than not, they grew up on farms in eastern Australia, where their parents and neighbors listened to country music on the radio and on 78-rpm discs. Keen to be part of a burgeoning local country-music industry that was largely based on recordings from the United States, they sang of prairies, of gray-haired mothers, of cabins in the pines, and of faithful old dogs. Some became recording stars, but sadly others missed out on commercial recognition. Lamentably, most had their singing careers abruptly terminated by marriage.

Australia, like the United States, had its share of yodeling cowgirls and female country artists during the 1940s and 1950s. Although their discs sold in smaller numbers than those of their male counterparts during those decades, female Australian country singers played a significant role in the development of country music "Down Under," and their enduring popularity has been borne out by recent reissues of their music.[1] Although not all of Australia's early female artists were yodelers, the popularity of the yodel in early Australian country music guaranteed that the most significant early Australian female artists featured yodeling on their recordings.

Australian country music had its origins in the 1920s, when discs from the United States made their way to Australia, where they were played on radio stations in rural areas.[2] "Nearly every country station had a 'hillbilly' session tucked away somewhere in its programming and these were sought almost fanatically by young dial twisters," wrote Australian country-music authority Eric Watson. "They were usually segregated into 15 or 30 minute sessions, once a day on some stations, once a week on others, and most often at 5 am or 6 am."[3] People in rural areas, in particular, identified with the sentiments of much early country music from the United States.

Discs of well-known artists from the United States and, later, from Australia were seminal influences in the development of country music in Australia. Unlike the situation in United States, however, the Columbia Graphophone Company virtually had a monopoly on country music during the 1930s and the early 1940s. Between 1927 and 1958, it released country music on the Regal Zonophone label. About 950 country-music records, featuring local talent and material from the United States and England, were released during those years. Although the majority of artists on the label were male, there were some releases by the Girls of the Golden West, who may have been role models for several of the first wave of Australian female country artists.

One of the first Australian country-music singers to record commercially was Tex Morton (Robert Lane), who was influenced by Jimmie Rodgers, Goebel Reeves and British yodeler Harry Torrani. Morton, who migrated to Australia from New Zealand in the early 1930s, made his first records for the Columbia Graphophone Company in Sydney, Australia, in 1936. By 1939, he was a huge success and fronted a traveling show that toured Australia and featured roughriding, whip cracking, singing and yodeling, hypnotism, and fancy shooting. The immense popularity of these shows and his phenomenal record sales clearly established Morton as the first star of Australian country music. His traveling companion at the time was Dorothy Carroll, who was given the sobriquet "Sister Dorrie," probably because the idea of a woman touring with a traveling western show was considered risqué by social standards of the time.[4] When she sang five duets with Tex Morton in 1941, she became the first female Australian singer to record country music.

Prior to her joining Morton, Sister Dorrie had been a member of the Ricketts family of entertainers, and had worked on the Tivoli circuit in Sydney. Although she recorded a further ten duets with Morton in 1949 or 1950, toured with him extensively, and recorded radio shows with him during the 1940s, their partnership ceased abruptly when he moved to the United States and Canada. She was briefly reunited with her old singing partner in 1972, some twelve years after he returned to Australia.

Perhaps to counter the popularity of Tex Morton and Sister Dorrie, Columbia had Bernie Burnett record two tracks with her husband, Buddy Williams, in 1941 and another two with Williams in 1943. By that time, Williams was Morton's main rival and Columbia had been having difficulties with the independent, freewheeling Morton, so they tended to use Williams as a competitor. The songs recorded by Williams and Burnett were among the most famous of Williams's 78-rpm discs. At the time, Williams was in the Australian Infantry Forces and recorded for Columbia while he was on leave. Burnett's ephemeral recording career ended soon afterwards, when she and Buddy were divorced.

Diana Milner narrowly missed the chance to become the first solo Australian female country artist to record commercially when she postponed a scheduled recording session in 1941. Milner, billed as "Australia's Only Yodelling Cowgirl," was born in 1924 in Melbourne. Later, her family moved to Brisbane, Queensland. She and her older sister, Freda, were both keen riders, and in 1935 Diana ran away home and tried to get a job as a boundary rider, but the police promptly apprehended her and sent her home. She and Freda, who was probably the better rider of the two, later toured with Ken Huntley's Wild West show, Freda as a roughrider and Diana as a singer and yodeler. She left the show in Sydney and sang on the radio station 2UE. Later she appeared on Australia's national radio network, the ABC, and made some vanity recordings. She was set to record for Columbia in March 1941, but she cancelled the session to marry a sailor who was due to be shipped overseas but was sent to Melbourne instead. Milner followed her husband to Melbourne, and thus gave up the chance to record.[5] Although she sang on radio during World War II, she withdrew from the entertainment business in 1942, when she was six months pregnant.

The first Australian female country singer to record solo was Shirley Thoms, who made her initial recordings in 1941 at the age of sixteen. Thoms's early influences were Tex Morton, Buddy Williams, Harry Torrani, and Elton Britt, although her grandfather later claimed that her yodeling ability was hereditary, as he grew up near the Swiss-German border. Thoms made her first public performance at the 1940 Radio 4BU (Bundaberg, Queensland) amateur trials, which she won, singing Harry Torrani's "Mocking Bird Yodel." After further radio success, she auditioned for Arch Kerr, the record sales manager for the Columbia Graphophone Company. Between 1941 and 1946, she recorded thirty-two tracks for Columbia. Her repertoire included songs about cowgirls ("The Cowgirl Yodel," "The Cowgirl's Life for Me," "I'm a Lonely Cowgirl")

Australia's first female country star was
Shirley Thoms, who began recording in
1941.

and compositions about her native Australia ("My Wonder Valley Home," "Australia, Land of My Dreams," "My Sunny Queensland Home"). In her recordings, "there was a complete identification with the then popular 'western' image, with its themes of 'moonlit prairies,' 'little homes in the west,' and 'darling mothers waiting back home in old log cabins,'" wrote Thoms's discographer Hedley Charles. "This rapport was shared not only by the hillbilly singers of the 1930s and 1940s, but millions of rural Australians and many of their city cousins as well."

Thoms made her final half-dozen 78-rpm recordings for the Australian Record Company in 1952, and the tracks were released on the Rodeo label. She toured the eastern states of Australia extensively and joined an army entertainment unit during World War II, but she gave up country music after she married and started raising a family. In 1970, however, she was coaxed out of retirement to record the first of two albums for the Hadley label in Tamworth. The second album was recorded in 1972. Thoms later stated that she thought the Hadley recordings better captured her voice, as she tended to pitch her songs higher and higher, owing to nervousness in the recording studios. (Her voice was once described as "small, even babyish.") Hadley also recycled all her 78s on three vinyl long-play albums, making her one of the first Australian country-music pioneers to have all her work reissued on long-play discs. In 1980, she was the first female to be elected to the Australian Country Music Roll of Renown. She battled Parkinson's disease and heart trouble during the 1990s and died in 1999.

The second solo Australian country-music recording artist was June Holm. She cut only six songs for Columbia in 1942, despite one critic's assertion that her yodeling and singing were "incomparable." Born in Brisbane, Queensland, on June 14, 1925, Holm probably learned to yodel and play Hawaiian steel guitar from her mother, Jessie May, who was, from some accounts, an excellent "alpine" yodeler. Holm may have played the steel guitar as a result of a Hawaiian music fad that swept the country during the 1930s, resulting in thousands of people learning the Hawaiian guitar at special music schools. A neighbor recalled that Holm was a lonely child who would practice her music for hours on end after school. She was also an accomplished rider. In 1934, she startled onlookers gathered to see the Duke of Gloucester traveling through Brisbane on a train when she jumped her horse over two level-crossing gates.

At the age of ten, Holm teamed up with two other young performers, Beverly Thorn and Roy Barton, as a steel guitarist and yodeler. When the group broke up, she toured with Thorn and gradually developed a liking

June Holm, the Australian
Yodeler, like many of her
contemporaries, appeared on
stage in full cowgirl attire
during the 1940s.

for hillbilly music. Her influences included Wilf Carter, who was extremely popular in Australia at the time, and Harry Torrani. Perhaps she heard some of their discs during the time she spent on a farm near the Clarence River, in the heart of New South Wales's country-music belt, or perhaps she was influenced by local releases of the Girls of the Golden West.[6] Holm was later billed as "The Yodelling Cowgirl," reinforcing her western image.

From 1935 to 1940, Holm sang on radio station 4BH (Brisbane, Queensland). In 1939, when she was thirteen, she and Thorn appeared together for the last time, at Brisbane's Town Hall. Holm sang "There's a Love Knot in My Lariat." In the same year, she left school and joined the Tivoli live-show circuit, which took her to Sydney and Melbourne. Holm usually commenced her Tivoli performances with "The Old Oaken Bucket," to which she had adapted a distinctive yodel.

Between the late 1930s and 1945, she made hundreds of transcription records for radio—some with Tex Morton—but none of these discs has survived to the present day. (Large numbers of transcription discs were destroyed in Australia in the 1950s, and some were even used as road fill.) In 1941, she joined the Red Cross as an entertainer and toured Australia and the Pacific Islands, entertaining Allied troops.

In 1942, Holm recorded six tracks—the only ones she made commercially—for the Regal Zonophone label. Four songs ("Happy Yodelling Cowgirl," "The Lullaby My Mother Sang to Me," "My Daddy Was a Yodelling Cowboy," and "Song of Queensland") were written by her, and reinforced the image of western cowgirls. In reviewing three of these tracks, Tony Russell wrote, "Holms [sic] sings and yodels with more vim than most of her American contemporaries . . . and is extraordinarily impressive."[7]

After this session, Holm disappeared from the recording scene, although she seemed to remain popular with country-music fans during the 1940s. She married in 1948, gradually withdrawing from the country-music industry; she eventually retired in 1960. After her husband died in 1965, she was treated for insomnia and depression. She died in 1966 from an inadvertent drug overdose, and was buried in an unmarked grave. Possibly because she made so few commercial recordings, Holm has arguably not received adequate recognition as a pioneer by Australia's modern country-music community.

Another Australian female country artist who had only a brief recording career was Joan Martin, who, with musical partner Eric Tutin, cut six sides for Columbia in 1942 as "The Sundowners," six months after Holm's session. A publicity photograph of the time shows Martin in full western dress, with cowgirl hat and vest. Some of the duo's songs ("My Pony, My Guitar and Me" and "Cabin in the Hills of Old Wyoming") yet again mirrored the western image that was becoming the norm for Australian country singers. The Sundowners' short-lived careers ended soon afterwards, however, when Martin married and left Australia.

Sixteen-year-old Cora Ruhle accompanied Martin to Sydney in 1942, and, like Diana Milner, narrowly missed the opportunity to become Australia's first solo female country recording artist. Although Columbia had wanted to record her as a solo singer, her worried mother asked her to return home. Previously, Ruhle had worked with Eric Tutin, calling herself "The Lone Star Cowgirl." Like Holm, her musical career had started during the Hawaiian music craze of the 1930s. She learned to play steel guitar at the age of fifteen, later developing a passion for country music. She made six solo vanity recording tracks in Brisbane while touring with "The Sundowners" and was asked to record commercially. In 1947, after the Sundowners had broken up, she toured with the Tex Morton and Buddy Williams Shows. She died in 1996.

The Sundowners, Eric Tufin and Joan Martin, made only six recordings before disbanding.

Lily Connors may well have been the first Australian country singer—male or female—to perform in the United States of America. In 1948, when she was seventeen, she accompanied her Canadian mother and her sister to California. After about six months, she appeared on KFI Television in Los Angeles, yodeling and singing. Then she joined a government-sponsored show that toured the war veterans' hospitals, traveling by train and bus. She even appeared on television shows with Spade Cooley.[8]

Connors returned to Australia about 1950 and recorded twenty songs that were released on the Regal Zonophone label, including "Chime Bells," which became her signature tune. On many of her records, she was accompanied by country bands, in contrast to many of her contemporary Australian singers, who tended to record with just guitar. To a large extent, record executives, who thought that full backings would have been too sophisticated for the country-music audience in Australia at the time, may have mandated the "solo-singer-with-guitar" sound. Columbia's Arch Kerr, for example, argued with Tex Morton over his using "The Roughriders" as accompaniment. Kerr also insisted that Buddy Williams record without a backing band.

Connors appeared on the Bonnington's Bunkhouse radio show (a mixture of comedy and country music),[9] but gradually withdrew from country music after her marriage in the late 1950s, retiring from show business completely in 1972.

When she was sixteen years of age, Queenslander Joan Ridgeway was also offered work in the United States based on a screen test, but she declined the offer, preferring to continue her career in Australia instead. Ridgeway was born in 1932, the daughter of an itinerant contract fencer and cattle-yard builder. An accomplished singer and yodeler, she won the Australian Hillbilly Championship in 1948 and formed her own traveling show with her parents in 1950. The family toured for about three years, but the show wound down after illness forced her to quit. She recorded a total of ten tracks, many of which featured yodeling, for Columbia in 1951, 1953, and 1955. She married in 1952, and ended her musical career afterwards.

The McKean Sisters, Joy and Heather, were Australia's first country-music sister recording act. Joy, born in 1930, and Heather, born in 1932, were the daughters of a schoolteacher who played Jimmie Rodgers and Carter Family songs on guitar, Hawaiian-style. Their mother played piano. In 1939, the family moved to the Blue Mountains, near Sydney. Joy learned to play piano, steel guitar, ukulele, and piano accordion, and Heather the ukulele. They were particularly impressed with the yodeling of Wilf Carter and Harry Torrani. Later, they listened to Vernon Dalhart and Carson Robison on their grandmother's gramophone, and were taught older-style songs by a neighbor. Surprisingly, perhaps, the Girls of the Golden West were not major influences on their music.[10]

The McKeans were taught guitar by Norm Scott at the Hawaiian Club in Sydney and appeared on Scott's radio program on 2GB (Sydney). Although Scott was then caught up in (and capitalizing on) the Hawaiian guitar craze, he had been influenced by hillbilly records from the United States and had performed Jimmie Rodgers songs as early as 1929. He and his brother, Arthur, recorded eight songs as "The Singing Stockmen" for Regal Zonophone in 1938 and 1939.

During the early 1940s, the McKeans performed for Australian troops and to raise funds for the war effort. By this time Joy had begun to write

The McKean Sisters, Joy McKean and Heather McKean, were the first sister act to record country music in Australia.

songs, and the girls had both developed into skillful yodelers. They turned professional in the late 1940s. In 1948, Joy entered Sydney University to train as a teacher, but later abandoned her studies in order to concentrate on performing. Between 1949 and 1956, she and Heather headlined the McKean Sisters Melody Trail Show, a weekly mixture of live performance and pre-recorded music, on radio station 2KY (Sydney). They made their first commercial recording in 1950, backing local country-music singer Tim McNamara on "Follow the Hilly Billys Down the Main Street." In 1951, they signed with the Australian Record Company and recorded eighteen sides, released on the Rodeo label, over the next few years. Their music was a mixture of Joy's compositions (thirteen songs, including "The Valley Where the Frangipannis Grow," "The Cowgirl's Lament," and "Yodel Down the Valley"), and American country songs ("I'm a Fool to Care," "Soldier's Last Letter," and "Bluegrass Waltz"). They toured briefly in 1951 with Shorty Ranger, Tim McNamara, and Gordon Parsons, but following Joy's marriage to country singer and bush balladeer Slim Dusty that year, the duo was forced to split as an act.[11] Heather married Australian country singer Reg Lindsay in 1954. The two sisters were reunited in 1983 and performed together, mainly as a part of the Slim Dusty show, for several years. They recorded an album in 1993.[12]

Following the dissolution of the McKean Sisters act, both Joy and Heather continued to play active roles in country music. Joy became a mainstay in the highly successful and influential Slim Dusty show, which toured Australia for over fifty years. She is generally acknowledged to be one of Australia's finest music songwriters. Her husband, Slim, has recorded many of her songs, including "Lights on the Hill," "Indian Pacific," and "The Greatest Disappointment." For many years, Heather managed the McKean Sisters' Melody Trail program while Joy was touring with Slim Dusty. She also co-produced and appeared on the Reg Lindsay Show, Australia's first weekly country-music television show. The program commenced in 1964 and ran for about seven years before it was terminated, despite good ratings. In the 1980s, Heather was involved in Country Music Australia, an industry organization.

Another early "sister" act was the Schneider Sisters, who, like the McKean Sisters, remained in show business after they withdrew from entertaining. Both Rita and Mary Schneider developed a passion for country music by listening to Carson Robison radio shows as children. The girls worked up a comedy act that parodied the rube/hillbilly image and showcased it on radio and at live performances. In 1950 they recorded eight sides for Columbia in Sydney. Although they recorded sporadically during the next two decades, they gradually drifted into television, Rita as a talent supervisor and copyright administrator and Mary as a production assistant. During the 1990s, Mary recorded some pop-country albums that showcased her powerful yodeling, and she is recognized today as one of Australia's best yodelers.

Dorothy Davidson and Lorna Whiteside had a short-lived career as country singers and yodelers when, as "The Bar BQ Girls," they recorded ten country-music tracks for the Rodeo label during the mid-1950s. Later they recorded pop music as "The Barry Sisters."[13] The duo had previously been successful as country singers and yodelers, and had worked in the

Bar BQ Club in Sydney.[14] Although their early recordings were in the tradition that combined country singing with yodeling, the advent of rock and roll during the late 1950s led to producers forcing the two to sing more pop-inspired material. When Whiteside became ill, the duo split up, though they both continued to be active in the country-music business—Whiteside as a songwriter, Davidson as a solo singer.

By the 1950s, female country singers were becoming more common in Australia, though many had short-lived careers. The Hickey Sisters, Kay and Margaret, recorded an impressive album of country music in the 1950s for the Viking label, but they withdrew from country music after they married. Kim Mahoney, billed as "a champion lady rough rider," performed in traveling rodeos with her husband Kid and recorded four sides for Rodeo in 1951 before vanishing into obscurity. Thel Carey, who was influenced by Tex Morton, toured Australia extensively and recorded with her husband, Rick, under the name Rick and Thel. Thel Carey was a mainstay of the Australian country-music scene and a talented songwriter: She wrote "Rusty, It's Goodbye," about a dog who sits at a railway station waiting for his master, who has been killed in battle. The song was a hit for Slim Dusty.

Although some Australian female country artists, like the McKeans, remained in the music business after they married, most, such as Thoms, Holm, Martin, Connors, and Ridgeway, wound down or terminated their involvement in country music after they married. Whether this situation reflected relatively poor economic prospects for female country singers of the 1940s and 1950s, or whether, instead, it was fueled by social beliefs about the merits of single women working in the country-music field has yet to be investigated. Certainly, the total recorded output of early Australian female country artists was much less than that of their male counterparts. A major reason for this was the early retirement of Australian female country singers, usually because of marriage and family considerations. To some extent, this paucity of recorded output might have limited the influence of local female artists on those who followed them. This was not the case with male country singers, who frequently cited their fellow male artists as influences. Buddy Williams, for example, stated that he was inspired by Tex Morton; as a teenager, Slim Dusty listened to both Morton and Williams while he was working on his family's farm. The relative longevity of male artists' careers meant that they had substantial recorded outputs that could, in turn, influence artists who followed them. In reading the accounts of Australia's pioneer female country singers, however, one is struck by the paucity of references to their being inspired by fellow Australian female artists. The rate at which female artists made records, however, was commensurate with that of their male counterparts. Between 1941 and 1946, for example, Shirley Thoms recorded roughly the same number of songs as Buddy Williams, although why June Holm made only six sides remains a mystery.

It is possible that discs by the Girls of the Golden West (Mildred and Dorothy Good) might have influenced some Australian female singers, although the McKean Sisters were not among them. British old-time music authority Tony Russell suggested that both Shirley Thoms and June Holm "carefully attended" records by the Good sisters.[15] Other female artists, however, seem to have been influenced instead by male performers, particularly yodelers like Jimmie Rodgers, Harry Torrani, Tex Morton, and Elton Britt. Two exceptions were Jean Calder, a New Zealand artist who recorded with her husband, Les Wilson; and Jacqueline Hall, who cut ten sides for Regal Zonophone during the 1950s, the first four in 1954 as a twelve-year-old. Calder and Hall were both influenced by Shirley Thoms and June Holm. For others, there may have been a realization of a void in record-company catalogs: June Holm told the *Launceston Examiner* that she decided to become a yodeling cowgirl because she failed to hear any females among the yodelers featured on records.[16]

The preponderance of yodelers amongst early Australian female country singers can be explained by the perception of record-company executives that country music sold better if it was accompanied by yodeling. In the mid-1940s, for example, Arch Kerr told Slim Dusty that Columbia "couldn't sell this country stuff without a yodel."[17] Consequently, nearly all of Australia's first wave of country artists, male and female, were yodelers. Some artists were not only influenced by yodeling on country-music discs from the United States, but by Swiss and Austrian yodeling as well.[18] Harry Torrani, an alpine-style yodeler from England, was a major influence on Australian country yodelers, and two of the first four songs that Tex Morton recorded featured alpine-style yodeling. To some extent, female artists might have been more influenced by alpine yodeling styles than their male counterparts. Both Thoms and Holm, for example, may have had hereditary links to alpine countries, and Mary Schneider yodels in both the Swiss and country-music style.

Limited touring might have been another factor that restricted the popularity of female artists. The major Australian male country singers all toured extensively. During the late 1930s, for example, Tex Morton headed a large (by Australian standards) traveling show that included bucking horses, roughriders, whip cracking, fancy shooting, and Morton's singing and yodeling. Indeed, the proprietors of traveling roughriding shows recognized the drawing power of "hillbilly" music as early as the 1930s. The Gill brothers, for example, included country music on their shows beginning in the mid-1930s. In 1937, their rodeo included Tex Morton.[19] Buddy Williams, Smoky Dawson, and Slim Dusty and Joy McKean also traveled the main highways and backroads of Australia to entertain country-music fans and to sell merchandise to supplement record sales. Reg Lindsay stated that in order to achieve airplay on radio in the 1950s, artists had to make personal contact with radio announcers in the country. Usually, making personal visits to local radio stations was an essential component of touring.[20]

Life on the road in traveling shows was hard—Smoky Dawson described it as "mostly one night stands made up of nine parts blood, sweat and tears, and one part the intoxication of being the centre of the universe to a packed audience for a few brief moments."[21] Although it had its high points, employment on the show circuit was often difficult and, at times, even dangerous: Stan Gill, the owner of a traveling rodeo, was fatally gunned down by a drunken spectator who had previously been evicted from a show. In addition, traveling showmen often had reputations (well deserved, from some accounts) of being somewhat immoral. Jenny Hicks stated that when Tex Morton and Lance Skuthorpe toured, "it was time to lock up your daughters." Teenage "groupies" or "buckle bunnies," as they'd be called today, frequently followed the shows from town to town.[22]

There is no research on the comparative extent of touring between male and female country artists in the 1940s, but it is tempting to speculate that perhaps the demanding regime of life on the road did not always suit young single females, who might have preferred to tour with well-known companies, such as the Tivoli Circuit, instead. Also, there may have been problems with the perceptions of the morality of young women touring with men. When Dorothy Carroll toured with Tex Morton, for example, she was known as "Sister Dorrie," probably to give the impression that she was Morton's sister.

During the war years, however, when the first wave of Australian female artists made their debuts, male artists were forced to cut down their touring, owing to gasoline rationing. Buddy Williams was even fighting in Southeast Asia, and Smoky Dawson was entertaining troops there in an army entertainment unit. So there may not have been the expectation for females to go on the road until after the war. During the 1950s and for decades afterwards, Joy McKean and Thel Carey both traveled across

Australia extensively in country-music shows with their husbands. Both remained popular with country-music fans, and both recorded commercially during those years. One could surmise that their popularity endured by their marrying "into" country music. In contrast, female country artists who married men who were not part of country music tended to retire from the music industry shortly afterwards.

During the past forty years, female singers have continued to play an integral part of Australian country music. Jean Stafford, who was influenced by Kitty Wells; Suzanne Prentice; Patsy Riggir, from New Zealand; Anne Kirkpatrick, Slim Dusty's daughter; Gina Jeffreys; Evelyn Bury; Norma O'Hara Murphy; and Kasey Chambers are some that come to mind. Sherrie Austin is perhaps an exception, as she has achieved a measure of success in the United States without having first made a name for herself within Australia. Olivia Newton-John, who began her career in Australia as a pop singer, was the center of a minor controversy in the United States when she was awarded the CMA Female Vocalist of the Year Award in 1974. This event may have been a pivotal factor in the formation of the Association of Country Entertainers (ACE), a group of "traditional" country artists who opposed developments in country music that they saw as pop-influenced.

Despite their importance in the development of Australian country music, many of Australia's female country-music pioneers have been largely overlooked or ignored by the modern Australian country-music industry. For example, between 1976 and 2002, only Shirley Thoms, the McKean Sisters, Thel Carey, and the Schneider Sisters were elected to the Country Music Roll of Renown (Australia's equivalent of the Country Music Hall of Fame), whereas, in the same period, two dozen male artists and broadcasters were similarly honored.

Today's Australian female country artists have, by and large, moved with the times, but they all owe a debt to the yodeling cowgirls of the 1940s and 1950s. Artists like Shirley Thoms, June Holm, and the McKean Sisters not only paved the way for other female singers to follow, but they were seminal influences on the development of Australian country music as well.

Notes

1. For example: *Down the Trail of Achin' Hearts* (National Film and Sound Archives, NFSA T0014); *Rhythm in the Saddle* (ScreenSound Australia CD0019). These releases feature Joan Ridgeway, Jacqueline Hall, Lily Connors, and the McKean Sisters.

2. For a more detailed account of the origins of Australian country music, see A. Smith, "Tex Morton and His Influence on Country Music in Australia during the 1930s and 1940s," in C. Wolfe and J. Akenson, *Country Music Annual 2002* (Lexington: The University Press of Kentucky, 2002), 82–103.

3. E. Watson, "How It All Began," in J. Smith, ed., *The Book of Australian Country Music* (Singapore: BFT Publishing Group, 1984).

4. The usual surname given for Sister Dorrie is Ricketts. This was her maiden name, but at the time of her joining Tex Morton, her married name was Carroll.

5. *Old Time Music* 43 (1986/87), 6.

6. See "Two Cow Girls on the Lone Prairie: The True Story of the Girls of the Golden West." *Old Time Music* 43 (1986/87), 6.

7. *Old Time Music* 29 (1978), 23.

8. E. Watson, *Country Music in Australia* (Cornstalk Publishing, 1983), 2:11.

9. See, for example, the CD *Laughter in the Air: A Selection of Australian Radio Comedy.* National Film and Sound Archive NFSA/RC0010

10. Joy McKean, personal communication, 4 June 1991.

11. Slim Dusty is the stage name of Gordon Kirkpatrick (born 1927).

12. *The McKean Sisters on Stage* (Nulla Records NUL 105).

13. The duo was also known professionally as "The Bar-Y Girls." The name "Barry" was derived from inserting an extra "r" into "Bar-Y".

14. Bill Walker, later a producer in Nashville, led the house band at the club.

15. *Old Time Music* 43 (1986/87), 6.

16. *Launceston Examiner*, 7 June 1946.

17. J. Lapsley, *Slim Dusty: Walk a Country Mile* (Rigby, 1984), 47.

18. Reg Lindsay interview, May 1990. Lindsay's rendition of *Streamline Yodel Song* was patterned on both Wilf Cater's style and Austrian yodeling.

19. J. Hicks, *Australian Cowboys Roughriders and Rodeos* (Angus and Robertson, 2000), 75.

20. Reg Lindsay interview, May 1990.

21. S. Dawson, *Smoky Dawson: A Life* (George Allen & Unwin, 1985), 127.

22. Hicks, 81.

TEACHING ABOUT WOMEN IN COUNTRY MUSIC

James Akenson

Introduction

In the introduction to *Finding Her Voice: The Saga of Women in Country Music* (1993), Mary A. Bufwack and Robert K. Oermann write: "The story of women in country music is a window into the world of the majority of American women. It describes poverty, hardship, economic exploitation, sexual subjugation, and limited opportunities. Sometimes it is self-defeating and reactionary, painful and despairing. But it also contains outspoken protest and joyful rebellion, shouts of exaltation and bugle calls of freedom. There is humor as well as sadness here, victory as well as heartache. The history of women's country music reveals a rich vein of positive images, self-assertive lyrics, and strong female performers" (x). Such eloquence seems inevitable in light of the continued interest in gender studies and gender issues within both academia and society as a whole. Women in country music merits serious study—both in the past and in contemporary life. A wide variety of scholarly articles, books, theses, and dissertations provides a substantive knowledge base, and it is growing. The proliferation of popular biographies, autobiographies, magazine articles, and web pages informs more academic analyses.

This discussion focuses upon teaching about women in country music from elementary school through college. Specifically, the discussion will focus on teaching materials and teaching strategies appropriate to the kindergarten through twelfth-grade curriculum, as well as dimensions of teacher training and undergraduate education in the liberal arts. Within the context of contemporary pressures on teachers, it may seem odd to advocate the use of country music as a content vehicle. Enormous pressures on teachers and schools to meet standards (Evans 2001; Lewis 1995) and to deliver superlative standardized test scores in high-stakes settings (Marker 2001; Ross 1999) suggest that country music would not serve this purpose effectively. In addition, the subject of women in country music provides a focus of great specificity, which, while significant, appears to constrain its potential application in schools.

However, this emphasis on women in country music is justified by the inclusion of gender study into the curriculum and increased diversification of curricula. The teaching strategies and materials discussed will be used to illustrate significant forms of thinking skills, including analogical reasoning and the varied set of skills developed through the use of graphic organizers. Graphic organizers, a generic term covering a large number of tools that stress the visual arrangement of information into conceptual hierarchies, provide a particularly effective and versatile way to involve students in factual and higher-order thinking. Specific examples of graphic organizers include concept maps, semantic webs, spider maps, series-of-events chains, problem/solution outlines, semantic differentials, fishbone maps, cycles, human interaction outlines, picture glossaries, scale diagrams, flow diagrams, timelines, and flow maps. Graphic organizer–based teaching strategies (Jones, Pierce, and Hunter 1989; Moline 1995) provide powerful teaching tools at all grade levels. Visualization strategies allow students to "better understand which ideas . . . are important, how they relate . . . show at a glance the key parts of a whole and their relations . . . help . . . to comprehend, summarize, and synthesize complex ideas" (Jones, Pierce, and Hunter 1, 2). By their very nature, such approaches encourage greater involvement in the learning process on the part of teachers. Research on graphic organizers focuses on a wide range of issues and subject matter, ranging from learning disabilities (Bos et al. 1989; Boyle and Wishaar 1997) to critical thinking (Cassidy 1992), mathematics (Braselton and Decker 1994), science (Simmons, Griffin, and Kameenui 1988; Spiegel and Barufaldi 1994), creative writing (Meyer 1995), and reading (Alvermann and Boothby 1986; Avery and Avery 1994).

Graphic organizers support a wide variety of basic thinking skills as well as higher-order thinking skills. As analogical reasoning offers an additional higher-order thinking skill for dealing with teaching about women in country music, it represents a domain of teaching meriting greater attention. Analogies provide a method for relating established skills and content to new skills and content as well as providing a manner for dealing with the relationships between varied phenomena (Salvucci and Anderson 2001; Silkebakken and Camp 1993); this method is explained by path-mapping theory. Typically, analogies fall into categories that emphasize relationships that can be characterized as association, purpose, cause-and-effect, part-to-whole, part-to-part, action-to-object, object-to-action, synonym, antonym, place, degree, characteristic, sequence, grammatical, and numerical. A wide variety of research suggests that analogies can be useful in teaching a variety of subjects and skills, including geography (Andrew 1997), science (Douglas and Newton 1995), and language skills (Plaister 1981). Castillo (1998) suggested that analogies could be helpful in teaching language arts skills of simile and metaphor. Indeed, simile and metaphor themselves are analogical forms in that both devices involve the comparison of unlike items. Rogers and Williams (2000) pointed out the use of metaphors in country music: "Part of this 'feel' of country music is due to the figures of speech popular in the music. They are often metaphorical figures, for country songwriters have always been particularly fond of them. Such metaphor is a way of expressing an abstraction in concrete terms and may reflect a discomfort with abstraction on the part of the songwriter and the audience" (48). Rogers and Williams identify further identify the use of metaphor in country music as two-sided figures that "break into halves with the two parts playing against one another" (49). This emphasis on the masterful use of words in figurative speech suggests significant instructional opportunities. Combined with the many forms of graphic organization as well as skill and content development in significant curriculum subjects related to language and social studies, the topic of women in country music in fact proves to be remarkably useful and appropriate for inclusion in the classroom. Finally, this discussion will also suggest ways in which teaching about women in country music may also address the current emphasis on standards. But first we turn to specific examples of teaching strategies that deal with women in country music.

Language Arts and Teaching About Women

The language arts curriculum provides a particularly appropriate starting point for dealing with women and country music. High school English students at Dobyns-Bennett High School in Kingsport, Tennessee, experienced instruction about women in country music. Author James Akenson and Dr. Suellen Alfred involved the high school students in country music to deal with figurative language and the ballad structure through the use of content based on women. This involvement first identified and reviewed the nature of metaphor and simile as major forms of comparisons in figurative language. After listening to country music selections, students filled out a graphic organizer and a response sheet, in which they symbolically represented key metaphors and similes. A graphic depicting two windows, one translucent and one opaque, was analyzed for its literalness and abstractness. Then students listened to the Suzy Bogguss song "Somewhere Between" (1989), which features lyrics that compare the thoughts and feelings of a loved one to a dark window that impedes vision. The selection permits a simple entry into the graphic representation of the content of "Somewhere Between" and the sample graphic representation. Students were also exposed to metaphorical representation with the line "There's a wall so high, it reaches the sky."

Another song that was used in this way was Michelle Wright's "One Time Around" (1992), which uses a metaphorical theme that life is a walk in the garden and that a person has but "one time around." Discussion before the students listened to the song led them to consider messages from religious teachings to which they had been exposed. The instructor's questions before the song was played implied neither approval nor disapproval of common religious dogma, but rather asked students to indicate whether they had ever been exposed to concepts regarding the nature of life or reincarnation, and the existence of life after death. The instructor concluded that most students had been exposed to a philosophy summarized as "While there may be life after death, they had but one time here on earth, in terms of common Christian teaching." Students then listened to and graphically represented "One Time Around," and then verbalized their understanding as represented in the graphic. Dolly Parton's "Eagle When She Flies" also provided a figuratively powerful song for analysis by the students of Dobyns-Bennett. In preparation to listening to "Eagle When She Flies," students answered the following questions: "Now that we are into the month of May what significant woman will you be honoring soon? Besides your mother, who are other women who have had an influence in your life? What types of strength do you see in women you admire? Do women you have admired show great strength, but have they shown that they can be hurt emotionally? If you are a young woman, do you see strength as well as vulnerability, an ability to be hurt, in yourself?" Then the following statement appeared on the screen: "In honor of the young women of Dobyns Bennett high school, their mothers, and other women who have influenced them in their lives." When "Eagle When She Flies" was finished, students created their graphic symbolization, and individuals shared their verbalizations and graphic representations of the metaphoric use of the eagle, the sparrow, stormy skies, the kaleidoscope, the shoulder, and the learning post and of the similes "as soft as feathers" and "as fragile as a child."

Alfred (1999) used ballads with strong women's content to reinforce the basic structure of ballads as well as a variety of analytical skills including point of view, identification of the gender of the narrator and characters, intended audience, and the nature of the relationships between characters. Students read and listened to "Long Black Veil" and responded to questions such as "In the refrains that occurs after stanza 2, who is 'she'? Did you have to read the rest of the poem before you could answer the question? In stanza 4, 'She sheds not a tear.' What does this tell you about the mysterious woman who has come to watch the hanging? Since 'She sheds not a tear' during the hanging, why does she now cry over the dead man's bones? How does this woman's reaction compare to the sweetheart's reaction in the 'The Hangman's Tree'?" After reading "The Hangman's Tree," Alfred emphasized the women's perspective with analytical questions such as "Why does the prisoner's sweetheart bring the gold to pay his fee when his father, mother, and sister do not? Compare the sweetheart's reaction to this hanging with the woman's reaction in 'Long Black Veil'?" Likewise, after reading and listening to "Barbara Allen," Alfred asked questions such as "If you were Barbara Allen's mother, how would you encourage her to embrace life rather than death? Does this ballad judge Barbara Allen too harshly? Is a woman obligated to be a man's sweetheart solely because being without her will cause him to become ill?"

Other ways of dealing with figurative language and women in country music include the use of symbolic data banks to guide the response. The "Graphix Portfolio," a "Collection of Visual Images for the Analysis of Women and Country Music," allows students to deal with the metaphorical content of country music. Students listen to a female country music artist and then circle or otherwise identify the visual image that corresponds to the metaphor. As already mentioned, "Somewhere Between" lends itself to students identifying the wall and window images. Questions include "Why is the use of metaphor effective in the song? How could the lyrics be altered to turn the metaphor into a simile? Would it change the power of the lyrics to shift from metaphor to simile? Does this song represent a particularly common point of view for women? Would it

Figure 1: Images and Metaphor

be significantly more common an experience for women than men? Does the fact that a man, Merle Haggard, wrote the song change your perception of the impact from a woman's point of view? Would the analogy Dark Window:Emotional Barrier::Transparent Window:Emotional Openness adequately represent the imagery of 'Somewhere Beyond'?" Similarly, Tanya Tucker's "Strong Enough to Bend" (1988) provides visual imagery with a metaphor about conflict resolution being similar to a tree that can bend in a storm. After identifying the visual image, a variety of questions assist analysis, among them, "Is a tree which bends in a storm a good metaphor for the problems in the relationship? What other types of living objects have to be literally able to bend in a storm? Is there evidence which suggests if men or women are more skilled at bending, compromising? Would a man or a woman be more likely to view bending, compromising as a sign of weakness? According to the song, what are the benefits of compromise, bending? Have you and another person ever reached a compromise in a disagreement? What were the results?" Lee Ann Womack's "I Hope You Dance" (2000) offers another metaphor to be identified. Analytical questions include "Is the graphic image suitable to what Lee Ann Womack means by dance? What other type of dance could she mean? Would a couple dancing still provide an appropriate metaphorical representation? Can the metaphor also deal with the need to let yourself participate in relationships with people as well as taking risks to become involved in school, jobs, travel?" A formally structured analogy, Taking Risks:Enjoying Life::Playing It Safe:A Dull Life, can be analyzed in terms of the accuracy with which it correctly identifies the metaphorical message of the lyrics. An analogy structured as I Hope You Dance:Taking Risks::Strong Enough to Bend:[Confrontation, Compromise, Indifference, Aloofness] provides an opportunity to compare the import of Tucker's and Womack's lyrics.

Women's Issues and Country Music

Bridgette Dempsey developed detailed procedures for dealing with women's issues through country music. She used the music and careers of Kitty Wells, Tammy Wynette, Dolly Parton, and Trisha Yearwood as the focus of her involvement. Dempsey delivered instruction through an mPower software presentation similar to PowerPoint. As seen in Figure 2, Dempsey delivered significant visual content supported by songs and student involvement with study questions and graphic organizers. Trisha Yearwood's song "XXXs and OOOs" (1995) provided content dealing with fundamen-

Figure 2: Four Women of Country Music: Multimedia Project

"Queen of Country Music"

➤ "It Wasn't God Who Made Honky Tonk Angels" is a song refuting claims made about women by Hank Thompson's in his song "Wild Side of Life."

➤ Began a line of strong independent female country music singers.

Tammy Wynette...

◆ "Stand By Your Man" is still the biggest selling single in the history of country music!

◆ Sings about topics of everyday life - divorce, lonelness, parenting, passion.

◆ No other female country singer conveyed the emotion of heartbreak like Tammy Wynette!

Dolly Parton.....

✢ "Dolly Parton is the most famous, most universally beloved, and most widely respected woman who has ever emerged from country music, a role model for not only other singers and songwriters, but for working women everywere."

✢ She is a superb singer, songwriter, actress, bestselling author and successful television and film producer.

Trisha Yearwood...

✳ She is a "self-assured, disarmingly candid, good-humored, a little sassy, and enormously likeable" young woman.

✳ She is the girl next door, with a little attitude!

✳ "I was taught it was OK to be independent and intelligent - that you could be all that and still be feminine."

tal tensions for women in contemporary culture, namely the balancing act between traditional desires (love, home, children) and money (professional success and the status of a once–exclusively male world). Students observe and listen to the multimedia presentation and then respond to the "Finding the Perfect Balance: Today's Woman" graphic organizer as well as responding to the following prompts:

1) Is this song representative of most working-class women in America today? Why or why not?
2) What is the ultimate balance that most women are trying to achieve and why do you think that they are trying so hard to achieve that balance?
3) Do you think that women are out in the work force because they want to be or because they have to be?
4) How does this song promote traditional gender roles? How does it challenge traditional gender roles?
5) Describe the two different worlds that are portrayed in the song (the differences in her mother's world and in her world).
6) How do you think that this song relates working-class people, country music, and the feminism/women's right movement?

Such analysis combines factual information with conceptual thinking while also dealing with significant sociological changes.

A similar set of exercises involves students with classic songs by Tammy Wynette and Kitty Wells. Dempsey created graphic organizers that allowed students to deal with the issues in "Stand By Your Man" and "It Wasn't God Who Made Honky Tonk Angels" with the help of supporting questions. Such questions for Kitty Wells included, among others, "This song has been hailed as a great Women's Liberation song. Do you agree? Keep in mind the time period that the song came out (1952)." For Tammy Wynette, questions included "How does this song promote traditional gender roles? How does it challenge traditional gender roles? Is 'Stand By your Man' a good representation of the women's movement in the 1960s and 70s?" Dempsey used a different approach to "Eagle When She Flies" than Akenson did, asking questions such as "The song is full of implications about women's roles in life. What do you think is the message about these roles?" and "Do you think the song describes women who would be attracted to the women's movement?" Each of Dempsey's four selections requires students to relate the song to the time period and the women's movement in the respective historical eras. As such,

Figure 3: Finding the Perfect Balance
Graphic Organizer

**Finding the Perfect Balance: Today's Woman
Trisha Yearwood's Song "XXX's and OOO's"**

Directions: Listen to Trisha's song. Begin to list the things that she is trying to balance in her life. After the song is over summarize what you think the message of the song is as well as the one overall balance that she is trying to achieve.

	Vs.	
_____	Vs.	_____
_____	Vs.	_____
_____	Vs.	_____

Main Overall Balance:

Message of the Song:

Dempsey's work integrates country music to the high school United States history curricula teachers are required to cover.

Other issues appropriate for secondary students include the controversial Dixie Chicks song "Goodbye Earl" (1999), which involves the murder of an abusive husband by a wife and her lifelong woman friend. "Goodbye Earl" raises ethical issues, including:

Figure 4: Equality or Inequality
Graphic Organizer

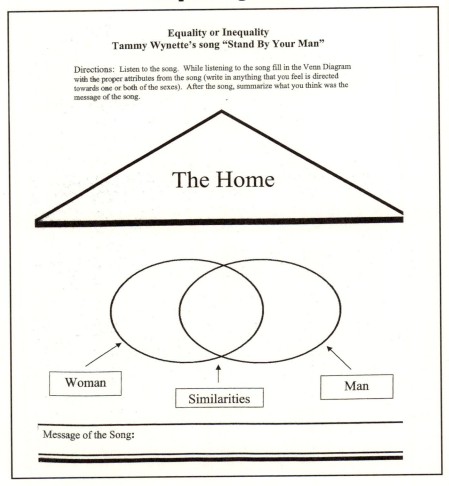

Is a woman ever justified in killing an abusive husband?

Would a defense of "justifiable homicide" be an appropriate defense if Mary Ann and Wanda were ever tried for the crime?

Why didn't Wanda go to a shelter for battered women instead of killing Earl?

Why didn't Wanda go to Atlanta and stay with Mary Ann?

Figure 5: Cause and Effect
Graphic Organizer

Cause and Effect
Kitty Well's song "It Wasn't God
Who Made Honky Tonk Angels"

Directions: Listen to the song. While listening to the song, fill in the cause and effect graphic organizer *(Keep in mind:* the cause(s) listed on the lines and the effect(s) listed in the circle; Cause = Why did it happen? Effect = What happened.). After the song is over, summarize what you thought was the message of the song.

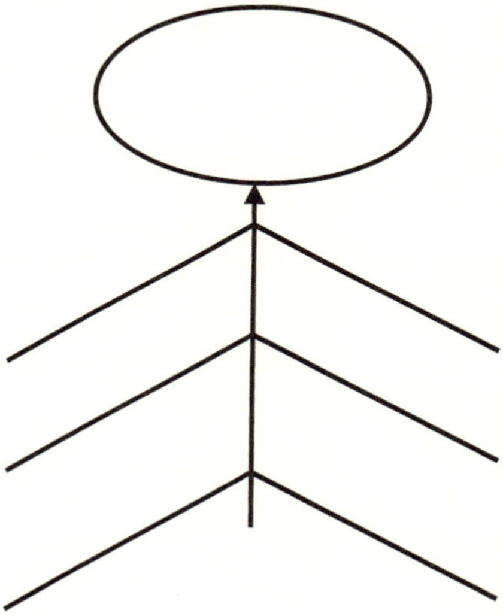

Message of the Song:

What organizations mentioned in "Goodbye Earl" might have taught Wanda things which could have made it harder to leave Earl?

Does "Goodbye Earl" reflect anything about the women's movement which you have studies in your United States history?

Graphic organizers such as timelines, decision trees, and polar opposite continua (justified vs. not justified, appropriate vs. inappropriate humor) provide additional options to organize and react to the events and issues in "Goodbye Earl." Analogies structured to make use of "Goodbye Earl" include "Mary Ann:Atlanta::Wanda:[New York, Los Angeles, Small Town U.S.A., Toronto], Mary Ann: [Independence, Fun, Work, Church]:: Wanda:Dependence, Powerless:Early Marriage::Power:[Divorce, Separation, Single, Older]. Such analogies invite discussion by focusing on the stated and implied relationships and messages in "Goodbye Earl" and their relationship to what students learn about the women's movement in United States history and other social studies courses. Thus, follow-up analysis of the analogies prompts questions such as "Does having a career in a major city always give a woman more power and freedom from abuse by men? Does an early marriage mean that a woman is subject to limited economic and social power? What role has urbanization played in the women's movement and increased power and freedom for women? Although Mary Ann lived in Atlanta, what problems as woman might she experience despite being a professional?"

Analogies further fit into teaching about such women's themes. Dempsey (2002) developed specific prompts to develop student-generated analogies. The prompt required students to brainstorm and write down facts they knew about women in country music. The follow-up activity required group work to "create analogies between the new information in this presentation and your prior knowledge of women in country music. Your group will be expected to explain your analogies to the rest of the class." The teacher-generated analogies based on issues of the women's movement and country music lend themselves to a variety of comparisons such as "It Wasn't God Who Made Honky Tonk Angels": Cheating in Marriage::["I Hope You Dance", "Goodbye Earl,", "XXXs and OOOs,", "Wrong Side of Memphis"]:Women Balancing Traditional and Non-Traditional Roles, Tammy Wynette:Gloria Steinem::Slow:[Happy, Fast, Up, Hot], and Dixie Chicks:Assertive::Women's Movement:[Submissive, Confrontational, Accepting, Ignoring]. Such analogies address women in country music content at the same time that they clearly relevant to historical and sociological content covered in United States history texts. The first analogy requires the ability to link specific song content to a specific women's issue. The second analogy puts Tammy Wynette in context with a major leader of the women's movement in an abstract relationship to the way their stances related to the pace and nature of social change. The Dixie Chicks' challenge to Sony reflects an industry-wide issue regarding royalty payments and length of contracts (Gunderson, D1-2) at the same time that it reinforces an independence of mind, confidence, and assertiveness in women that would not have been possible in the 1950s, when Kitty Wells was performing.

Assertiveness and achievement can be addressed through the careers of women in country music. The career of Frances Preston offers students of all grade levels an opportunity to deal with mobility toward and through the glass ceiling. Preston became the chief operating officer of the performance rights organization Broadcast Music Incorporated (BMI) in 1986. The use of a ladder-like graphic organizer allows students to plot Preston's rise from working in the newsroom at the Nashville radio station WSM-AM to her initial employment with BMI and the rise that followed. Likewise, the appointment in 1994 of Donna Hilley as chief executive officer of Sony Tree Music offers evidence that can be symbolically plotted on a ladder or on an incline plane graphic organizer: "Hilley is the first woman in Nashville's music industry to carry the title president, and she recently became the first woman elected to the board of ASCAP, one of three performing rights agencies" (Roland E1).

The Dixie Chicks provide opportunities to evaluate young women who appear traditionally rooted, hip, self-confident, and assertive. The Dixie Chicks challenged the accuracy of the royalty payments Sony was paying them: "Now it's war. In a town and an industry where political decorum and public restraint are the rule, the Dixie Chicks have laid out a bitterly worded indictment of Sony . . . claiming a pattern of fraudulent accounting" (Havighurst E1). The Sony–Dixie Chicks dispute allows students to be involved with the economic and legal dimensions of the music business. Graphic organizers such as Venn diagrams allow students to compare the Dixie Chicks dispute with Sony to a marriage. Both arrangements are legal in nature, have economic consequences, include points of dispute involving money and power, and sometimes result in conflict resolution.

In the case of the Dixie Chicks and Sony "marriage," a reconciliation took place and the relationship continued. As an article in the business section of *The Tennessean* reported: "The Dixie Chicks, who accused Sony Music of cheating them out of millions of dollars in royalties, have reconciled . . . and will release their next record under a new label jointly created by the group and Sony" ("Dixie Chicks, Sony Make Up," June 18, 2002, E1). Placed in the context of women's issues, the Dixie Chicks' legal challenge also allows students to react to their actions on a graphic organizer that uses polar opposites to evaluate their actions. Polar opposites such as strong-weak, assertive–non-assertive, and independent-dependent allow students to respond to the Dixie Chicks in their dealings with Sony. A variety of questions can be used, such as "Would the Dixie Chicks have

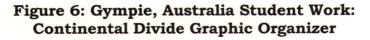

**Figure 6: Gympie, Australia Student Work:
Continental Divide Graphic Organizer**

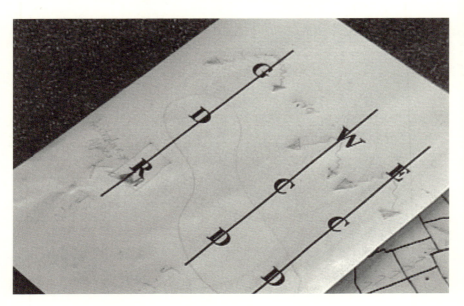

been able to be so assertive if they were recording in 1950? How has the women's movement since World War II made it possible for women in the early twenty-first century to challenge a powerful corporation like Sony? How does the onstage behavior and dress of the Dixie Chicks reflect their confidence to challenge Sony? If the Dixie Chicks weren't a major act with millions of sales, could they have taken on Sony in a lawsuit?"

Women and Geography

Elementary as well as middle school students may be involved with women and country music at the same time they study geography. Akenson involved fifth, sixth, and seventh grade students in Gympie, Queensland, in Australia as well as eighth grade students in Tennessee with varied versions of a lesson based on Patsy Montana's signature piece "I Want to Be a Cowboy's Sweetheart." Some variations included comparative Australian content using Slim Dusty's version of "The Man from Snowy River." A graphic organizer helped direct students in Gympie to conceptualize significant geographic comparisons between Australia and the United

**Figure 7:
Gympie, Australia,
Student Does
"The Great Divide"**

States. The introductory discussion focused on questions such as "How many of you have ever ridden a horse or wanted to ride a horse? How many of you have ever gone camping? Of the girls, how many of you have ever been told you can't do something because you're a girl?" The focus then shifted to the graphic organizer, in which students placed their writing instruments on the vertical lines, verbalized the three letters vertically arranged on each line, identified the letter D as common to all three vertical lines, and then grouped the letter D together by drawing a line enclosing the three Ds. Students then identified the basic mathematical operation that begins with the letter D—division. Students at Gympie South State School plotted symbols on the organizers for river systems dividing the three mountain ranges. The Australian Alps and Mt. Kosciusko were also presented symbolically to highlight content from the Slim Dusty version of "The Man from Snowy River." Symbols for mountains were then drawn on each vertical line and a map of Australia and a map of the United States presented with analogous geographic features. Students identified and plotted the Great Dividing Range and then the Eastern Continental Divide and the Western Continental Divide. Patsy Montana's

"I Want to Be a Cowboy's Sweetheart" was then played in segments, with students learning the lyrics and performing appropriate motions for the sections dealing with roping, riding, sweetheart, and the sun setting in the west. Most significantly, Patsy Montana mentions "out west of the Great Divide," at which point the students raised their index fingers vertically and pointed in opposite directions, as they were instructed to do.

Students plotted the sun symbol in the west and a figure on a horse appropriately placed west of the divide. Students then listened to Patsy Montana with instructions to raise their hands if Patsy Montana wanted to do some things that might have not been seen as proper for a young woman. Students raised their hands and identified that girls and women would have been discouraged from roping and riding and sleeping out under the stars on a cattle drive. The instructor further reinforced the role of women by having the students subtract 1935 from 2002, pointing out that some sixty-six years ago restraints on women were greater than they are now. Discussion also reiterated that even today girls are told that they shouldn't do certain things because of their gender. In lesson variations, which include Slim Dusty's version of "The Man from Snowy River," comparative questions include "Would young boys or men be told they shouldn't want to ride in an effort to catch the runaway horse?"

Geography skills may be further developed by the use of touring schedules provided in country music magazines, artist websites, and organization websites. The Country Music Association of Australia provides touring schedules, which include numerous women such as Leslie Avril, Audrey Auld, Crystal Bailey, Cyndi Boste, Kel-Anne Brandt, Catherine Britt, Lindsay Butler, the Byrnes Sisters, Kasey Chambers, Tanya Self, Those Gals, and Jeanette Warmald. In October 2002 Kasey Chambers toured extensively:

2 - Empire Theatre, Toowoomba, Qld

3 - Nambour Civic Centre, Qld

4/5 - Twin Towns Services Club, Tweed Heads, NSW

6 - Brisbane Convention Centre, Qld

9 - Enmore Theatre (Sydney), NSW

11 - Evan Theatre, Panthers Leagues Club, Penrith, NSW

12 - Newcastle Civic Theatre, NSW

23 - Canberra, Llewellyn Hall, ACT

25 - The Palais, Melbourne, Vic

(http://www.countrymusic.asn.au/ontour.html)

Plotting these Kasey Chambers performance dates develops specific geographical content knowledge set in the context of the five major geographic conceptual themes: movement, region, location, place, and man-land interaction (Hardwick and Holtgrieve 1996). Such plotting and related analysis also fits in with the need to meet eighteen geography standards in terms of the six essential elements identified by the Geography Education Standards Project: 1) The world in spatial terms, 2) Places and regions, 3) Physical systems, 4) Human systems, 5) Environment and society, and 6) The uses of geography (33–35). The level of difficulty can also be adjusted for age and ability. Such plotting thus may fit geography standards at all grade levels. At the kindergarten through fourth grade level, the plotting would help address the standard to "Organize Geographic Information," which includes the skill to "prepare maps to display geographic information" (47).

As with other content, geographical content provides opportunities for the creation of analogies. The study of Patsy Montana generates analogies based on the concept of the continental divide. Thus, The Great Dividing Range:Australia::Western Continental Divide:[France, Russia, Peru, United States] or Patsy Montana:Western Continental Divide::Slim Dusty:[Eastern Continental Divide, The Great Dividing Range, Andes, Urals]. Comparison of women's touring schedules in the United States and Australia results in numerous opportunities for analogies, such as Tamworth:Australia::[Austin, Ames, Nashville, Seattle]:United States or Kasey Chambers:Brisbane::Lee Ann Womack:[Myrtle Beach, Asheville, Clearwater, Denver]. Such analogies require comparisons involving cultural capitals and state capitals. Tamworth and Nashville function as the respective capitals of country music, and Brisbane and Denver are two state capitals.

A Collegiate Course

Teaching about women in country music can also be effective at the collegiate level. A special-topics undergraduate seminar "Women in Country Music" served as the course focus at Tennessee Technological University. The team included faculty from the English, education, music, and sociology departments, so the seminar provided multiple perspectives. Bufwack and Oermann's *Finding Her Voice* served as the course text, and the class involved lectures, discussion, and written presentations by students. The initial seminar provided an overview of women in country music with emphasis on its strong roots in the southern United States. To emphasize the role of women, Akenson provided an interview video with Elsie Williamson McWilliams, sister-in-law of Jimmie Rodgers, known as the "Father of Country Music." McWilliams discussed her role as a songwriter for Jimmie Rodgers, recording sessions in the 1920s and 1930s, and contextual material regarding southern culture. The overview provided video and audio examples of women in country music history, including Kitty Wells, Holly Dunn, Tanya Tucker, and Reba McEntire. Assignments for the course included a presentation on a selected topic about women in country music and short position papers. One position paper required students to combine the introductory overview presentation by Akenson with the course text:

> In 5 typewritten pages, or equivalent, react to the following statement:
>
> The text *Finding Her Voice: The Saga of Women in Country Music* reinforces the concept of southern roots and continuing southern identity in country music as emphasized in the overview presentation.
>
> Please use specific examples drawn from the pre-commercial, early commercial (1920s-1940s), and modern (1950s-90s) country music. Feel free to agree and/or disagree with the above statement.

One student responded, in part, as follows:

> As a pure-bred Southerner, I was raised on country music. I had always felt no one else in the world had even heard a country music song except us hillbilly southern folks. looking back I realize how terribly naive that was. Country music is a world wide institution that was created and respect in many regions. Our text, *Find Her Voice: The Saga of Women in Country Music* demonstrates this . . . and helps us realize that although Nashville is "the country music capitol of the world," Tennessee is not country music's birthplace, or at least not it's only birthplace. (Graves 1)

Graves's discussion developed points about the Hutchinson Family from New Hampshire which developed a country music sound as early as 1838, about the WLS Barn Dance based in Chicago, about Atlanta's failure to become "Music City U.S.A.," as well as the middle-class origins of many artists.

An additional component to the "Women in Country Music" course included special lectures; a Tennessee Humanities Council (THC) grant enabled Patsy Montana and three guest scholars to take part. THC funding involved a public-access component in the course billed as "From

Figure 8:
Women in Country Music Symposium.
Art by Wayne Hogan.

Honky Tonk Angels to Mainstream Artists: The Saga of Women in Country Music." As seen in Figure 8, the public attended course lectures titled "Gender Roles in Country Music," "The Saga of Women in Country Music," and "Being a Woman in Country Music," as well as a performance by Patsy Montana with a children's chorus and university chorus, and a round-table discussion. Each public symposium lecture included a study guide for students and general public alike. The "Gender Roles and Country Music" study guide (Akenson 1994) included an overview and specific questions designed to focus on significant content and issues:

> Gender roles, the attitudes and behaviors which society teaches are correct and appropriate for males and females, represent a major cultural feature in all societies. Ideas about gender are often deeply held and transmitted through virtually every institution from church, family, and school to government, corporations, and even music. Change concerning what is appropriate and desired behavior for males and females occurs over time, creates controversy, and is resisted by those who feel threatened by the changes advocated by various individuals and groups.

> Country music provides a mirror on the nature of gender and related issues in the United States and abroad. Dr. Lundy will provide insight to the typical messages found in country music concerning the role of women. She will identify changes in thematic emphasis in country music songs which reflect broader changes in society and within the country music audience itself. You might also listen for her discussion of changes in the roles of women country music artists regarding their stage behavior, behavior in their personal lives, and the variety of roles which women now occupy within the country music industry.

> You may want to ask Dr. Lundy questions such as the following:

> 1. Do changes in country music lyrics just reflect change in the attitudes of the country music audience, or do changes in the lyrics themselves help cause further change?

> 2. To what extent are country music lyrics still very traditional and conservative in comparison to mainstream thought?

> 3. To what extent do the numerous songs extolling the virtues of family (such as Holly Dunn's "Daddy's Hands") counteract songs with lyrics which project and/or advocate expanded roles for women?

> 4. To what extent are women who take charge of their careers and have multiple business interests (such as Reba McEntire and Dolly Parton) typical or the exception in today's country music?

> 5. Given the limited number of women in the Top 10 of the country music popularity charts, how can women expect to gain greater success as artists?

6. How can attitudes that women cannot headline a country music concert without a male co-headliner be changed?

7. How does the "tight playlist" which favors men over women restrict the advancement of women artists in country music?

8. Many radio station program directors and concert promoters honestly believe that men country music artists draw bigger audiences than do women country music artists. What evidence is there to justify this belief or is it "dead wrong?"

9. Tanya Tucker has two children out-of-wedlock. How has she been able to flaunt such a traditional norm and find success with the conservative country music audience?

10. Looking at album covers, attending concerts, and watching television suggests that a woman cannot be overweight and a country music artist. How are these physical expectations determined and maintained?

11. Was "Stand By Your Man" any worse than many of the songs in popular, rock, rap, or blues music which express traditional concepts or even degrade women?

Similarly structured study guides prepared students and the public for a presentation by *Finding Her Voice* co-author Mary Bufwack, Wayne Daniel's presentation "Patsy Montana and the WLS Barn Dance," and Patsy Montana's discussion "Being a Woman in Country Music." Patsy Montana also made an appearance in a graduate-level education course about country music and went to an elementary school in addition to performing in concert with a children's chorus and a university chorus. As a result of a collegiate course, a wide variety of audiences were touched by the saga of women in country music as well as the conventional student audience, which took the course for credit.

Conclusion

The history and contemporary status of women represents a remarkably broad and complex topic for inclusion into the curriculum. This discussion merely scratches the surface of the numerous applications that may enrich the curriculum. The role of women in country music legitimately stands on its own merits as a worthwhile topic for inclusion in curricula. Teachers and those who design curricula for the elementary schools, middle schools, and high schools face enormous pressures related to public scrutiny and expectations brought about by standardized testing. The topic of women in country music lends itself to enriching, elaborating, and sustaining the focus on conventional content while contributing to the development of basic and higher-order thinking skills. The emergence of standards for each curriculum subject can also be accommodated as content about women in country music finds its way into the classroom. In so doing, the remarkable complexity of country music and the country-music culture as a whole receive increased attention. The role of women in country music points to another dimension of the much-needed diversity for all students to be culturally literate.

Works Cited

Akenson, James E. "Study Guide for Dr. Karen S. Lundy. Genders Roles in Country Music." In *From "Honky Tonk Angels" to Mainstream Artists: The Sage of Women in Country Music.* Cookeville, Tennessee: Tennessee Technological University, 1994.

Alfred, Suellen. "Using Country Music to Teach the Ballad Form." Project presented at Dobyns-Bennett High School, Kingsport, Tennessee, 4 May 1999.

Alvermann, D.E., and Boothy, P.R. "Children's Transfer of Graphic Organizer Instruction." *Reading Psychology: An International Quarterly* 7 (1986): 87–100.

Andrews, A.C. "The Concept of Analogy in Teaching Geography." *Journal of Geography* 76 (1977): 167–69

Avery, C.W., and Avery, B.F. "Merging Reading and Cooperative Strategies Through Graphic Organizers." *Journal of Reading* 37, no. 8 (1994): 689–90.

Bos, S., Anders, P.L., Filip, D., and Jaffe, L.E. "Effects of an Interactive Instructional Strategy for Enhancing Reading Comprehension and Content Learning for Students with Learning Disabilities."*Journal of Learning Disabilities* 22 (1989): 384–90.

Braselton, S., and Decker, B.C. "Using Graphic Organizers to Improve the Reading of Mathematics." *The Reading Teacher* 4, no. 8 (1994): 3276–3281.

Bogguss, Suzy. "Somewhere Between." *Somewhere Between.* Capitol B 44270 82790. 1994.

Bufwack, Mary A., and Oermann, Robert K. *Finding Her Voice: The Saga of Women in Country Music.* New York: Crown Publishers, 1993.

Cassidy. J. "Using Graphic Organizers to Develop Critical Thinking." *Gifted Child Today* 12, no. 6 (1989): 34–36.

Castillo, Lisa C. "The Effect of Analogy Instruction on Young Children's Metaphor Comprehension." *Roeper Review* 21, no. 1 (1998): 27.

Country Music Association of Australia. "On Tour." http://www.countrymusic.asn.au/ontour.html.

Dempsey, Bridgette. "Teaching About Women in Country Music: Analogies and Graphic Organizers" (paper and multimedia demonstration presented at Tennessee Technological University). CUED 692 Topics: Country Music. Tennessee Technological University. Cookeville, Tennessee, 2002.

Dempsey, Bridgette. "Using Analogies to Teach About Women in Country Music." Unpublished paper and multimedia presentation. CUED 692 Topics: Teaching Analogical Reasoning. Tennessee Technological University. Cookeville, Tennessee, 2002.

Dixie Chicks. "Goodbye Earl." *Fly*. Monument CTDP 098642. 1999.

"Dixie Chicks, Sony Make Up." *The Tennessean*. 18 June 2002. E1–2.

Evans, Ronald W. "Thoughts on Redirecting a Runaway Train." *Theory and Research in Social Education* 29, no. 2 (2001): 330–39.

Geography Education Standards Project. *Geography for Life: National Geography Standards*. Washington, D.C.: National Geographic Research and Exploration, 1994.

Graves, Heather. "Country Music: More Than Just the South." Unpublished paper. Tennessee Technological University. Cookeville, Tennessee. 1994.

Gunderson, Edna. "Rights Issue Rocks the Music World." *USA Today*. 13 September 2002. D1–2.

Hardwick, Susan, and Holtgrieve, Donald. *Geography for Educators: Standards, Themes, and Concepts*. Upper Saddle River, New Jersey: Prentice Hall, 1996.

Havighurst, Craig. "Dixie Chicks Fire Back at Libel in Money Dispute." *The Tennessean*. 30 August 2001. E1

Jones, Beau Fly, Pierce, J., and Hunter, Barbara. "Teaching Students to Construct Graphic Representations." *Educational Leadership* 46, no. 1 (1989): 20–25.

Lewis, Anne. "An Overview of the Standards Movement." *Phi Delta Kappan* 76, no. 7 (1995): 745-50.

Marker, Perry. "Standards and High Stakes Testing: The Dark Side of a Generation of Political, Economic and Social Neglect of Public Education." *Theory and Research in Social Education* 29, no. 2 (2001): 357–62.

Moline, Steve. *I See What You Mean*. York, Maine: Stenhouse Publishers, 1995.

Montana, Patsy. "I Want To Be a Cowboy's Sweetheart." *Patsy Montana and the Prairie Ramblers*. Columbia Historic Edition FCT 38909. 1984.

Meyer, D.J. The Effects of Graphic Organizers on the Creative Writing of Third Grade Students. Unpublished Masters Project. Kern College of New Jersey, 1995.

Parton, Dolly. "Eagle When She Flies." *Eagle When She Flies*. Columbia CK 46882 ADD. 1991.

Rogers, Jimmie, and Williams, Miller. "Figure It Out: The Linguistic Turn in Country Music." In *Country Music Annual 2000*. Lexington: University Press of Kentucky, 2000.

Roland, Tom. "New Sony Tree CEO To Take Show On Road." *The Tennessean*. 24 January 1994. E1.

Ross, E. Wayne. "Resisting Test Mania." *Theory and Research in Social Education* 27, no. 2 (1999): 126–28.

Salvucci, Dario D., and Anderson, John R. "Integrating Analogical Mapping and General Problem Solving: The Path-Mapping Theory." *Cognitive Science* 25 (2001): 67–110.

Silkebakken, Gail P., and Camp, Donna J. "A Five-Step Strategy for Teaching Analogous Reasoning to Middle School Students." *Middle School Journal* 24, vol. 4 (1993): 37–50.

Simmons, D.D., Griffin, C.C., and Kameenui, E.J. "Effects of Teacher Constructed

Press and Post Graphic Organizer Instruction on Sixth Grade Science Students' Comprehension and Recall." *Journal of Educational Research* 28, no. 1 (1988): 15–21.

Spiegel, G.F., and Barufaldi, J.P. "The Effects of a Combination Text Structure Awareness and Graphic Post Organizers on Recall and Retention of Science Knowledge." *Journal of Research in Science Teaching* 31, no. 9 (1994): 913–32.

Tucker, Tanya. "Strong Enough to Bend." *Strong Enough to Bend.* Capitol B-44188 82574. 1988.

Womack, Lee Ann. "I Hope You Dance." *I Hope You Dance.* MCA 068170 0992. 2000.

Wright, Michelle. "One Time Around." *Now and Then.* Arista 07822-18685-2. 1992.

Yearwood, Trisha. "XXXs and OOOs (An American Girl)." *Thinkin' About You.* MCA 11201. 1995.

CONTRIBUTORS

WAYNE W. DANIEL, retired Professor Emeritus at Georga State University, is the author of many articles on country, bluegrass, and gospel music and is the author of *Pickin' on Peachtree: A History of Country Music in Atlanta, Georgia*, published by the University of Illinois Press in 1990.

CHARLES WOLFE is a professor of English at Middle Tennessee State University, near Nashville. He is the author or coauthor of some twenty-one books on American culture and music, including *Kentucky Country, The Devil's Box: Masters of Southern Fiddling,* and *A Good-Natured Riot: The Birth of the Grand Ole Opry.*

ELLEN WRIGHT is a rhythm guitarist, as well as a college lecturer in the Writing Program at Northwestern University. Almost entirely self-taught, she has emerged with a rhythm guitar style that resembles most closely that of the pre-war old-time guitarists; she occasionally takes lead breaks in a style reminiscent of the Carter Family. She has delivered scholarly papers on humor in bluegrass and on the parallels between learning to write and learning to play the guitar. She is currently working on an as-told-to biography of Roni Stoneman.

GLORIA NIXON-JOHN is the director of the Oakland Writing Project and a Red Cedar Writing Project Teacher consultant. She lives on a small ranch in Oxford, Michigan, and is currently working on a biography of poet Bronwen Wallace.

KRISTINE McCUSKER is an assistant professor of history at Middle Tennessee State University. She has published widely in World War II history, women's history, and mass media. Her country music interests include Lily May Ledford, Minnie Pearl, and other early women pioneers in country music.

TRACEY E.W. LAIRD is an assistant professor of music at Agnes Scott College. Her research and teaching interests include grassroots music in the southern United States, popular music, jazz, western European music history, and ethnomusicology.

MICHAEL ANN WILLIAMS is director of folk studies and anthropology at Western Kentucky University. She is currently working on a book on Sarah Gertrude Knott, founder of the National Folk Festival, and John Lair, creator of the Renfro Valley Barn Dance.

JOCELYN NEAL is an assistant professor of music at the University of North Carolina at Chapel Hill. Her primary area of research involves early recorded country music and blues. She has also written on the interaction of country music and country dancing.

REBECCA THOMAS was born in 1965 and began her education in southern music and culture on an Ozark farm. She received her Ph.D. in American history from the University of Missouri in 2000. She has published articles on regionalism and music in *Newsweek* and the *Midwest Quarterly*. Dr. Thomas currently teaches at California State University, Long Beach.

KATHLEEN HUDSON teaches in the English Department of Schreiner University. She writes a weekly newspaper column on Texas music for the *Kerrville Daily Times*, and is the founder/director of the Texas Heritage Music Foundation. Her first book, *Telling Stories, Writing Songs: An Album of Texas Songwriters*, was published in 2001. She is currently working on a second volume, *Voices of Women in Texas Music,* for University of Tennessee Press.

LINDA JEAN DANIEL earned a Doctor of Education degree from the University of Toronto in 2000 with a thesis entitled *Singing Out! Canadian Women in Country Music.* Her love for country music began on a farm on Daniel Road in southwestern Ontario where she spent the first ten years of her life. She teaches for a school board in Mississauga, Ontario.

ANDREW SMITH works as an educational statistician and has been collecting country music for over thirty years. He is currently researching the life of Tex Morton.

JAMES AKENSON is a social studies education specialist in the Department of Curriculum and Instruction at Tennessee Technological University. His current research involves integrating country music into K-12 curricula. He helped found the International Country Music Conference, is an officer in the Tennessee Folklore Society, and is the executive director for the Tennessee Council for the Social Studies.